THE RADICAL RIGHT

Studies in Critical Social Sciences Book Series

Haymarket Books is proud to be working with Brill Academic Publishers (www.brill.nl) to republish the *Studies in Critical Social Sciences* book series in paperback editions. This peer-reviewed book series offers insights into our current reality by exploring the content and consequences of power relationships under capitalism, and by considering the spaces of opposition and resistance to these changes that have been defining our new age. Our full catalog of *SCSS* volumes can be viewed at https://www.haymarketbooks .org/series_collections/4-studies-in-critical-social-sciences.

THE RADICAL RIGHT

Politics of Hate on the Margins of Global Capital

EDITED BY
FABIO LUIS BARBOSA DOS SANTOS
CECILIA LERO
TAMÁS GERŐCS

Haymarket Books
Chicago, IL

First published in 2022 by Brill Academic Publishers, The Netherlands
© 2022 Koninklijke Brill NV, Leiden, The Netherlands

Published in paperback in 2023 by
Haymarket Books
P.O. Box 180165
Chicago, IL 60618
773-583-7884
www.haymarketbooks.org

ISBN: 979-8-88890-022-2

Distributed to the trade in the US through Consortium Book Sales and
Distribution (www.cbsd.com) and internationally through Ingram Publisher
Services International (www.ingramcontent.com).

This book was published with the generous support of Lannan Foundation,
Wallace Action Fund, and the Marguerite Casey Foundation.

Special discounts are available for bulk purchases by organizations and
institutions. Please call 773-583-7884 or email info@haymarketbooks.org for more
information.

Cover design by Jamie Kerry and Ragina Johnson.

Printed in the United States.

Library of Congress Cataloging-in-Publication data is available.

Contents

Acknowledgements

The chapter on Hungary was co-financed by the project "From developmental states to new protectionism: changing repertoire of state interventions to promote development in an unfolding new world order" (OTKA FK_124573), supported by the NRDIO (NKFIH) in Hungary.

Cecilia Lero would like to thank the Centro de Estudos da Metrópole (CEM) and the Fundação de Amparo à Pesquisa do Estado de São Paulo (FAPESP).

Aparna Sundar would like to thank Fabio Luis Barbosa dos Santos for his patience and support and Nandini Sundar for her timely assistance, and to both for thoughtful comments that have greatly helped to improve her chapter.

Ilhan Can Ozen would like to acknowledge the love and support of his dear wife, Pinar Acar Ozen.

The Editors would like to thank Alison McClymont for generously copy-editing the chapter on Hungary.

All chapters that were not written by native English speakers were copy-edited by Cecilia Lero. Her patience, sensitivity and competence were invaluable, and the authors wish to register their deepest gratitude.

Figures and Tables

Notes on Contributors

Fabio Luis Barbosa dos Santos
is Latin American Studies Professor at Federal University of São Paulo (UNI-FESP) and Research Associate at the Society, Work and Politics Institute at University of Witwatersrand. Author of *Power and Impotence. A History of South America under Progressivism* (Brill, 2019).

Daniel Feldmann
is a lecturer at the Economics Department at the Federal University of São Paulo (UNIFESP).

Ágnes Gagyi
is a sociologist, working on East European politics and social movements in the context of the region's long-term world-economic integration. She is a researcher at the University of Gothenburg, and member of the Budapest-based Working Group for Public Sociology "Helyzet".

Daniel Geary
is Mark Pigott Associate Professor in American History at Trinity College Dublin.

Tamás Gerőcs
is a political economist who has currently finished his Ph.D. at the Corvinus University of Budapest in Hungary. His research field of interest is semiperipheral dependent development. Gerőcs is an external research fellow at the Institute of World Economics, Centre of Economic and Regional Studies and a member of the Budapest-based Working Group for Public Sociology "Helyzet".

Şefika Kumral
is an Assistant Professor of Sociology at University of North Carolina-Greensboro. She has published articles on fascism; far-right; global labor; democracy and violence.

Cecilia Lero
is the lead researcher at Build-A-Movement. She received her Ph.D. in Political Science at the University of Notre Dame (2019) and was a post-doctoral fellow at the Centro de Estudos da Metrópole at the University of São Paulo and Brazilian Center for Analysis and Planning.

Devika Misra

is an Assistant Professor at the Jindal School of International Affairs, OP Jindal Global University, India.

Ilhan Can Ozen

graduated from the Economics Department of Bilkent University in 2004, and received his M.A. and Ph.D. degrees in Economics from Johns Hopkins University Economics Department. His work focuses on development economics, political economy and health economics.

Aparna Sundar

is a political scientist affiliated with the Asian Institute at the University of Toronto, Canada, and the School of Development, Azim Premji University, Bengaluru, India.

CHAPTER 1

Introduction

The Radical Right: Politics of Hate on the Margins of Global Capital

Cecilia Lero

This book is the fruit of several years of discussion among scholars from five countries outside the centers of global capitalist development: Turkey, Hungary, India, the Philippines, and Brazil. All these countries have experienced a dramatic and disheartening phenomenon under their political leaders: Recep Erdoğan in Turkey (since 2003); Viktor Orbán in Hungary (since 2010); Narendra Modi in India (since 2014); Rodrigo Duterte in the Philippines (since 2016); and Jair Bolsonaro in Brazil (since 2019). The phenomenon goes by many names: strongman politics, extreme-right nationalism, neo-fascism, illiberalism, exclusionary regimes, and, perhaps most commonly, populism and authoritarian populism.

The precise meanings and usefulness of these terms have been discussed at length and with much expertise elsewhere (e.g. Norris and Inglehart 2019; Müller 2016; Mudde 2021) and this book will not seek to enter the debate on particular concepts. Rather, the purpose of this book is to describe and analyze the political, economic, and social roots of these regimes; their strategies for legitimation; and the role of the opposition, especially the progressive opposition. It is no coincidence that these leaders find themselves in power at the same time in history and we cannot explain them away as merely gaffes or temporary errata as countries continue on their supposedly inevitable paths towards peace and democracy. Rather, we draw a direct line between the nature of global capitalist development combined with the unfulfilled promises of liberal democracy in the late 20th and early 21st centuries and the rise of popular authoritarian regimes across countries with great differences in history, culture, and political institutions.

This relationship will not appear new for those familiar with similar political movements in the United States and Western Europe. However, we believe it is important to pay particular attention to developing countries. The rapid and unbridled nature of capitalist expansion has affected developing countries differently than industrialized democracies. The push towards modernization and development has shifted subjective class relations as billions of people find themselves out of extreme poverty and new middle classes have emerged, but with enhanced tensions of relative deprivation and precarity. At the same time as these economic changes and class shifts, social changes and perceived challenges to social hierarchies further fanned tension. Projects to define modern nations in the wake of colonialism, authoritarian regime collapse, and changing geopolitical dynamics found themselves in conflict with traditional values and power interests. A constant contradictory relationship with the Global North/West, characterized by the simultaneous emulation, yet desire for self-assertion, has resulted in inconsistent and opportunistic forms of chest-thumping nationalism, characterized by 'reactionary exclusionism' (Evans 2020). The consequences of these regimes are arguably more dire as immature government institutions and norms leave those very institutions and vulnerable populations at heightened risk.

We began this process by asking three central questions: First, how similar are these regimes, really? To what extent can we identify similar characteristics and patterns? Second, how can we explain the rise of similar regimes in such different countries? Third, how to compare these regimes to the wave of authoritarianism during the Cold War?

1   Popular and Authoritarian Regimes of Hatred Politics

The five leaders analyzed in this book have defining characteristics in common. They are *popular*, having legitimately won democratic elections (multiple national elections, in the cases of Erdogan, Orbán, and Modi). They ascended to power based on popular support and continue to maintain sizeable and vocal bases. These are not leaders who reached high office based on skilled deal-making among elite camps or armed coups. Rather, they won elections riding on waves of popular sentiment, often to the initial dispassionateness if not outright dismay of the established political and economic elite. This is important for our analysis because beyond understanding what these leaders have done to make themselves appealing to voters, we must also understand what it is about the situations, perceptions, desires and frustrations of voters that make them open to strongman leadership.

They are *authoritarian*. All five countries, although far from democratic apogees, had achieved some basic establishment of democratic institutions and norms and respect for civil liberties. Many observers expected the countries to be on their way, arduous as it was, to better quality democracy. Many in-country activists themselves took it for granted that democracy was the accepted system and that the challenge over the next generations would be expanding the breadth and inclusivity of democratic principles. Yet, these regimes have been characterized by the purposeful capture and dismantling of democratic institutions and norms. The country chapters will detail how these five leaders have sought to concentrate power and resources in their offices; attacked or co-opted other supposedly independent government branches and state agencies; discredited, harassed, and in some instances jailed, exiled, or killed figures of the political opposition; treated security forces as personal militias; and attacked independent media through physical threats and legal harassment, as well as through the proliferation of fake news and conspiracy theories. Although the five regimes differ in ideology and purpose of their respective 'national projects,' all of their projects include as a cornerstone the undoing of any norms or mechanisms that could be used to restrict their powers or make them subject to accountability.

These leaders thrive on *hate and fear*. What allows them to dismantle democratic and social protections and freedoms while maintaining popular support? Creating an existential threat and the ambiance of continuing crisis not only distracts the public and political opposition from misgovernance, but also presents a veneer of justification for a wide range of extreme and offensive actions in the name of 'defending the nation.' These leaders, in particular, took advantage of already existing bigotry and fear in their societies as a central strategy of their electoral campaigns and ruling styles. Here we depart somewhat from the traditional concept of populism. Whereas most definitions of populist leadership styles focus on the drawn dichotomy between the 'real people' and the 'corrupted elites,' the leaders included in this study also focus their hate against already marginalized groups in society, painting them as the central obstacles to safety and development. The groups primarily include, but are not limited to, the poor, black slum-dweller in Brazil; refugees in Hungary; Muslims and other religious minorities in India; the slum-dwelling, drug user in the Philippines; and secularists, then later Gülenists and Kurds in Turkey. The elites, in turn, are also constructed to be enemies of the people because they enable these groups. According to these leaders' narratives, the corrupt oligarchs and traditional politicians have created a system so inept that it stacks the deck against the honest citizen giving unfair advantages to the unscrupulous ones. That many of these leaders themselves belong to traditionally privileged classes and social groups is an inconsequential irony. Furthermore, these leaders extend their demonization efforts to human rights activists, liberal democracy defenders, and communists, whom they paint as more concerned with protecting the bad citizen than the good citizens, thus making them, too, existential threats to the nation.

Finally, for all their anti-elite rhetoric, these leaders are *right-wing*. They range from ideologically culturally conservative and economically neoliberal (as in Bolsonaro's case) to only opportunistically so (as in Duterte's case). Nevertheless, on the whole they have embraced capitalism in its most exploitative forms. Addressing systemic inequality, improving the quality of and access to social services, strengthening labor, and regulating abusive and extractive businesses practices are not goals of these regimes. Rather, these regimes have actively worked to weaken organized labor, provide unfair advantages to friendly capitalists, dismantle movements towards universal social services, and reinforce inequality and patronage. This position also distinguishes these leaders from similar movements in the Global North. While Trump in the U.S. and the wave of European nationalist parties have rallied against globalization and championed some protectionist measures, these five leaders (with the exception of Orbán) have continued if not accelerated their countries' openness to the global economy as a central strategy for development. Despite promises to uproot the system in favor of the 'common' man, these leaders have largely bought into neoliberal capitalism, doing little to transform the economic systems of their respective countries beyond carving out places for their own cronies to participate in rent extraction.[1]

2   Why These Leaders Now?

In recent years, numerous authors have written about this sharp turn away from liberal democracy.[2] A large body of literature in the Global North centers on the 'losers of globalization' argument. This argument posits that globalization and technical advancement have fundamentally reshaped the nature of work. Transferring jobs to the developing world where wages are lower and there are less labor regulations, as well as the replacement of manual tasks with automation has led to job losses and economic insecurity, particularly in the low-skilled manufacturing sector. At the same time, recent decades have seen major waves of migration to the developed world fueled by both the globalized economy and regional conflicts. This influx of migrants has resulted in nativism and xenophobia in receiving countries, resulting in backlash (Rodrik

---

1   While Orbán has focused more on developing domestic capital, his regime has also been receptive to Chinese and Russian investments in order to offset the influence of Western and especially German capital.
2   A simple definition of liberal democracy could be systems of government where competitive elections are accepted as legitimate and civil liberties such as the freedoms of speech, assembly, and political affiliation, and the right to due process under the law are respected.

2018; Roth 2017; Diamond 2019; Spruyt et al 2016; Kriesi 2014; and Stiglitz 2018; McVeigh and Estep 2019).

Another argument stems from the growing influence of supranational bodies and international standards and regulations that have made citizens feel that too many rules affecting their daily lives were made by 'faceless' bureaucrats in Brussels or Washington DC. At the same time, they felt unrepresented by mainstream political parties as the parties maneuvered within the confines of often convoluted procedures and established economic arrangements. Berman and Snegovaya (2019) describe how socialist and social democratic parties' moved towards the center on economic issues in the late twentieth century. This move, in no small part due to international pressures, left them ill-prepared to take advantage of the discontent created by economic changes and exacerbated by the 2008 global economic crisis. Research by Gold (2015), Boxell, Gentzkow and Shapiro (2022), and Rodden (2021) reveals that since the 1990s, Americans have developed more negative feelings about the political party system in general, more animosity towards members of the opposing party, and feel personally distant from their own party (see also Drutman 2021).

Finally, 'cultural backlash' theory builds on modernization theory to argue that as societies become wealthy, younger generations become less concerned with material security and more amenable to post-materialist and socially-liberal values. As the older generations die out and more of the population is sympathetic to post-materialist values, society reaches a tipping point where those adhering to the old values begin to feel threatened, resulting in backlash (Norris and Inglehart 2019).

We find these explanations inadequate to explain the rise of far-right hatred regimes outside the centers of global capital. By the most obvious measures, the countries included in this study appear to be net winners in the global economy. Gross domestic product has increased, extreme poverty has reduced, and a burgeoning middle class appeared (Hungary is an exception to this trend).[3] Furthermore, all countries had undergone several cycles of generally legitimate democratic elections and basic respect for civil liberties was codified in law and appeared to be steadily expanding in practice – what most political scientists would consider telltale signs that democracy had been 'consolidated,' or established as the only acceptable political regime type. None

---

3   Post-socialist Hungary faced economic crisis at a scale comparable to the Great Depression in Europe. GDP and poverty incidence did not begin to improve until the early 2000s.

of the countries experienced significant waves of in-migration or rapid demographic changes.[4]

Cultural backlash theory appears to have some resonance in the countries
included in this study, as we do observe strong conservative reactions to social
modernization efforts, and especially the inclusion of historically marginalized
groups. However, it is important to highlight that modernization theory, developed with the Global North/West in mind, distinguishes between survival ver-
sus self-expression values: survival values emphasize physical and economic
security, including economic redistribution, whereas self-expression values
include religious, ethnic, and gender diversity and participation in economic
and political decision-making (Norris and Inglehart 2019, 33; Inglehart and
Welzel 2005). In the Global South/East, however, the line separating these two
concepts is not so clear. Movements to recognize and include minority groups
(or the majority group, in the case of Brazil's black population) are inextricably
tied to physical and economic security. Beyond mere identity and expression,
economic and democratic inclusion in these contexts is about the very right of
hundreds of millions of people to exist. Furthermore, when we analyze voting
data, the correlation between age and support for these leaders is not nearly as
clear as it is for their counterparts in the North and West (Lero 2022).

This presents us with a puzzle: If GDPs have been growing, new middle
classes rose out of poverty, and, though far from perfect, people arguably had
more access to civil rights and protections for civil liberties than at any time
in their countries' histories, why the sharp turn towards right-wing authoritarianism? What has made people vulnerable to hate politics in the 21st century?
To answer this, we must look at who within these societies have been the big
winners and who has been relatively left behind, patterns of social disembeddedness and polarization, and how liberal democratic regimes and institutions
were ultimately unable to address or mediate the grievances that came to be
exacerbated and mobilized by the radical right

Scholars who study both the developed and developing world have offered
explanations that reach beyond patterns found in the centers of global capital. Evans (2020), Curato (2016), Garrido (2020), Heydarian (2018), Souza
(2018), Jayasuriya (2020), and McVeigh and Estep (2018), among others, have
focused on how these leadership styles have exploited longstanding concerns
with security, justice, and punishment to build popular images for themselves
related to order, discipline, corruption, and violence. Curato refers to this style

---

4 Although Hungarian authorities sought to politicize an influx of refugees from the Syrian
civil war, most of these refugees were passing through Hungary to get to Western Europe and
so should not be considered migrants to Hungary.

as 'penal populism.' Its narrative is directly related to the politics of hate and existential threat. Liberal democracy's approach of 'reformism' and 'good governance' is not enough to deal with the economic and physical threat that the undisciplined 'others' (however they may be defined by the leader) pose to the more 'deserving' members of society. The leader thus gains popularity by taking a tough-on-crime stance that promises to protect the people while actively demonizing and dehumanizing the targeted group. That this group is even present in society indicates that society is not ready for democracy or universal respect for civil liberties. Rather, establishing order and disciplining or cleansing society of the miscreants is a necessary prior step before democracy can be established.

Once the demand for regressive, punishment-focused politics is present, institutional weaknesses can enable these kinds of leaders to come to power. Levitsky and Ziblatt (2018) argue that beyond written, enforceable rules, much of what keeps liberal democratic regimes in place are norms of acceptable behavior. When leaders who are willing to violate these norms appear and with popular (even if not majority) support, it can be surprisingly easy to disregard these norms. Teehankee and Thompson (2016) and Avritzer (2019) describe how recently democratized countries can oscillate between periods of seemingly calm moments of democratic procedural reformism that respects said norms and episodes of authoritarianism when these norms are disregarded. This oscillation is because of the tension between the desire for institutional stability and the desire for immediate solutions to pressing social problems, as well as democratic and authoritarian features that exist side by side within state institutions.

Bello (2018) chooses to center his analysis on the concept of 'counterrevolution.' He draws parallels between periods in history when a progressive revolution was followed by a wave of regressive recoil. While we would not necessarily categorize the precursors to the regimes studied in this book as 'revolutions,' we do observe that the authoritarian leaders rode on waves of recoil against their precursors' approaches to development and political systems: neoliberal economics and liberal democracy.

3   Right-Wing Hate Politics as a Result of 20th Century Capitalism and Liberal Democracy

This book argues that the rise of these far-right, authoritarian leaders is not an historical coincidence. Strategies of hate politics, violent penal populism, and the exploitation of weak institutions have been made viable by the frustrations brought about by neoliberal capitalist development and the inadequacies of liberal democracy. Neoliberal development strategies have exacerbated extreme inequalities by catering to the desires of finance capital and selling the promise of meaningful social mobility and security, while simultaneously eroding the same. Attacks on independent workers' organizations and social protection schemes and the general commodification of life have contributed to social disembedding[5] and the reconfiguration of class relations that these leaders were then able to exploit.

At the same time, the myth of meritocracy sends the message that wealth comes to those who deserve it, rather than being largely the result of long-ingrained and unjust systems of social reproduction. The poor are therefore undeserving, unworthy of empathy and likely morally inferior, and individualism is to be valued over communities and society. We find that the middle classes are often the most susceptible to these narratives and they play pivotal roles amidst class reconfigurations. As a new middle class rises, its members are eager to differentiate themselves from the 'undeserving' poor from whose ranks they came. In some cases, new middle classes seek to also distinguish themselves from cosmopolitan elites by clinging to traditional moral values and identity markers (such as ethnicity and religion) while in other cases, it is the established middle classes that invoke traditional values and identities to try to maintain an air of superiority as their social and economic status are challenged by new middle classes.

In all cases, the failure of liberal democratic regimes and institutions to deepen widespread participation and accountability accelerated patterns of de-socialization that engender fear, hate and indifference, thus paving the way for different shades of the politicization of resentment. Far right leaders have consequently co-opted liberal democratic institutions to erode democracy from the inside, while simultaneously pursuing extralegal and often violent strategies of social and political control from the outside. In other words, the social and economic effects of neoliberal capitalism as practiced in the late 20th and early 20th century, combined with the failure of democratic regimes to adequately mediate social tensions and address populations' urgent needs, have produced the subjective and objective conditions for hate politics and authoritarianism. The great irony is that liberal democracy's embrace of neoliberal capitalism created the conditions for the undoing of liberal democracy. Yet, neoliberal capitalism continues to thrive under authoritarian leadership.

---

5 By "social disembedding" we mean lifting social relations out of their local and temporal contexts, often resulting in weaker social ties and communities. See Giddens 1991.

4   Book Outline

We intend this book to be accessible to those who have no prior knowledge about the countries included, and thought-provoking for those already familiar with them. The following chapters will analyze these five popular authoritarian leaders' strategies for legitimation and power consolidation, particularly the ways they have sought to change formal political institutions in ways that will have a lasting impact. Beyond that, it will look at the societies that brought them to power, paying attention to social schisms, cultural and historical legacies, changing class relations, and shifting relationships with geopolitical power configurations. Importantly, this book will look beyond the new authoritarians themselves and include analyses of the political opposition and resistance movements.

Şefika Kumral's chapter on Turkey presents Erdoğan's regime as a reaction to the Kemalist power structure that emphasized secularism and a professional bureaucratized military and judiciary. The evolution towards an increasingly repressive and Islamist-nationalist regime has been aided by changing class relationships, particularly at the local level. Tamás Gerőcs and Ágnes Gagyi's chapter on Hungary focuses on the country's transformation from a state socialist to a post-socialist neoliberal regime and then, after 2010, an authoritarian conservative regime based on the rise of the national bourgeoise. These transformations fueled capital reconfigurations and class tensions as Hungary sought to define a new space for itself amidst shifting power configurations between the United States and European Union, Russia, and China. In Aparna Sundar's chapter on India, the Bharatiya Janata Party (BJP) stands out as the most organized and ideologically established authoritarian force among the five cases. The BJP and Nahrendra Modi's rule are based on a strong identity of Hindu nationalism and the strong rejection of the vision of a pluralist India that dominated the country's early years of independence. Economic liberalization in the 1990s combined with the desire to be a more influential global player help explain the BJP's rise to become a significant political player by 2014. Cecilia Lero's chapter on the Philippines focuses on the tensions between the optimism of the democratic period (1986-), especially the 2010s when the Philippines was experiencing record economic growth and a flood of consumer goods and credit, and latent fears and frustrations with petty crime, corruption, and inequality. Duterte's rhetoric of fear took advantage of class-based loathing – loathing against the poor who were painted as drug-addicted criminals, as well as loathing against the hypocrisy of the political, economic, and social elite – to make violence appear to be an acceptable development strategy. This rhetoric found supporters across classes, but most fervently and significantly among the new middle class that came out of poverty during the democratic period. Fabio Luis Barbosa dos Santos' chapter on Brazil analyzes how as the Worker Party's (PT) lost popularity, the national capital class saw that it no longer needed a relationship of convenience with the party in order to protect its interests. At the same time, then-candidate Bolsonaro's brusque style, drawing heavily on racist, misogynistic, and violent tropes, gained him popular support among a very vocal subset of the population (including notably the expanding Neo-Pentecostal movement) while his strongly neoliberal economic agenda gained him a marriage of convenience with economic elites.

Following the individual country chapters, we include an analysis compiled by Daniel Feldmann, et al. of how each government has responded to Covid-19. The Covid crisis that unraveled as we were writing this book allowed us to observe how these leaders govern in times of intense crisis when competence and efficiency were both necessary and atypically well-documented across countries. We see that for all their desires to centralize power, their responses to Covid have been ineffective and characterized by passing on authority and responsibility, while taking advantage of the crisis for corruption. Daniel Geary then bridges the rise of authoritarianism in these five countries with its perhaps most well-known counterpart in the Global North, in the chapter "It Can't Happen Here: Trump Viewed from the Margins". The concluding chapter provides a comprehensive comparative analysis of these five regimes, aiming to further understand the historical roots of this global trend, how it operates and ultimately, how to confront it.

Finally, it is important to acknowledge that this book has a point of view. We strive to be objective in our analyses, but we are not dispassionate. We identify as progressives who believe in democracy, human rights, and social and economic equality. We strongly reject the notion that the 'free market' should be the arbiter of morality and social good or that economic growth as an end justifies any means to achieve it. We strongly lament the paths our respective countries have taken towards unapologetic authoritarianism, exploitation, and violence. We hope that this book may be our small contribution towards an effective resistance and a future without fear.

References

Avritzer L (2019) *O Pêndulo da Democracia*. São Paulo: Todavia Livros.
Bello W (2018) *Counterrevolution: The Global Rise of the Far Right*. Halifax: Fernwood Publishing.

Berman S and Snegovaya M (2019) Populism and the Decline of Social Democracy. *Journal of Democracy*, 30(3): 5–19.

Boxell L, Gentzkow M and Shapiro JM (2022) Cross-Country Trends in Affective Polarization. The Review of Economics and Statistics 2022.

Curato N (2016) Politics of Anxiety, Politics of Hope: Penal Populism and Duterte's Rise to Power. *Journal of Current Southeast Asian Affairs*, 35(3): 91–109.

Diamond L (2019) *Ill Winds: Saving Democracy from Russian Rage, Chinese Ambition, and American Complacency.* New York: Penguin Press.

Drutman L (2021) Why the Two-Party System Is Effing Up U.S. Democracy. *FiveThirtyEight.* Available (Confirmed 1 April 2022) at: https://fivethirtyeight.com/features/why-the-two-party-system-is-wrecking-american-democracy/.

Evans P (2020) Introduction: The rise of twenty-first century exclusionary regimes. *International Sociology* 35(6): 581–589.

Garrido M (2020) A conjunctural account of upper- and middle-class support for Rodrigo Duterte. *International Sociology* 35 (6): 651–73.

Giddens A (1991) The Consequences of Modernity, Cambridge: Polity Press.

Gold HJ (2015) The Polls – Trends: Americans' Attitudes Toward the Political Parties and the Party System. *The Public Opinion Quarterly*, 79(3), 803–819.

Heydarian R J (2018) *The Rise of Duterte: A Populist Revolt against Elite Democracy.* Singapore: Palgrave Macmillan.

Inglehart R and Welzel C (2005) *Modernization, Cultural Change and Democracy.* New York: Cambridge University Press.

Jayasuriya K (2020) The Rise of the Right: Populism and Authoritarianism in Southeast Asian Politics. *Southeast Asian Affairs*: 43–56.

Kriesi H (2014) The Populist Challenge. *West European Politics*, 37(2): 361–378.

Lero C (2022, *forthcoming*) Voting for Violence. In: Pereira (ed.) A *Right-Wing Populism in Latin America and Beyond.* London: Routledge.

Levitsky S and Ziblatt D (2018) *How Democracies Die.* New York: Penguin Books.

McVeigh R and Estep K (2019) *The Politics of Losing.* New York: Columbia University Press.

Mudde C (2021). Populism in Europe: An Illiberal Democratic Response to Undemocratic Liberalism (The Government and Opposition/Leonard Schapiro Lecture 2019). *Government and Opposition.* 56(4): 577–597.

Müller J (2016) *What is Populism?* Philadelphia: University of Pennsylvania Press.

Norris P and Inglehart R (2019) *Cultural Backlash: Trump, Brexit and Authoritarian Populism.* New York: Cambridge University Press.

Rodden J (2021) Keeping Your Enemies Close: Electoral Rules and Partisan Polarization. In: Rosenbluth F and Weir M (eds.), *Who Gets What?: The New Politics of Insecurity.* Cambridge: Cambridge University Press.

Rodrik D (2018) Populism and the economics of globalization. *Journal of International Business Policy*, vol 1 (1–2): 12–33.

Roth K (2017) The Dangerous Rise of Populism: Global Attacks on Human Rights Values. *Journal of International Affairs*: 79–84.

Souza J (2018) *A classe edia no espelho: sua história, seus sonhos e ilusões, sua realidade.* Rio de Janeiro: Estação Brasil.

Spruyt B, Keppens G and Van Droogenbroeck F (2016) Who Supports Populism and What Attracts People to It? *Political Research Quarterly*, 69(2): 335–346.

Stiglitz J (2018) *People, Power, and Profits: Progressive Capitalism for an Age of Discontent.* New York: W. W. Norton & Company.

Teehankee J and Thompson M (2016) Electing a Strongman. *Journal of Democracy*, 27(4): 125–134.

CHAPTER 2

Right-Wing Authoritarianism in Turkey

Şefika Kumral

This chapter analyzes the rise, transformation and consolidation of the Erdoğan regime in Turkey with a focus on (1) its historical background, (2) changing class relationships at the local level and (3) political strategies used by Erdoğan and Erdoğanist cadres. I discuss various regime legitimation strategies used by Erdoğanism including the making and unmaking of socio-political coalitions, selective oppression and violence, neoliberal developmentalism and new nationalism, the centralization of authority, and the transformation of political violence. I conclude by discussing how transformations at each level have produced contradictions and an emergent resistance on the ground.

1 Introduction

The Justice and Development Party (AKP) came to power in the 2002 general elections as a newcomer political party. The party and its leader, Recep Tayyip Erdoğan's rule have been intact since then. What was then called by U.S. foreign policymakers and the mainstream media as a 'moderate Islamist party' would remain in power for two decades while securing a majority vote in nearly all elections and transforming the political structure into an authoritarian regime.

From the very beginning and until this day, Erdoğan's master narrative has been to create a 'new Turkey' through the unmaking of the old Kemalist power structure that mainly dominated the country's bureaucracy – particularly the military and the judiciary – and to reconstitute the 'will of the people'. While this rhetoric initially took a moderate form as the AKP and Erdoğan championed European Union (EU) membership, currently the party has formed a *de facto* one party and one-man regime with very little room for opposition parties and groups to operate.

In this chapter, I examine socio-economic transformations in Turkey during the turn of the 21st century and discuss how the making (and unmaking) of new classes during Erdoğan's neoliberal regime, i.e., the emergence of a new faction of the Turkish bourgeoisie, a new middle class and new factions of the working-class, helped consolidate Erdoğan's mass support. I also discuss various regime legitimation strategies used by Erdoğan and the Erdoğanist cadres including pragmatic socio-political coalition building, selective oppression and violence, partisan welfare distribution, and the constant politicization of the population. After bringing these layers together, I conclude by discussing how transformations at each level have produced contradictions and an emergent resistance on the ground.

2   Historical Background

Erdoğan's rise and appeal to large segments of Turkish society when he first came to power in 2002/2003[1] cannot be fully grasped without taking a long historical approach to the main foundations of the Turkish Republic. Founded in 1923, the new Turkish state was the only state to emerge as an independent state after the 'post-war settlement in the Middle East' (Zürcher, 1992: 237–238). The founding cadres of the emergent bourgeois republic abolished the Sultanate in 1922 and the Caliphate in 1924. The new Republic was founded upon the rejection of the Ottoman political and Islamic cultural lineage, and it strove to become a member of the newl inter-state system by producing a new 'civilized nation. It embarked upon a radical cultural, socio-political, and economic transformation of Turkish society with the goals of creating a secular and modern society that was modeled after modern European societies. The ideology of the new Turkish state became inseparable from Mustafa Kemal Ataturk, one of the leaders of the 'Independence War' who established his political and symbolic rule over the new state soon after its formation in 1923.

One of the central goals of the new state was to transform society, which had been the *tebaa* (subjects) of the Ottoman Sultan, into a modern *nation*. The Turkish 'nation' was defined as including anyone living in Turkey and are 'happy to call themselves Turks'. Despite this seemingly 'civic' conception of nationhood, which appeared to exclude religion as a definitive character of Turkishness at first sight, most non-Muslim minorities continued to be excluded and expelled from the new nation and society through active state policies such as the population exchange between Greece and Turkey in 1923, the infamous Wealth Levy of 1942, and sporadic societal violence targeting

---

1 In 1998, Erdoğan was convicted for inciting people to violence and religious hatred due to a poem he wrote, and he was subsequently banned from holding public Office. That is why although the AKP came to power in the aftermath of the 2002 elections, Erdoğan only became a prime minister in 2003, when the AKP government led by Abdullah Gul ended Erdoğan's political ban.

non-Muslims. The top-down modernization and transformation of society further cemented the status of non-Muslim minorities as socially alienated 'others' throughout the 20th century.[2] As part of the strong state tradition, the military became a key political actor in this paradoxical democracy, whereby a new parliamentary republic engaged in a process of creating its own modern nation/people. Hence, throughout the 20th century, "the military assumed the role of the guardian and the vanguard of the Turkish revolution with its nationalist and secular ideology" (Gürsoy, 2012: 736). This role entailed three *coup d'états* in 1960, 1970 and 1980, as well as a post-modern coup in 1997[3] (Bardakç 1 , 2013) which aimed to eliminate what the military viewed as *threats* to the secular Turkish nation-state.

2.1   *Political Economy of Turkey in the Long 20th Century*
Although it had also temporarily established pragmatic ties with the U.S.S.R, especially from 1929 to 1949, the new Turkish State was a clearly bourgeois republic which aimed to climb the ladders of the political and economic hierarchy of the capitalist world-system. Despite state-led efforts to modernize its industry (and agriculture), the Turkish economy was securely anchored in a semi-peripheral position during the U.S. world hegemony. As a typical semi-peripheral regime, the Turkish political economy has been characterized by periodic structural crises that take place almost every two decades as illustrated by in Figure 2.1.

Partly as a response to these crises, the economic governance regimes in Turkey have switched back and forth between state-controlled/regulated and market-driven/liberal economic regimes since its foundation in 1923 – i.e., from a state controlled economy in the 1930s to a liberal market period in the 1950s, to an import substituting industrialization (ISI) period in the 1960s, to a mixed economic model in the 1970s and a neoliberal model in the 1980s. Despite these changes, there has also been a high degree of continuity and overlap between these different economic governance models as illustrated by

---

2   On the one hand, the forceful inclusion of the Kurdish minority in the Turkish nation through forced language policies and a lack of cultural, social, and political recognition led to waves of Kurdish mobilization, which culminated in the post-1980 Kurdish unrest. On the other hand, the Muslim majority population increasingly became alienated and excluded from the state due to the top-down modernization and secularization of the society. These two groups would become the mass base of the two strongest social movements in post-1980s Turkey.

3   It refers to the process which started with the 1997 Military Memorandum and ended up with the resignation of Islamist *Refah Partisi* (Welfare Party) Prime Minister from his position. Unlike ordinary coups, the 1997 Military Memorandum did not involve the military's takeover of politics from the civilians.

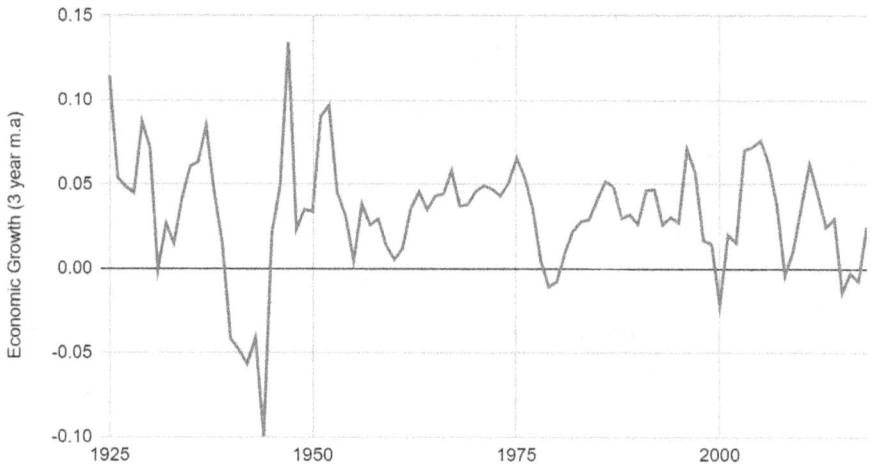

FIGURE 2.1   Per capita GDP growth from 1924 to 2018
SOURCE: AUTHOR'S CALCULATIONS FROM MADDISON TABLES, 3 YEAR
MOVING AVERAGE

the fact that the state bureaucrats who oversaw the planned economy during the ISI period in the late 1960s were also in charge of preparing Turkey's transition to neoliberalism in the 1980s (Öniş, 2010; Karatasli, 2015).

As the military coups of 1960, 1971, 1980, the 'post-modern coup' of 1997 and the recent failed coup attempt of July 15, 2016 illustrate, the development of Turkish politics has also been crisis-driven. Since the introduction of the multi-party elections after the Second World War, Turkey experienced a major *coup d'etat* almost in every decade until the 1980s and one major military intervention in almost every two decades since then. On the contrary, it is a manifestation that, in a semi-peripheral country like Turkey, similar to economy, bourgeois politics also faces periodic structural crises in the course of its development. One of the key dynamics behind these interventions is military commanders' and officers' belief that the prolonged political crisis cannot be resolved through existing political channels. Put differently, the Turkish military seems to share Joseph Schumpeter's (1942) dictum that "without protection from some non-bourgeois group, the bourgeoisie is politically helpless and unable not only to lead its nation but even to take care of its particular class interest" (p. 138).

Historically, the Turkish military has played this Schumpeterian 'protection' role by suppressing sections of new ruling elites whom they found 'deviant' (as in 1960 and in 1997) or by suppressing radicalized anti-systemic movements from below which existing ruling elites could no longer contain (as in 1971 and

1980). In these interventions, military commanders ousted existing govern-ments (as in 1971 and 1997) or temporarily took control of the state (as in 1960 and 1980). Periodic military coups in Turkey, then, played the role of 'tempo-ral fixes' aiming to resolve structural political crises, stalemates and political obstacles facing the development of bourgeois politics by containing radical-ized movements, transforming existing regime of governance, and sometimes by realigning Turkey within the sphere of influence of the world-hegemonic power in the international system. Similar to Harvey's (2005) 'temporal fixes' of capitalism, which temporarily solve the crisis of profitability by transform-ing the existing regime of accumulation, but by doing so prepare conditions of a deeper crisis, military coups in Turkey temporarily solved existing struc-tural political crises only by planting the seeds of a deeper crisis in the political sphere.

2.2 Neoliberal Transition and the Dual Crisis of the Turkish Republic

Like Chile's transition to neoliberalism in 1973, Turkey's transition to neolib-eralism in 1980 also occurred in the aftermath of a military coup. The 1980 coup aimed to end not only the escalation and violent confrontation of anti-systemic movements in Turkey, but to also end the deep economic crisis of 1978/9. Turgut Özal, who used to work in the State Planning Organization that was responsible for coordinating the ISI-based developmentalist policies fn the 1960s, became the key architect of Turkey's transition to neoliberalism. This first phase of Turkey's neoliberal transition under the Özal decade was left incomplete, as the privatization of state enterprises, the rapid commodi-fication of land, labor and services, and the opening of the capital account in 1989 triggered a vicious cycle of inflation, economic stagnation and political instability. This instability also strengthened Necmettin Erbakan's radical con-servative Islamist movement in the late 1990s, which demanded a return to industrial growth focused on an Islamist developmentalist model as opposed to Özal's neoliberal model. When Erbakan became the prime minister of Turkey (in 1996–1997) and signaled that he wanted a transformation of the secular Turkish nation-state towards an Islamist direction, it triggered a series of decisions expressed in a military memorandum in 1997 (aka the 'postmod-ern coup'). The 1997 coup had two major consequences. First, it escalated the vicious cycle of the 1990s by deepening the political and economic instabil-ities and preparing the preconditions for the 2001 economic crisis. Second, it prepared the preconditions for the ascension of Erdoğan's AKP. After the 1997 memorandum, a reformist section within Erbakan's Welfare Party with close links to the rising Anatolian-based 'Islamic bourgeoisie' abandoned the party. In a couple of years, this segment established the AKP as a center-right conservative party advocating a liberal market economy, globalization, an export-oriented growth strategy, and integration into the European Union.

As a newly formed political party, the Justice and Development Party (AKP) came to power after a deep economic and political crisis in Turkey. In 2001, Turkey was hit by a severe financial and currency crash. This led to the worst economic crisis in Turkey's history, resulting in a radical decline in GDP and employment (see Öniş, 2009; Ghoshal, 2006). The economic crisis had already been preceded by a political crisis and instability in which partners of the coalition government – the social democrat Democratic Left Party (DSP), ultra-nationalist Nationalist Action Party (MHP), and center-right Motherland Party (ANAP) – were in acute disagreement. The economic crisis further exacerbated the political crisis in Turkey and eroded the trust in the existing political parties, particularly those that were part of the coalition government (Figure 2.2).

This dual crisis paved the way for the unstoppable rise of the AKP, led by Recep Tayyip Erdoğan, in the early 21st century. Shortly after the disastrous 2001 economic crisis, the newly-founded AKP won a sweeping victory in November 2002, gaining 34.26% of the votes and a two-third majority of seats in parliament. All parties that belonged to the previous coalition government failed to win seats. Since then, the AKP has won almost all elections in Turkey by securing the majority of popular votes, which in turn has granted them executive power for over two decades. These two decades have been critical for Erdoğan to sustain his popular power while fundamentally transforming

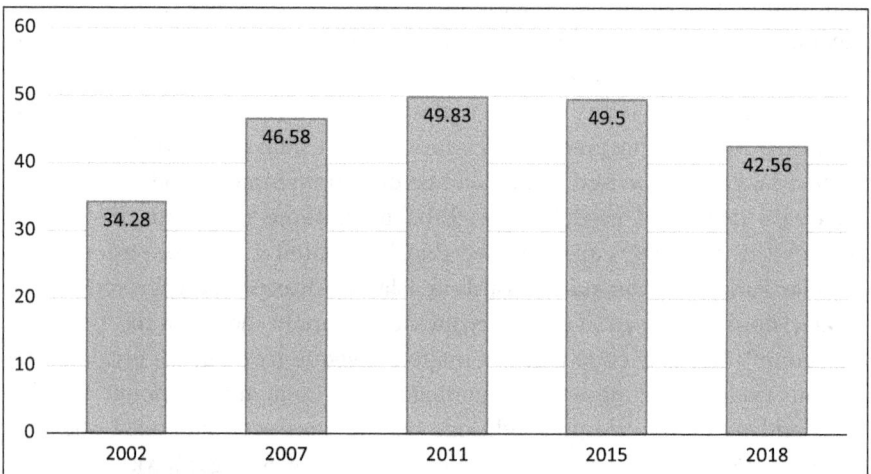

FIGURE 2.2   Popular votes for the AKP in general elections, 2002, 2007, 2011, 2015, 2018
SOURCE: TURKISH INSTITUTE FOR STATISTICS

the regime. In the following sections, I will discuss various strategies of legitimation of Erdoğan's new mass-based authoritarianism.

3   Strategies of Legitimation

3.1   *Building Consent through Anti-elitism, Neoliberal Developmentalism, New Nationalism, and Strategic Coalition Building*

In the 2002 elections, the AKP was not the only new party in the electoral arena that was trying to capitalize on the dual crisis. Yet, it was the only party that successfully managed to do so. This is precisely why the AKP's rise and consolidation of power cannot be explained through macro-structural dynamics alone. To explain this phenomenon, we need to have a closer look at various strategies used by the AKP.

One of the fundamental characteristics of Erdoğan's AKP has been sustaining the popular support it received from the population, both in the electoral arena and beyond. The AKP, and particularly Erdoğan as its leader, was able to garner a stable and committed following from the popular masses. Frequently administered opinion polls not only revealed the growing support for Erdoğan and the AKP throughout the 2000s and 2010s, but they also revealed a deep level of commitment from the populace. Various crises, such as the Gezi uprising in 2013 and, also in 2013, a great corruption scandal known as the 17–25 December 2013 events, were unable to shake this popular support. The reaction to the 2016 military coup attempt against the AKP government showed the violent aspect of this committed popular support as thousands of Erdoğanist supporters lynched and beheaded soldiers in the streets. While this popular support has started to decline with Turkey's most recent economic crisis (the 2018–2022 currency and debt crisis) that is still unfolding, Erdoğan's and the AKP's long term popular support has defined the last two decades of Turkish politics.

Erdoğan's AKP utilized a variety of strategies to garner and sustain this majority popular support to remain in political power. Different from mainstream political parties that engage in electoral politics, it sustained the constant politicization of its support base beyond elections through combining (1) anti-elitism with popular mobilization, (2) neoliberal developmentalism with a new nationalist rhetoric centered around creating a new Turkey as a global rising power, and (3) political and ideological flexibility with strategic coalition building with diverse political groups in subsequent elections.

3.1.1   Anti-elitism and Popular Mobilization

From the onset, Erdoğan's political discourse and political style were marked by a combination of anti-elitism and popular mobilization. Even before his so-called authoritarian turn, Erdoğan exhibited a strong anti-establishment and anti-elite rhetoric that framed him as the real representative of ordinary people. Even before the 2002 elections, in political rallies, he did not hesitate to highlight this rhetoric anytime he had a chance.

> My story is the story of this people. Either the people will win and come to power, or the pretentious and oppressive minority – estranged from the reality of Anatolia and looking over it with disdain – will remain in power. The authority to decide on this belongs to the people. Enough is enough, sovereignty belongs to the people!
>
> ERDOĞAN, quoted in AYTAÇ and ÖNIŞ, 2014:45

Who constitutes this 'people' that has hitherto been ruled by a pretentious and oppressed elite? To answer this question, Figure 2.3 shows different dimensions of Erdoğan's and the AKP's social base. As Figure 2.3 shows, Erdoğan and the AKP managed to attract the support of many oppressed, exploited and excluded sections of Turkish society as its support throughout the 2000s was mainly composed of the economically vulnerable (bottom 50 percent income-earners), the least educated populations and religious conservatives. Erdoğan and the AKP also managed to attract more votes from women, and – especially in AKP's initial years in power – the Kurdish minority population. Also,

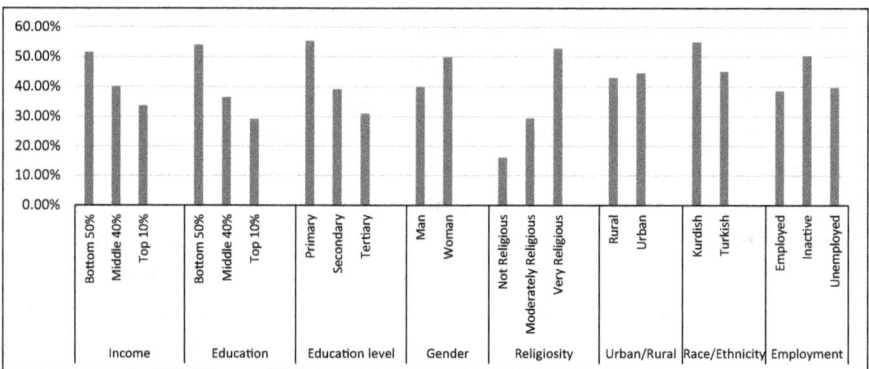

FIGURE 2.3   Categorization of popular support for the AKP
SOURCE: AUTHOR'S CALCULATIONS FROM WORLD POLITICAL CLEAVAGES AND INEQUALITY DATABASE, WPID.WORLD. (GETHIN, MARTINEZ-TOLEDANO AND PIKETTY, 2021)

Erdoğan and the AKP managed to attract more votes from the economically inactive populations, i.e., the elderly, the disabled etc.

Erdoğan championed himself as the representative of these oppressed groups, whom they see as the 'losers' of Kemalist cultural modernity – such as low-educated, pious Muslims – and as excluded from the economic and political privileges enjoyed by the urban, secular and educated minority under the Kemalist regime. According to a nation-wide survey, only 11% of the AKP voters/supporters view themselves as 'modern.' (Konda, 2018). The intersection of this modern lifestyle and class/income level is expressed by an AKP supporter as follows: "I think modern means the life of the rich. Because their rich activities cannot help me ... it means more expenses." (Male, 48)[4] Erdoğan's populist rhetoric was aided by his unusually populist political style. This populist political style, which enabled him to forge strong bonds with ordinary people, was grounded in his movement background. As mentioned earlier, Erdoğan came from the ranks of Erbakan's Islamist *Refah Partisi* (Welfare Party), a grassroots Islamist social movement that forged strong networks among working-class neighborhoods throughout the 1980s and 1990s. Erdoğan's community-organizer background was already visible during his unusual electoral campaign for mayor of Istanbul in 1994. Quite different from a regular politician, he knocked on the doors of people from all walks of life during the campaign. He expanded on this strategy by maintaining dynamic and direct interactions with ordinary people during the 2022 general elections and afterwards. Erdoğan skillfully mobilized his support base through the *constant politicization and polarization of the population* (see Altınörs and Akçay 2022). Erdoğan, from his first day in power, has constantly utilized a Manichean world-view (Elçi, 2019) and strategy towards his political competitors and engaged in active political propaganda against his political 'enemies.'[5]

---

4   KONDA, 2018.
5   Initially, the *political enemy* was the political and bureaucratic representation of Kemalist politics in Turkey. More specifically, Erdoğan engaged in a dynamic and never-ending political campaign against the Republican Party and its then and current leader, Kemal Kilicdaroglu. Since then, they mobilized masses through a constant political campaign against political enemies by explicitly targeting different political groups and mobilizing nationwide political campaigns against these groups. Political enemies came from diverse camps. Kemalist bureaucrats, army officials and politicians were targeted through a politicized trial process entitled Ergenekon trials (2008–2016) against what was claimed to be an organization to overthrow the government. Kurdish political parties and politicians were more openly targeted particularly after the 2014 Kobani Protests and the failure of the peace process. Furthermore, an Islamist organization associated with Fethullah Gülen, an old-time close ally of the government and now called as "Feto", became the main political enemy after the coup attempt in 2016.

The AKP's populist politics, marked by anti-elitism, resonated with large segments of the working class. Erdoğan also championed himself as the protector of the 'poor' through the massive yet informal distribution of resources to working class districts, which enabled him to forge patrimonial links with informal workers, the unemployed, and the precariat through neoliberal developmentalism.

3.1.2 Neoliberal Developmentalism and New Nationalism

The AKP's neoliberal developmentalism, particularly in its first decade in power, was key to building the economic foundations of the new regime. This economic model not only enabled the AKP to gain the support of a cross-class alliance that it needed in its initial years in power, but it also enabled Erdoğan to consolidate his social base.

Upon coming to power in 2002, the AKP continued and further deepened Turkey's neoliberal transition through the complete privatization of state-owned enterprises, further integration into the global economy, and the increasing flexibility of labor markets (see Öniş, 2011; Akçay, 2018; Erol, 2016). In this first decade of the AKP/Erdoğan regime, Turkey became a major location of global capital flows and was framed as a model of Muslim capitalist democracy. In this period, economic performance was characterized by "good growth coupled with single digit inflation for the first time for several decades" (Öniş and G ü ven 2011: 55). The economic stability of this decade was in complete contrast to the 1990s, which was marked by low growth, high inflation, and economic instability linked to the debt crisis. Furthermore, while unemployment levels rose in this first decade of AKP rule due to privatizations and labor reforms, income inequality actually declined (Karatasli 2015), mainly due to cash transfers (Akçay, 2018, Karatasli, 2015) as well as the informal welfare and redistribution that the AKP pursued through its patrimonial ties. Finally, international credit was channeled to large scale construction projects, which formed the basis of Erdoğan's construction-based growth regime that entailed some of world's largest public-private partnership schemes (see Kumral, 2022).

The particular regime of accumulation and distribution during the Erdoğan era, coupled with social and political transformations, enabled Erdoğan to secure the support of the masses as well as to transform the class structure that was key to create his hegemonic bloc. First and foremost, the AKP was able to secure the support of the working-class masses despite rising unemployment and precarity thanks to economic growth during the AKP's 'golden years,' informal redistribution schemes, and cash transfers. Relatedly, the AKP's neoliberal developmentalism also led to the rise of a new aspirational middle class in Turkey. This group mainly comes from the aforementioned underprivileged and often excluded conservative populations. In addition to benefiting from rising levels of income and consumption, this new middle class also bene-fited from the socio-political re-distribution of resources and status as part of Turkey's political and social transformation under AKP rule. For the first time, this particular group, which did not fit in with the conventional 'modern' and secular citizens/middle classes, found it possible to obtain state employment and become bureaucrats, judges, and teachers, and finally replicate the con-sumption patterns of the secular middle classes in their own ways.[6]

The AKP regime also undersaw a major transformation in Turkey's bour-geoisie. While Turkey's secular Istanbul-based bourgeoisie (mainly from the industrial and financial sectors) supported the AKP in its initial years due to the party's commitment to neoliberal economic policies, this support was not long-lived. The increasing rift between big capital and Erdoğan unfolded espe-cially during the anti-governmental uprising in 2013, whereby some of the key capitalists openly supported and participated in the protests. While in power, as part of its construction-based growth regime, Erdoğan's AKP produced its own loyal bourgeoisie through enabling five companies (i.e. Cengiz, Limak, Kolin, Kalyon, MNG), also known as the 'gang of five' (Kumral, 2022) to rapidly accumulate wealth.

While Erdoğan's neoliberal developmentalism and construction-based growth regime helped him to gain the support of the large masses, the limits and contradictions of this model were crucial to the regime's eventual authori-tarian turn. In direct contrast with its first decade, AKP rule in its second decade witnessed low growth, high inflation, and one of the biggest currency crises in the history of modern Turkey. As Altınörs and Akçay (2022) argue, AKP's 'authoritarian neoliberalism' eventually led to a crisis, resulting in the authori-tarian fix and consolidation of the regime in its second decade in power.

An important pillar of Erdoğan's neoliberal developmentalism is economic nationalism coupled with geopolitical aspirations. In a global context of declining US hegemony and changing economic and geopolitical power struc-tures, the AKP framed itself as the first party that can actually make Turkey a global economic power and a regional hegemon in the Middle East. High

---

6 The secular/modern middle classes also rose in this period, mainly in big cities like Istanbul, with Turkey's increasing integration with global economy. As opposed to the "new/rising" middle classes, this secular/modern middle class felt increasingly threatened that they may lose their positions in social and cultural arenas despite growing in numbers in this period. This uncertainty regarding the future of the secular/modern middle classes guided their vast participation in the Gezi Uprising of 2013, which was the biggest anti-government uprising in the history of modern Turkey.

growth rates in the first decade of the AKP rule were often presented as proof of Turkey's rise as an economic power and mega-construction projects (such as Europe's largest airport, etc.) were presented as its physical manifestations. Growth-related promises and large-scale construction projects are often utilized as propaganda materials in Turkey's race with the developed world.

Furthermore, the AKP's first decade in power was a period when Turkey adopted the image of the new leader of the Middle East in a newfound neo-Ottomanism (also see Arat-Koç and Sundar, 2021; Kumral, 2022). This was a period when U.S. policy-makers also believed that the 'Turkish model' (Tuğal, 2016) could be a model of Muslim-democracy to be exported to other countries in the Middle East. Various societal and geopolitical crises in the Middle East, such as the Arab Spring, the Syrian Civil War and the Civil War in Libya, provided further opportunities for Turkey to showcase Erdoğan's AKP as a counterpoint, thus increasing its influence. In one such instance, Erdoğan clashed with Israeli President, Shimon Peres, over Gaza during Davos meetings in 2009. This symbolic and pragmatic move made Erdoğan "a hero in the Muslim world, where he is seen as the new Nasser" (Rosen 2010). Turkey also became an active party in the civil war in Syria by providing crucial support for the formation of the anti-Assad *Free Syrian Army* (Hinnebusch, 2015). In the course of the civil war, Turkey engaged in various cross-border operations in Syria, mainly targeting the autonomous Kurdish region formed during the Syrian Civil War. Erdoğan even skillfully utilized the Syrian refugee crisis to increase his power over international relations. Aside from Syria, Turkey became militarily involved in the Libyan Civil War. Erdoğan also utilized various social uprisings in the region to extend his symbolic populist influence over broader Muslim communities in the Middle East. This active and symbolic involvement in regional politics enabled Erdoğan to be viewed as a strong leader, not only in Turkey, but also among the broader Muslim regional community.

3.1.3   Political Flexibility and Strategic Coalition-Building

While Erdoğan's neoliberal developmentalism in his early years in power enabled him to gain the substantial support of the working-class and 'neo-middle classes', his quest for the majority of votes in elections led him to make temporary coalitions with a variety of competitive political parties and groups. These included unlikely allies such as the secular bourgeoisie, the Kurds, and certain sections of the Left in the early years; some sections of the nationalist Kemalists in the later years; and the ultra-nationalist Nationalist Action Party (*Milliyetçi Hareket Partisi*, MHP) around a common cause. This pragmatic coalition-building approach was not alien to the AKP, which itself was formed by bringing together different elements of the Turkish right in a new political party. The AKP, in its formative years, incorporated reformist elements of the Islamist movement and its political component, the Welfare Party (Refah Partisi, RP), as well as cadres of major center-right political parties of the 1990s and cadres from the ultra-nationalist MHP.

In its initial years, the AKP was able to get electoral support from the wider middle classes as well as the Istanbul-based, big industrial and financial bourgeoisie due to its commitment to neoliberalism and the EU accession process. AKP's commitment to the EU accession process entailed the implementation of democratic reform packages which pertained to the limiting the military's role as well as expanding the rights of minorities, particularly Kurds. The AKP's short-lived moves towards expanding democracy and a 'Kurdish opening' temporarily attracted Kurdish votes, which was critical for the AKP to secure a majority of seats in parliamentary elections.

In addition to the support that Erdoğan received from these different groups, AKP's first decade in power was marked by its partnership with the *Gülen movement*. It can also be argued that the military memorandum of 1997 prepared the conditions for the Erdoğan-Gülen alliance, which was instrumental to the rise of the AKP. Centered around a reformist Muslim preacher named Fethullah Gülen, the Gülen movement (aka the Hizmet movement or Cemaat/ Jamaat in popular language) started to organize in the 1970s and extended their operations during the 'Ozal decade' after the 1980 military coup. By the 1990s, it managed to become the largest Islamic network in Turkey. In the course of its slow but steady development, the Gülen movement gained control over many resources that Erdoğan and his circle never had, including informal networks of people in the state bureaucracy, judiciary, police and military. In addition, the Gülen movement gained command over well-connected grassroots organizations in urban and rural neighborhoods, influence over thousands of schools and businesses in Turkey and around the world, and vast financial resources based on export-oriented business enterprises (establishing the backbone of the Islamic bourgeoisie) in Anatolia.

The Erdoğan-Gülen alliance was mutually beneficial in the early years of the AKP. To secure a degree of protection from the state bureaucracy, Erdoğan needed Gülen, and to expand its political influence beyond its own organizational network, Gülen needed Erdoğan. Consequently, during the early AKP rule, Erdoğan and his circle embraced the Gülen movement and opened unprecedented opportunities in the political sphere for their organization, capital accumulation, and further penetration in state apparatus (including Turkish intelligence, the police, and the military). The Erdoğan-Gülen alliance also became one of the factors that brought the AKP towards a pro-U.S. line and securing U.S. support in the AKP's early years.

More importantly, however, this alliance played a key role in the eradication of high-ranking hardline secularist commanders and officers from the Turkish military. According to the claims of the Erdoğan-Gülen alliance, some of these top military commanders were a part of a clandestine organization – named 'Ergenekon' – and they planned a series of military conspiracies against Erdoğan in 2003–2004, including the alleged Balyoz (Sledgehammer), Sarıkız, Ayışığı, Yakamoz, and Eldiven coup d'état attempts. Based on these allegations, starting in 2007, the Erdoğan-Gülen alliance began arresting and expelling many top secularist military commanders and officers from the Turkish military and installing a new section of military officers, many of whom were close to the Gülen community.

The partnership with the Gülen movement petered out in the second decade of the AKP rule. The tension between these partners first became publicly visible during the 2013 Gezi uprising, where Erdoğan pointed towards the Gülen movement's role in stirring up anti-government sentiments through police violence. The tension escalated during the government corruption scandal in December 2013, where the Gülen movement played a key role by leaking recordings that implicated top ranking AKP officials in corruption, including Erdoğan. The tension reached its peak during and after the coup attempt, which was led by Gülen-associated military officials. After the coup attempt, the government declared the Gülen movement the 'Fethullah Teror Orgutu' (FETO, Fethullah Terror Organization) and people suspected to be associated with the movement were detained.

The 2016 coup attempt started a new period for the Erdoğan regime in terms of his political alliances. From 2016 onwards, the *Nationalist Action Party* (*Milliyetci Hareket Partisi, MHP*) became Erdoğan regime's junior ally. They engaged in an electoral coalition since 2018, known as the Cumhur İttifakı (People's Alliance). As an ultra-nationalist far-right party, the MHP used to be one of the ardent opposition figures to Erdoğan in his first decade in power. As Erdoğan had already lost his vote base among the Kurdish population, the votes of the MHP have been central for Erdoğan to gain an electoral majority in both parliamentary and presidential elections. Furthermore, this far-right coalition went beyond the electoral coalition between the AKP and MHP and incorporated ultra-nationalist politicians and patriotic organizations that have key positions within the state bureaucracy. These coalition partners gave further impetus to the nationalist and authoritarian tendencies of the Erdoğan regime and intensified the crackdown on the Kurdish movement and the left. As the former ally, Gülen, became the new enemy, Erdoğan managed to reestablish links and to secure a pragmatic alliance with Ergenekonist military commanders who had been previously imprisoned by the Gülenist cadres within the state bureuacracy. Finally, to sustain his electoral hegemony, Erdoğan further strengthened his relationship with the various *tariqas*, i.e., religious organizations/networks, giving way to their increasing presence and influence. While the prominent nationalist and religious personalities of Erdoğan regime were present even from the beginning of his rule, the post-coup alliances further intensified their influence, and they came to dominate the increasingly religious ideological framing of the new regime. The pragmatic approach to ideology as well as coalition-building led the AKP regime to transform through time and frame itself in different forms.

3.2   *Exercising Coercion: Rise of the Authoritarian Democracy*
3.2.1   Centralization of Power and Repression of Opposition
Sharing the characteristics of modern populists, Erdoğan targeted the power of the parliament and the judiciary, gradually centralizing power (see Finchelstein, 2019). Despite the importance he attributed to electoral support and popular legitimacy for his power, Erdoğan radically transformed existing political institutions to enable the centralization of power in the hands of the executive vis-à-vis the parliament, local governments, and the bureaucracy (particularly the judiciary and military). In the introduction to his victory speech following the AKP's electoral victory in the 2014 local elections, Erdoğan was described as "the loud voice of the oppressed in this world, [and ...] the leader that recognizes no one but the [will] of the nation." (Topçu, 2014). This description shows how Erdoğan, as the leader, is perceived as the embodiment of the will of the nation and is considered above all institutions and actors in a democratic regime. Within this framework, Erdoğan undertook a slow but radical transformation of the political structure in Turkey while keeping the electoral process intact.

Though a long and gradual process, this centralization was formalized by a constitutional referendum in 2017, which replaced Turkey's parliamentary system with a presidential system and gave Erdoğan massive powers as the chief executive. Executive control over the judiciary further strengthened in 2018, when the president gained the new power "to rule by decree and appoint judges" (Freedom House, 2019). In this process of centralizing power, Erdoğan also solidified his power within the Justice and Development Party and embraced a patrimonial form of leadership where he appointed his close family members to key posts within the party, while expelling the old cadres.

Parallel to this transformation of existing political institutions to centralize decision-making power in Erdoğan's hands, the political opposition has increasingly been treated as enemies of the state and subjected to persecution. The leaders and MPs of some opposition parties, mass democratic

organizations, independent media outlets, and journalists are marked as enemies and imprisoned without legal charges or trials. The group that has been
most affected by this repression has been the Kurds. While Kurdish parties
faced party bans and mass arrests throughout the 2000s, the crackdown on
the Kurdish movement increased as Kurdish political parties increased their
electoral support and political power. On the one hand, elected local officials
(at the municipal level) from opposition parties, mostly in the Kurdish regions,
were purged and were forcefully replaced by individuals appointed by the government. Selahattin Demirtas, the presidential candidate of the pro-Kurdish
People's Democracy Party (HDP) whose campaign in the 2015 elections was
built around the slogan "We will not make you the President", obviously referring to Erdoğan, was detained along with most of the other Kurdish MPs.

Erdoğan's crackdown on opposition politicians gained momentum after
the 2016 coup attempt and the state of emergency declared afterward. This
period witnessed mass arrests of the Gülen movement, whose members in
the military were key in organizing the coup attempt. This conflict between
old allies became an excuse for Erdoğan to further persecute other groups in
the political opposition. Political arrests went beyond those affiliated with the
Gülen movement/FETO, and the repression of all forms of opposition further
became increasingly common and associated with 'terror'. As of 2020, 58,409
people have been on trial for terrorism linked to the Gülen movement, "25,012
were held in prison on remand," and at least 8,500 people, including elected
politicians, were on remand for alleged links to the PKK (Human Rights Watch,
2021). To summarize, Erdoğan has increasingly secured his absolute power by
undermining the role of state institutions, political parties (both opposition
parties and his own Justice and Development Party), and civil society and mass
organizations, while keeping the electoral process intact.

3.2.2   Extension and Diversification of Violence

In addition to state repression towards actual and possible opposition from different groups, Erdoğan's regime has radically transformed the forms of political violence in Turkey. Key tenets of this process have been the unmaking of
the military as an institution, Erdoğan's attempt at building new security forces
he can control, and finally, the institutionalization of paramilitary violence.

Erdoğan and the AKP's first decade in power was marked by the unmaking
of the power of the military over Turkish politics. Responsible for three military coups and a post-modern military coup in the 20th century, the military
has considered itself to be the "greatest supporters and devoted guardians of
Turkey's Kemalist, modern, secular, democratic character," as stated by the
Chief of the Turkish General Staff in November 2006 (Karabelias, 2009: 57).

In its early years, the AKP passed constitutional amendments limiting the power of the military. As the tension between the AKP government and the military escalated, high-ranking military officials were imprisoned as part of the 'Ergenekon Terror Trials,' and a coup plot against the government.[7] Despite decreasing the role of the Kemalists within the military, Erdoğan was not successful enough to maintain his own power over this key institution, as revealed by the 2016 coup attempt. Furthermore, the police forces also were infamously filled with *Gülenist* cadres. Hence, a key obstacle limiting Erdoğan's power was the lack of committed support from the military and security forces.

No revolution, even passive ones, can be won without the power of the military and security forces. Erdoğan utilized multiple strategies to build new security forces which radically transformed institutions and forms of political violence in Turkey. This new security regime incorporated a "network of security structures that includes military contractors, political party clubs, and a newly militant and mobilized AKP base" (Eissenstat, 2017: 1). Not surprisingly, this new structure resembled other tenets of Erdoğan's new regime, such as its close links with private companies and civil mobilization. On the one hand, Erdoğan trained and raised security forces that are loyal to his political project through the help of SADAT, a Turkish military contractor that upholds Islamist and nationalist ideals (see Eissenstat, 2017; Karmon and Barak, 2018). Not being part of the formal armed forces, the new paramilitary groups trained by SADAT played significant roles not only in domestic politics but also in Turkey's involvement in the conflicts in Syria and Libya (Taş, 2020), aiding Erdoğan's neo-Ottomanist project. While often compared to Iran's Revolutionary Guards (see Karmon and Barak, 2018) due to its expansionist-Islamist discourse and its active involvement in regional conflicts, the SADAT company and its relationship with Erdoğan regime have a more striking resemblance to Putin's Private Army.

Erdoğan's regime further enabled, supported, and formed organizations that promote civil and paramilitary violence towards the domestic political opposition. It would not be an exaggeration to state that Erdoğan has started to emulate the fascist strategy, by directing horizontal violence against mass movements that challenge his authority (see Kumral 2018). He started to openly embrace civilian and paramilitary violence during the 2013 Gezi uprising, when he praised shopkeepers who attacked protesters, calling them "the police, the soldier, the guardian of the neighborhood, when necessary" (Cumhuriyet, 2014).

---

7   Despite the problematic judicial process, most sections of Turkish society welcomed the outcome of a decreased military role over politics, which has been the Achilles heel of Turkish democracy since its foundation.

The 'riot strategy' was particularly visible in post-election anti-Kurdish riots in September 2015, whereby Erdoğan incited riots to activate anti-Kurdish hostility before the elections. In various cities, the violence was led by a relatively new organization called Osmanlı Ocakları (Hearths of the Ottoman) formed in 2009, which has organic links with the AKP and considers its members to be 'soldiers of Recep T. Erdoğan' (Kumral, 2018; also see Eissenstat, 2017). The increasing salience of this new paramilitary organization bears a remarkable resemblance to *ülkü ocakları* (Hearth of Idealists), the youth branch of quasi-fascist Nationalist Action Party (Milliyetci Hareket Partisi, MHP, see Kumral, 2017), who has been Erdoğan's ally in power since 2016. This organizational and strategic emulation further indicates how Erdoğan has started to copy fascist organizational forms. Erdoğan's directing popular masses and semi-organized groups towards political violence was most visible in the 2016 coup attempt, whereby popular demonstrations against the soldiers led to lynching and public beheadings of soldiers that participated in the coup attempts.

4   Conclusion: Cracks and Resistances

There seems to be almost a consensus among media pundits and the general public about the increasing strength of Erdoğan and the AKP. Unlike as is widely assumed, however, Erdoğan's increasing authoritarian tendencies are rooted not in its increasing strength, but rather in the radical weakening and alienation of the AKP in both the national and international spheres. A clear indicator of this weakening is the dissolution of alliances the AKP had established with other factions of ruling elites and international powers.

Today, the AKP seems to have lost almost all support it used to receive from great powers in the international arena. In its first decade, the United States and other Western allies promoted the AKP as a champion of democracy and an ideal model for Middle Eastern countries (see Tuğal, 2016). In return, Erdoğan's AKP did its best to play the role of a useful ally for Washington. Turkey helped the U.S. armed forces and NATO in various military operations in North Africa and the Middle East, gladly played the role of a negotiator between the United States and many Middle Eastern countries, reinforced the idea that political Islam and global capitalism were not incompatible, and aimed to contain the 'Kurdish threat' in the region through partially extending democratic rights and liberties.

These trends, however, have completely changed. Starting with 2008/9, but more explicitly since the 2013 Gezi protests, Erdoğan has been perceived by the U.S. and most of the Western world as an unpredictable ruler with authoritarian tendencies. The United States and Turkey find their interests in conflict in many key geopolitical issues in the Middle East, including the Syrian crisis, how to fight against the ISIS, how to deal with Kurds in Rojava (Syria) and in Turkey, and the Israel-Palestine conflict.

While Erdoğan's AKP continues to lose support from its international allies, its polarizing politics and increasing authoritarianism have led to resistance from different groups domestically. The most notable resistance to Erdoğan's AKP has been the Gezi Uprising in 2013, which was the biggest anti-government uprising in the history of modern Turkey. Despite its scale, this anti-government/ anti-Erdoğan revolt was crushed and was followed by increased repression of the opposition. Another major source of opposition to Erdoğan's rule came from the Kurdish movement in Turkey. On one hand, the vibrant Kurdish movement ceased to be a party that merely emphasized the political inclusion of the Kurdish minority, but rather came to represent a wider democratiza-tion project through an alliance with some elements of the Turkish left. Since the 2000s, the Kurdish democratic movement increased its political power and mobilization in various parts of Turkey, including those beyond Kurdish-dominant provinces. Through social movement mobilization and coalition-building with the Turkish left, feminist movement, and the LGBTQ movement, pro-Kurdish political parties have been significant challengers of the Erdoğan regime. The pro-Kurdish Halkin Demokrasi Partisi (People's Democratic Party, HDP) became the center of the opposition to Erdoğan's quest to centralize executive power. With the campaign 'We will not make you [Erdoğan] become the President,' the HDP succeeded in gaining 13.12% of the popular vote in the June 2015 general elections and 10.76% of the votes in the November 2015 elec-tions; surpassing the 10% electoral threshold which enabled the party to send representatives to the parliament. The HDP continued to sustain its electoral success, gaining 11.70% of the popular vote in the 2018 parliamentary elections and becoming the third-largest party in parliament. The regime's response to this electoral success was the repression and imprisonment of HDP party lead-ers and members, and the constant threat of a party ban.

Erdoğan's increasing authoritarianism created a specific form of reaction in the Kurdish provinces. In what was called the 'City Wars' in 2015, major cities in the Kurdish region experienced violent clashes between state forces and the Kurdish youth that created units to defend themselves against the Turkish military and regime-backed paramilitary organizations as well as push for autonomy. The massive military operation led by the Turkish military and Erdoğan's newly formed paramilitary groups – composed of ultra-nationalists and Islamists – brutally repressed this revolt, leading to the near destruction of whole districts and towns in the Kurdish region, civilian deaths, and the forced migration of thousands of people. This brutal repression in the Kurdish region created reactions from different segments of Turkish society. A group of academics wrote and signed a petition, the *'Academics for peace petition'* calling for an end to the war in the Kurdish region. They have since become victims of the largest academic witch hunt in the history of Turkey, with hundreds of academics removed from their positions and exiled while many others were arrested.

Signals of opposition strength, in most cases, has further led Erdoğan to repress the opposition and social movement mobilization. This has led to a visible decline in social protest action in the Turkish socio-political scene. Despite the decline in overall protest mobilization, popular protest continues sporadically in the form of strikes and workplace unrest, large-scale March 8 International Worker Women's Day demonstrations, and LGBTQIA+ pride marches. People are filling various 'cracks' in the system to manifest their opposition in other ways as well – including organizing against arbitrary firings and unlawful arrests and establishing cooperatives in the middle of cities to build solidarity around creating a more sustainable and democratic way of life. Mobilization around discontent has also been on the rise among AKP's electoral base. The catastrophic outcomes of AKP's neoliberalism led to rural-based environmental protests led by villagers to protect their land, water, and natural resources from AKP-backed private companies. Finally, the recent economic crisis with declining growth and skyrocketing inflation has led to increasing discontent among AKP's electorate, though this growing discontent has not yet turned into popular mobilization. In recent years, a new coalition of center-right parties that includes the Republican Party is trying to tap into this discontent for the eventual electoral defeat of the AKP. Despite this growing discontent at many layers, the Turkish political scene still lacks a viable progressive alternative to garner support from these different groups and provide a strong response to Erdoğan's authoritarianism.

References

Akçay Ü (2018) Neoliberal Populism in Turkey and Its Crisis. *Institute for International Political Economy Berlin, Working Paper 100.*

Altınörs G and Akçay Ü (2022) Authoritarian neoliberalism, crisis, and consolidation: the political economy of regime change in Turkey. *Globalizations*: 1–25. https://www.tandfonline.com/doi/full/10.1080/14747731.2021.2025290?casa_token=k6gADdGaffwAAAAA%3ArIX7yjLvsVvCDvpqkty_Y3vChL9vl7P7OiQbetCehKB4aCoKa6lkBZLxvFH-NKfbWHdvJ5jvIwh9rCw.

Arat-Koç S and Sundar A (2020) Rising Powers and Authoritarian Populism. *Augmenting the Left.* Halifax: Fernwood.

Aytaç S E and Öniş Z (2014) Varieties of populism in a changing global context. *Comparative Politics,* 47(1): 41–59.

Bardakçi M (2013) Coup plots and the transformation of civil–military relations in Turkey under AKP rule. *Turkish Studies,* 14(3): 411–428.

Cumhuriyet (2014) Erdoğan vicdansızlığını bir kez daha gösterdi. *Cumhuriyet Gazetesi,* 26 November 2019. Available at: https://www.cumhuriyet.com.tr/haber/erdogan -vicdansizligini-bir-kez-daha-gosterdi-150279

Eissenstat H (2017) Uneasy Rests the Crown: Erdoğan and 'Revolutionary Security'In Turkey. *Project on Middle East Democracy, December 2017,* Available at: https:// pomed.org/wp-content/uploads/2017/12/Eissenstat_171220_FINAL.pdf.

Elçi E (2019) The rise of populism in Turkey: a content analysis. *Southeast European and Black Sea Studies,* 19(3): 387–408.

Erol M E (2016) Authoritarian but Flexible: Turkey and recent labour market reforms. *SPERI. 6 June, 2016,* Available at: http://speri.dept.shef.ac.uk/2016/06/06/authoritar ian-but-flexible-turkey-and-recent-labour-market-reforms/.

Finchelstein F (2019) *From Fascim to Populism in History.* University of California Press.

Freedom House (2019) *Freedom in the World 2019: Turkey.* Retrieved from: https://freed omhouse.org/country/turkey/freedom-world/2019.

Gethin A, Martínez-Toledano C and Piketty T (2021) *Political Cleavages and Social Inequalities: A Study of Fifty Democracies, 1948–2020.* Harvard University Press.

Ghoshal A (2006) Anatomy of a currency crisis: Turkey 2000–2001. *International Journal of emerging markets,* 1(2): 176–189.

Gürsoy Y (2012) The changing role of the military in Turkish politics: democratization through coup plots? *Democratization,* 19(4): 735–760.

Harvey D (2005) *A Brief History of Neoliberalism.* Oxford: Oxford University Press.

Hinnebusch R (2015) Back to enmity: Turkey-Syria relations since the Syrian Uprising. *Orient, Journal of German Orient Institute,* 56(1): 14–22.

Human Rights Watch (2021) "Turkey: Events of 2020". Available at: https://www.hrw .org/world-report/2021/country-chapters/turkey.

Karabelias G (2009) The military institution, Atatürk's principles, and Turkey's Sisyphean quest for democracy. *Middle Eastern Studies,* 45(1): 57–69.

Karataşlı S (2015) The Origins of Turkey's "Heterodox" Transition to Neoliberalism. *Journal of World-Systems Research,* 21(2): 387–416.

Karmon E and Michael B (2018) Erdoğan's Turkey and the Palestinian Issue. *Perspectives on Terrorism,* 12(2): 74–85.

Konda (2018) *KONDA Secmen Kumeleri -AK Parti.* https://konda.com.tr/wp-content/ uploads/2018/05/KONDA_SecmenKumeleri_AkParti_Secmenleri_Mayis2018.pdf.

Kumral Ş (2017) Ballots with bullets: Elections, violence, and the rise of the extreme right in Turkey. *Journal of Labor and Society*, 20(2): 231–261.

Kumral Ş (2018) Democracy, Crisis and Geopolitics. *The Return of Geopolitics*. Liverlag.

Kumral Ş (2022) Globalization, crisis and right-wing populists in the Global South: the cases of India and Turkey. *Globalizations*: 1–30.

Öniş Z (2009) Beyond the 2001 financial crisis: The political economy of the new phase of neo-liberal restructuring in Turkey. *Review of International Political Economy*, 16(3): 409–432.

Öniş Z (2010) Crises and transformations in Turkish political economy. *Turkish Policy Quarterly*, 9(3): 45–61.

Öniş Z (2011) Power, Interests and Coalitions: The Political Economy of Mass Privatisation in Turkey. *Third World Quarterly*, 32(4):707–724.

Öniş Z and G ü ven A B (2011) Global Crisis, National Responses: The Political Economy of Turkish Exceptionalism. *New Political Economy*, 16(5): 585–608.

Rosen S J (2010) Erdoğan and the Israel Card. *Wall Street Journal, June 10, 2010*, Available at: https://www.wsj.com/articles/SB10001424052748703302604575294523287747404.

Schumpeter J (1942) *Capitalism, Socialism and Democracy*. New York: Harper Torchbooks.

Taş H (2020) The New Turkey and its Nascent Security Regime. *GIGA Focus Nahost, 6. Hamburg: GIGA German Institute of Global and Area Studies – Leibniz-Institut für Globale und Regionale Studien, Institut für Nahost-Studien*. Available at: https://nbn-resolving.org/urn:nbn:de:0168-ssoar-70612-3.

Topçu Ö (2014) Türkler onu neden seviyor? *Zeit Online. 11 April 2014*. Available at: https://www.zeit.de/politik/ausland/2014-04/Erdoğan-tuerkei-wahl-tuerkisch?utm_referrer=https%3A%2F%2Fwww.google.com%2F.

Tuğal C (2016) *The fall of the Turkish model*. Verso.

Zürcher E J (1992) The Ottoman Legacy of the Turkish Republic: An Attempt at a New Periodization. *Die Welt des Islams 2*: 237–253. Available at: https://www.jstor.org/stable/pdf/1570835.pdf?refreqid=excelsior%3A4c1c2172dee554a459ae6be7b83f9392&ab_segments=&origin=.

CHAPTER 3

Global Crisis and the Realignment of Eastern European Capitalist Class Alliances

The Case of Hungarian Illiberalism

Tamás Gerőcs and Ágnes Gagyi

This chapter discusses how Hungary's present authoritarian regime has emerged as a result of a transition that began with a state socialist, then post-socialist neoliberal regime transformation. This transformation affected state-class relations, political control of the state, and the reconfiguration of geopolitical relations with the European Union, Russia and China. The chapter examines how class tensions brewing under previous forms of neoliberal democratic parliamentary politics have been utilized to build the new illiberal hegemony, and how the present regime suppresses those tensions to sustain a reconstituted national bourgeoisie through the institutional centralization of political power.

1   Introduction

In the following chapter, we analyze the formation of Hungary's present authoritarian regime in terms of a reconfiguration during the country's integration into the present dynamics of a global capitalist crisis and transformation. Instead of merely focusing on the post-2010 Orbán regime's rollback of specific democratic institutions or its ideological tactics of legitimation, we analyze the regimes attempts to reconfigure internal-external capitalist class relations, with a view to global integration. We analyze this recent reconfiguration as part of a longer process of Hungary's global economic integration since the second half of the state socialist period, which, through different political regimes, has transformed Hungarian class relations as part of the "long downturn" (Brenner 2006) of the post-WWII global capitalist cycle (Arrighi 1990). Similar to Kumral and Karatasli (2020) or Jeffery Webber (2021), we do not approach the Hungarian case from the perspective of an ideological battle between democracy and authoritarianism, but more in terms of a socio-political history of semi-peripheral capitalist development whose typical tensions are exacerbated by its dependent integration into a crisis phase of global capitalism (cf. Gates 2018; Bello 2019). Unlike narratives that celebrate postsocialist liberalization as the victory of democracy over dictatorship, and then interpret the Orbán regime in terms of democratic backsliding; we want to show how both the socialist and post-socialist liberal regimes worked as temporarily effective ways to suppress social tensions arising from capitalist integration. Similar to Nicos Poulantzas' (1974) interpretation of fascism, we interpret Hungary's postsocialist authoritarian turn as a pragmatic buildup of cross-class alliances, social fragmentation and oppressive social control, which have enabled the authoritarian state to carry out a reconfiguration of global integration to the benefit of a (somewhat reorganized) internal-external capitalist alliance.

2   After 1956: A State Socialist Regime Built on Incorporating Labor and a Fragile East-West Trade Balance

Whilst the state socialist economy had already been embedded in relations of world trade and finance,[1] the direct reintegration of Hungary into the capitalist world-economy started with the crisis of the 1970s. In the 1960s, Hungary's post-war regime of accumulation was based on the "bridge-position" that the country occupied in international trade. The "bridge model" targeted trade specialization between Western capitalist and Comecon state socialist international commerce (Gerőcs and Pinkasz 2018a) and was also closely tied to a new economic paradigm built around a reconfiguration of the socialist regime after 1956 Revolution. This new economic stance integrated concessions to popular classes, with a compromise among the major economic factions in the country which were comprised of agrarian, industrial and energy lobby groups.

The reconfiguring of forces in the post-revolutionary period was a peculiar feature of the bridge-model. Historians generally refer to the model as the consolidation of the Kádár regime, referencing the socialist leader of Hungary from 1957 to 1989. The political compromise sought to fix the internal contradictions inherited from the Stalinist industry-heavy accumulation regime, by easing political pressure on opposing factions and promising better living standards for workers by focusing more on their consumption needs. The Hungarian Thaw, or as the western media mocked it "Goulash Communism," was a specific model of state socialist accumulation, built around an East-West trade-orientation and a political compromise of the major economic

---

1 State socialist regimes entailed social formations significantly different from capitalist ones, however these did not develop outside the confines of the capitalist world-system (cf. Bettelheim and Dobb 1965; Frank 1977; Chase-Dunn 1980).

lobby groups, including the Western-oriented agriculture. The incorporation of large segments of the working population by ideological, as well as material provisions, was another important feature of this model. The model, however proved in the long run to be very fragile owing to the complex and contradictory interests of its stakeholders. As the word-economic conditions deteriorated from the 1970s onwards, the fragility of the model culminated in evolving internal crises, both in the economic sphere as well as with regards to the political compromise. The latter half of the Kádár era was characterized by constant adjustment to changing economic circumstances in order to sustain the fragile balance among the major economic actors.

One peculiarity of the bridge model was Hungary's specialization in technology imports from the West. This exposed the country to international partners who demanded payment in convertible currency, while other Comecon members sustained more autarchic economic models, like the Soviet Union (Ban 2012; Gerőcs and Pinkasz 2018a, 2018b). Whilst Hungary's manufacturing exports also targeted the Comecon market, it was unable to produce enough currency to compensate for financial payments made to Western interests. To solve this problem, the bridge model prioritized the re-export of subsidized Soviet crude oil alongside traditional agrarian exports, as the most convenient way to produce convertible currency. International trade with the Global South was also favored in the 1960s and 70s, especially with allied countries in Africa and South-East Asia. Profitable terms of trade were a crucial requirement for the financial balance upon which the bridge model rested, meaning that the re-export of the Soviet crude oil had to produce a sufficient amount of currency to cover the costs of Western technology-imports. Without these financial arrangements the country would have had to rely on international loans to pay its trade bills.

As mentioned earlier, the bridge model rested upon the political compromise between three major economic lobby groups, the most dominant of which were the so-called industrial and agrarian factions (Berend 1996). It is worth noting that this type of economic structural division was a peculiar feature in the history of industrialization within the global semi-periphery during the early twentieth century (Wallerstein 1976). The roots of this structural division lay between the large agrarian exporters, such as those in Latin America, and large-scale urban industries who were commonly the product of the interwar protectionist tendencies (Cardoso 1972; Boatcă, 2006). The industrial oligarchy, supported by organized labor, usually favored state support in the form of subsidies and resource allocation, to nurture infant industries. The protectionism they developed during the early phase of import-substitution industrialization (ISI) during the 1930s-1940s was a favored policy tool. In contrast, the export-oriented agricultural and extractive sectors preferred liberal trade policies that aimed to sustain deeper integration in the capitalist world-economy (cf. Gereffi and Evans 1981).

In the case of the majority of the Comecon member states in the post-war era of the early 1950s, industrialization remained influenced by Stalinist war-preparation, and as a result, it came largely at the expense of agricultural production. Exploitation of the peasantry and the transformation of large estates into nationalized *kolkhoz*, were meant to serve the needs of industry and urbanization, both in terms of surplus extraction from agricultural production as well as the forceful transformation of the peasant class into a semi-proletarian labor force (Vigvári and Gerőcs 2018). As already mentioned, the post-revolution compromise was meant to appease the contradictory needs of both agriculture and industry and also pacify and reintegrate workers after their short-lived revolutionary initiatives. The agrarian lobby represented the needs of large state farms, agricultural collectives, and the growing number of informal entrepreneurs in the so-called second or informal economy; these groups were more interested in liberalized trade with their traditional Western partners.[2] Large industrial conglomerates were not necessarily opposed to international trade, but their products were usually marketable only within the Comecon and in the Global South (Bideleux 1996). The industrial faction was important not only because of the Comecon trade, but also because it was backed by the trade union confederation which was responsible for the pacification and incorporation of industrial workers – an important pillar of the political compromise in the Kádár era.

The compromise embodied in the 'bridge model' was highly sensitive, both in its external trade relations, as well as in the fragility of the agreement among the major political factions. The balance of payments and the terms of trade on which this model rested, were relatively favorable both in the Comecon and Western markets throughout the 1960s. The model however was ultimately overturned by the oil price shocks and the interest rate hikes of the 1970s. The economic impact of these crises resulted in negative terms of trade in both accounts – the socialist and the non-socialist –, creating a large gap in the country's overall balance of international payments.[3] The inevitable result of

---

2   They faced difficulties not only because of restrictive Comecon trade policies, but also because of barriers erected around the European Common Agricultural Market in the late 1960s.

3   Hungary's net foreign debt stood at 0.5 billion US dollar in 1971 but it quickly piled up to 14.9 billion USD by 1989. According to Lóránt's estimations Hungary managed to withdraw 1.2 billion USD for its fiscal needs, the rest of the money was spent on interest and debt

such an economic blow was the greater accumulation of foreign debt,[4] which caused changes in the balance of power towards a more Western-aligned trade outlook. This shift led to economic liberalization and better access to Western markets and credits, as both Western markets and Western credits proved a necessary condition for the bridge-model to continue to be sustainable post-1979.

The political transition of 1989 superseded a long process of economic reforms and subsequent shifts in the balance of social and economic forces that undermined the ISI model in the long-run. The main trigger behind this shift was the unsustainable debt acquired, and the austerity terms Hungary adopted after joining the IMF in 1982.[5] The economic reforms of the 1980s opened up space in the so-called 'property vacuum' (Böröcz 1999) for various groups of monetarist technocrats and corporate managers to gain relative autonomy in coordinating the process of privatization (cf. Gagyi 2015). Further benefits of liberalization were shared amongst entrepreneurs from the informal (or second) economy (Szelényi 1988) and the growing number of foreign investors whose activities were previously regulated by the joint venture act in the mid-1970s. Meanwhile, the economic effects of austerity were temporarily buffered by the legalization of the second economy (Galasi and Kertesi 1985), which allowed households to compensate for declining purchasing power and cuts in state investments through working second shifts in their private small enterprises and informal reproductive work (Vigvári and Gerőcs 2018). Despite the successful buffering effect of the newly legalized second economy, hidden unemployment and poverty grew throughout the last decades of the Kádár era.

This shift in the balance of forces culminated in a new alliance between managers of state-owned companies, members of the younger generation in the politburo, urban intellectuals and semi-formal entrepreneurial groups.[6]

---

repayments: costs on higher interest rates hit 11 billion USD, while losses caused by unfavorably FX-rate cost 2.2 billion USD between 1971 and 1989 (Lóránt 2010:2–3).

4   The Hungarian Central Bank did not acknowledge the country's foreign debt obligations which was inherited from the interwar period (part of which had been rolled over from the Hapsburg Monarchy) until the dispute was settled with Western donors. The settlement was required for the new installments from the IMF.

5   Hungary – with fellow Comecon members and other states in the Global South – was compelled to join the IMF in 1982 and launch a neoliberal austerity program under the supervision of a domestic alliance of monetarist technocrats, intellectual dissidents and state socialist "reform bureaucrats" (Gagyi 2015, Fábry 2019).

6   This alliance of a nascent class of quasi-property owners in the period of late state socialism was referred by Böröcz (1999) as the "property vacuum" before the formal codification of private property in the 1990s.

There was a diverse group of elites at the time of the state socialist liberalization comprised of international lenders (e.g. monetarist technocrats) and the nascent propertied classes. These factions converged into a domestic capitalist class alliance, supported by trade union leaders who were afraid of foreign investors' growing dominance in the economy[7] (Stark 1996; Burawoy and Lukács 1994; Böröcz 1999). The bifurcation between the two competing groups (one oriented towards foreign trade and the other on protecting internal markets) escalated during the post-socialist transition period.

3   Postsocialist Neoliberalization: Western Capitalist Dominance and the Marginalization of Labor

The regime change occurred in Hungary against a backdrop of mounting external debt and an urgent need for foreign direct investment (FDI). During this period international organizations and Western capital played a pivotal role in the process of liberalization. As a consequence, Hungary was fully integrated into Western export markets through specializing in low value-added manufacturing dominated by foreign corporations. However, the presence of these foreign corporations in the economy was conditioned by full-fledged privatization and economic shock therapy (Böröcz 1999; Gille 2010). The FDI-based model demanded neoliberal policies that prioritized foreign capital inflow, over the protection of domestic ownership, a common structural dilemma for semi-peripheral states (Gerőcs 2022). During this period of the 1990s, two forms of foreign investments entered the economy: 'brownfield investment', fire-sale privatization tenders that targeted state assets, and 'greenfield investment' from multinational automotive and electronic companies. Greenfield investment brought assembly production to the country's customs-free export zones in a structure that bore similarities to Mexico's maquiladoras.

Hungary's successive governments in the 1990s – whether conservative or liberal – introduced shock therapy-type economic policies that were aimed not only at privatization, but also at the deregulation of labor laws, as well as at the continuation of trade and financial liberalization (Haney 2002; Bohle and Greskovits 2012). The major beneficiary of this mixed policy approach was foreign capital, and among them mostly those from within the automotive and electronic industries who operated in the special export-zones. The

---

7   The sociological origin of the Hungarian nascent bourgeoisie went back to the 1980s, either in the informal second economy or as the managerial elite of large public enterprises (Burawoy and Lukács 1994; Stark 1996).

nascent domestic capitalist classes were subjugated into a subordinate position, including even those segments of the economy which were not directly exposed to international trade such as the retail, media, telecommunication and construction industries (Gagyi and Gerőcs 2022).

The majority of workers who were employed by stated-owned companies lost their jobs after the collapse of the Comecon in 1991. This allowed for their subordinated integration into the new industrial structure. Political parties of the regime change – including new parties formed by former dissident professionals and the reformed socialist party – combined in alliance with different capitalist factions formed a cross-party consensus to prohibit workers' organizations to avail of democratic means to hinder capitalist interests in the process of marketization. This consensus included a pre-election liberal-conservative agreement on banning political strikes and exempting workers' collective property from the privatization process (Thoma 1998). While institutionalizing political democracy was a common interest among new parties, blocking the representation of labor's interests within the marketization process was also a vital common ground.

In the political process, two major power blocs formed throughout the regime change that were tied into different social alliances (Gagyi 2016): the conservative MDF party and the alliance of liberal parties (SZDSZ, the Socialist party and Fidesz). MDF promoted a model of national capitalism, while the liberal parties, promoted a fast-track Euroatlantic integration, with the Socialist party remaining the major advocate of the postsocialist propertied classes. Ideological conflict between these blocs defined the framework of public discourse during the post-socialist period: while conservatives spoke of defending "national interests" from Western capital and its internal allies, the liberal-socialist bloc promoted Western-type open markets and liberal democracy as a developmental paradigm and favored fast-track admission to the European Union. Criticism of the change of regime, voiced from left positions, was effectively muted by a cross-party anti-communist consensus (Krausz 1998). This structure of the political debate created a discursive space that either muted the expression of workers' interests in the name of prioritizing Western-style democracy or included workers' interests in attacks against Western-led liberalization in the name of protecting national interests. In the long term, popular discontent against the social effects of the post-socialist neoliberal shock therapy was successfully channeled towards supporting conservative political projects (Gagyi 2016).

Liberal democracy in Hungary was consolidated after 1994 when shock-therapy economic practices eased, and the opposition parties engaged in a coalition government. Privatization continued under the liberal-socialist period; but certain factions of the domestic capitalist classes enjoyed limited subsidies from the government in protected circuits of accumulation, such as housing, construction, and media. During this period, an inevitable confrontation emerged between the domestic capitalist classes hoping to secure access to the remaining elements of state-owned enterprises, and foreign capital which continued to gain access to untapped domestic markets, relatively well-preserved infrastructure, and a cheap labor force. Because the domestic classes did not have sufficient financial capacity to save their position in the economy at a time when the indebted state was in an urgent need of currency inflow, foreign capital had the upper hand in the privatization. Despite the overall disadvantage for domestic capitalist groups,[8] the majority remained loyal to the Socialist party until as late as the early 2000s, mostly due to their long-existing although weakened informal linkages with old members of the politburo. The Socialist party was also able to mobilize the main successor of the trade union confederation after the latter's disintegration in the early 1990s.

A significant point of discord between the opposing factions was the two blocs differing relationships with workers' demands during the period of privatization. The main liberal and conservative parties, SZDSZ and MDF, made an official pact to rule out political strikes and workers' collective ownership of property. However, the MDF approached the renewed workers' council movement throughout the 1990s and promised state support as part of a political alliance. For the MDF, this alliance served to build leverage against big company managers who aligned themselves with the Socialist party and larger trade unions. While this political assistance resulted in limited benefits, by 1998 the workers' council movement declared itself a Christian union, giving up aims of workers' collective property ownership. It has continued to work in alliance with the conservative bloc up until the present day. Liberals however, supported the formation of a new trade union alliance (LIGA), hoping to weaken the existing national trade union alliance, inherited from state socialism. LIGA participated in the National Roundtable discussions of the regime change, but in accordance with liberal interests', they focused on issues of political transition, rather than issues related to workers' interests (Thoma 1998).

---

8 A small number of well-connected individuals could profit from this period largely due to their exceptional managerial skills, accumulated experience of the spontaneous privatization in the late 1980s as well as political connections that helped them secure and rollover loans from state-owned banks (Voszka 1994).

4   The Crisis of Neoliberal Hegemony

By the second half of the 1990s, Fidesz, an originally liberal party, took an ideological turn, explicitly taking up the role earlier occupied by MDF. This came
after the first full-scale structural adjustment program that the socialist-liberal
coalition government introduced as the "Bokros package".[9] Fideszs' ideological
position was expressed as moderate nationalism with the promise of national
capitalism. It brought the party to an electoral victory in 1998.

The first Fidesz government continued the MDF strategy of breaking up alliances between domestic capital and the Socialist party, with a view to realign
these entities to a conservative core. However, Fidesz's ability to mass mobilize
of the middle-classes against austerity measures by invoking historical notions
of 'national embourgeoisement' (Vigvári and Gerőcs 2018) proved to be a significant difference. As it invoked symbolic gestures of national unity, Fidesz
reallocated social funds from lower classes to the upper middle-classes and
introduced a disciplinary labor regime that complemented neoliberal austerity.
Despite successfully building a base of party-related national capitalist firms,
the first Fidesz government was unable to break the bond between domestic
capital and the Socialist party. Fidesz subsequently lost the 2002 elections to
the socialist-liberal governments, and Hungary became a full member of the
European Union. In reaction to the electoral loss, Fidesz launched a national
project for organizing "Civic Circles" successfully integrating much of the
popular anti-neoliberal energy into its political networks (Greskovits 2020).
The 2000's popular right-wing, anti-neoliberal wave of politicization (which
relied on the political discourse of the conservative power bloc in the 1990s)
had another major political beneficiary: the new far-right party Jobbik, which
worked next to Fidesz to penetrate and publicize this movement. Jobbik managed to enter parliament by 2010 (Szombati 2018).

The second phase of the neoliberal accumulation regime showed signs
of exhaustion as privatization temporarily slowed down in the mid-2000s.
Furthermore, the regulatory capacity of the state to subsidize domestic capital
became more limited because of the European Union's competition law framework. Problems with the public budget attracted inspection by international

---

9   In March 1995 the finance ministry introduced a gradual devaluation of the Hungarian cur-
    rency to cope with the growing deficit in the balance of accounts. The "Bokros package"
    aimed a full liberalization of the balance of payment and the convertibility of the Hungarian
    currency. To keep the account in control, social benefits were curtailed, university fees intro-
    duced, and nominal wages in the public services were capped. In addition, the privatization
    process was accelerated.

lenders, while the cumulative effects of financial liberalization and the austerity policies introduced by the "Bokros package" led to growing public discontent. The socialist-liberal governments attempted to alleviate their own political delegitimation by encouraging private households to take loans in foreign currencies, thus increasing their consumption power in the short term. In the early 2000s, this created the temporary illusion of neoliberalism with social benefits.

By the late 2000s, the debt incurred by the neoliberal accumulation regime's dependence on international lending (including IMF loans) in comparison to foreign direct investment (Figure 3.1) bound the governments to austerity policies that were met with rising social and political discontent from disillusioned middle-classes. Fidesz was able to articulate this discontent with the party's national agenda (cf. Gagyi 2016; Scheiring and Szombati 2020).

Disillusionment further intensified when domestic capitalist groups were affected by hardening austerity measures that the coalition governments were forced to implement upon the demands of successive IMF packages. By the time of the world economic crisis in 2008, approximately 30 percent of private households and small-enterprises that held mostly foreign currency debt, went bankrupt due to exchange rate fluctuations (Pellandini-Simányi and Vargha 2018; Pósfai 2018).

As the result of the exhaustion of the FDI-based neoliberal model in combination with strict compliance with EU and IMF rules, the national bourgeoisie slowly distanced itself from the Socialist party and re-grouped around

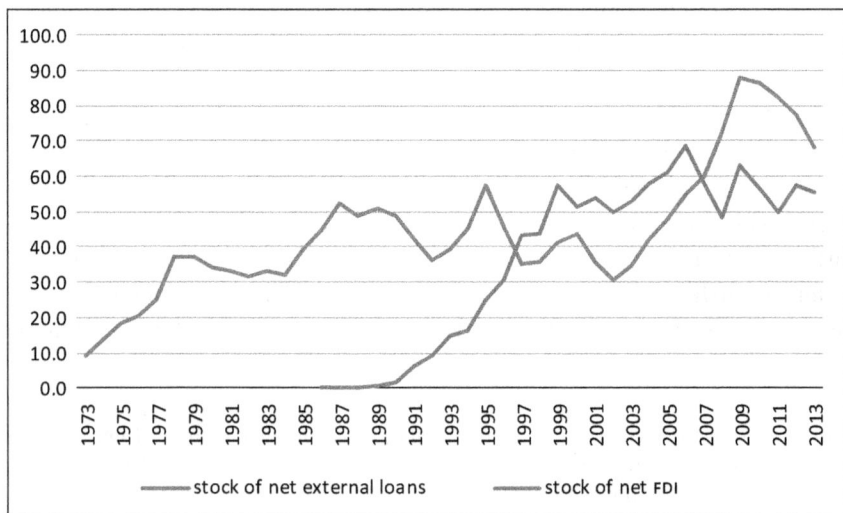

FIGURE 3.1   Stock of net loans and direct investment in comparison (percentage of GDP)
SOURCE: GERŐCS AND PINKASZ 2018

the contender Fidesz (Wilkin 2016; Fábry 2019; Scheiring 2020; Scheiring and Szombati 2020). By the same token, the largest trade union, which had been a close ally of the Socialist party, officially declared its separation from any party politics. Moreover, Fidesz reorganized its network of local organizations, the Civic Circles Movement, that was affiliated to the party leadership and was easy to mobilize for local causes. Members of the Civic Circles Movement were comprised not only of middle-class participants, but also an increasing number of blue-collar workers who became advocates of the party's national agenda. In 2006, violent demonstrations broke out in Budapest, sparked by the leaked speech of Socialist premier Ferenc Gyurcsány, in which he hinted that his party had lied to voters about the state of the budget, and that the 'human face' of neoliberalism came up short. Aggressive repression by the police under the Socialists' rule marked the events as the endpoint of a liberal-socialist political hegemony. Although the demonstration themes were initially dominated by far-right movements led by Jobbik, Fidesz most successfully utilized their political aftermath, positioning itself as the leader of a popular national revolt against neoliberal domination.

Fidesz' victory in the 2010 election, where it won two-thirds of the vote, can be seen as the result of the massive delegitimation of the socialist-liberal coalition in combination with the very harsh effects of the world economic crisis of 2008. The Fidesz government used the opportunity provided by the global crisis to reconfigure the post-socialist power block by renegotiating economic and financial relations with international capital on behalf of the national bourgeoisie. However, elements of neoliberal austerity policies, in combination with subsidizing foreign capital, remained in place. Thus, neoliberalism did not end with the rise of Fidesz but rather carried over to the illiberal hegemony.

5   "Illiberal" Hegemony after 2010: A New Authoritarian Capitalist Reconfiguration

Viktor Orbán dubbed his second government "illiberal." This concept was aimed to express its general ideological opposition to "liberal democracy", as he explained in one of his annual speeches at the summer gathering of his conservative Fidesz party in Bálványos, Transylvania in 2015.[10] Hungary's national bourgeoisie achieved a more prominent role in a newly formed power block

---

10   https://visegradpost.com/en/2019/07/29/orbans-full-speech-at-tusvanyos-political-phi losophy-upcoming-crisis-and-projects-for-the-next-15-years/.

within Orbán's illiberal regime and its institutional centralization of political power (Melegh 2018). As part of the political centralization, a new constitution was inaugurated in 2012. Fidesz also subsequently redefined the electoral system several times in order to maintain the party's two-third majority in the parliament. At the same time, a series of economic reforms was introduced, including reforms in a wide array of industrial, educational and taxation policies, labor market flexibilization, and a public workfare initiative. This series of reforms was targeted at some important factions of the neoliberal power block which had dominated the previous accumulation regime. In addition to passing constitutional amendments, since the introduction of these political and economic reforms, successive Fidesz governments have faced no serious challenge to their power at the national level. However, opposition parties have achieved some success at the municipal level.

Unprecedented control over the media has followed the centralization of political power and economic reforms that weakened the neoliberal power bloc. Fidesz' governments have systematically undermined the environment for independent media through regulatory, as well as market interventions. Fidesz built its own camp of media oligarchs during its first term during the late 1990s and after 2010 it gained control over large sways of Hungary's independent media outlets (Wilkin 2016).[11] Its control of the majority of public and private media outlets has allowed the government to convert them into a state propaganda machine. This machine has been frequently used against targeted groups and on carefully selected issues. Significantly, its infamous anti-migration campaign, which it launched 2015 during the European refugee crisis. The campaign was initially a move to counterbalance the party's sinking popularity ratings after the 2014 elections but has since been maintained as a main theme of its communication. Other campaigns include the anti-LGBT, anti-homeless, and anti-feminist, all of which serve to symbolically re-create the notion of a "national unity" that supposedly universally benefits from Fidesz politics.

In terms of soft power struggles for international recognition, state propaganda often targets prominent European politicians who have publicly criticized Orbán. A more frequent target is Hungarian-born billionaire George Soros who contributed to the consolidation of liberal democracy through his philanthropic donations to independent NGOs during the post-socialist transition. The so-called "Stop Soros" legislation is one of the most restrictive

---

11   Two of the biggest independent (liberal-left) outlets including a print magazine called *Népszabadság* and an online magazine called *index.hu* have been overtaken or closed down by Fidesz-affiliated media oligarchs.

regulations towards civilian organizations in the EU, as the law has banned NGO's from accepting foreign donations without state approval. Another element of the anti-Soros campaign involved pressurizing the Central European University – originally founded by Soros – to relocate from Budapest to Vienna. Other autonomous cultural institutions, such as the University of Theatre and Film Arts (SZFE) were reorganized by a newly appointed management, whose head is a former lieutenant of the Hungarian military. The reorganization of the university was followed by the resistance of students of the University of Theatre and Film Arts who also occupied the university campus. The Hungarian Academy of Sciences was also targeted by the state apparatus and by 2020, most Hungarian higher educational institutions had been transferred to Fidesz-affiliated private foundations, triggering demonstrations among urban middle-classes and the intelligentsia. The curriculum has often been redesigned in line with the government's industrialization goals, and humanities departments have been curtailed or rendered unnecessary. A crisis in the education sector was marked by a nation-wide teacher's strike in March 2022, joined by secondary school students in a second strike wave in September 2022.

Moreover, state-controlled media plays a pivotal role in attacking the leadership of opposition parties; the remaining socialist-liberals, and the far-right party Jobbik. Despite the very harsh media attacks on opposition figures, the opposition has not been criminalized in the same way as in other authoritarian regimes such as Turkey or the Philippines. Throughout its first and second terms, Jobbik grew to be the main political challenger of Fidesz due to its ability to acquire a considerable amount of popular support among those who were alienated by Fidesz's reforms. Jobbik's 2018 electoral campaign "You work. They steal." illustratively sums up this political rhetoric (Szombati 2018). As a response, Fidesz stepped up its own far-right narratives, and took efforts to destroy Jobbik both symbolically and organizationally, though criminalization was not part of the strategy. Amidst this conflict, an interesting change of political positions took place in the mid-2010s: Jobbik moved from the far-right closer to the political center, while Fidesz moved from its moderate center-right position, towards the far right. Simultaneously, Fidesz helped to create the "Our Homeland Movement", an anti-Jobbik faction which has attracted far-right elements and sets the tone for symbolic identity politics which aligns with the state's ideological goals. This movement emphasizes a so-called "moral discourse" that has an anti-LGBTQ, anti-Roma, and pro-state violence orientation.

The remaining strategy of the liberal and socialist parties is to invoke notions of "Europeanness" and values of "Western civilization" in opposition to the strong nationalist rhetoric of the state propaganda, relying on mostly symbolic gestures of alliance with Western liberal powers. This long-term strategy

of political communication has been at the heart of the post-socialist neoliberal regime since the years immediately following the regime change and is
thus less appealing to the majority of the population. While liberal opposition
parties' electoral base could not be recovered after the implosion of the neoliberal hegemony in the late 2000s (despite various splits in the incumbent
party, and a new generation of liberal parties, e.g., the Momentum party), the
liberal pro-Western frameworks of the previous neoliberal power bloc have
dominated much of the post-2010 demonstration waves against the consolidating illiberal regime. These protests, dominated by educated middle-class
constituencies of the previous neoliberal hegemony (Szabó and Mikecz 2015),
criticize the regime's rolling back of democratic freedoms, including reforms
of the media, the judicial system, cultural financing, and higher education. In
this new movement phase of liberal politics, social issues have been included
as a political argument against the illiberal regime, and groups representing
social claims (from housing, Roma advocacy groups or unions) are invited to
speak at demonstrations. However, these issues remain subordinated to civil
liberty claims, and instead of penetrating popular constituencies like Jobbik
did prior to taking its centrist position, the liberal strategy has remained within
the conventional middle-class confines of post-socialist politics.

Social movements' energy is used to support opposition coalitions during
electoral mobilizations. A new development in this respect was the cross-party
opposition alliance (including Jobbik) that was formed ahead of the 2019 local
elections. Due to the alliance, opposition candidates gained some seats in a
few local governments, including the Budapest Municipality. This raised hopes
to break Fidesz's supermajority at the 2022 parliamentary elections. However,
due to the political and ideological incoherence, a fragmented electoral base
of the opposition, as well as to the escalating energy price crisis followed by
the sudden outbreak of the war in Ukraine, against which Fidesz promised to
shield the population (stating that Hungary should not take part in the conflict, while the opposition urged for helping Ukraine) Fidesz was able to secure
its supermajority once again.

6   The Post-2010 Capitalist Power Block

In terms of economic policy, despite its anti-Western symbolic rhetoric,
Orbán's illiberal regime was not entirely hostile to international capital due to
the country's persistent dependence on external financing. Instead, it sought
to form new international alliances outside of the Transatlantic geopolitical
space to help the regime diversify away from the European Union's Structural

and Cohesion Funds and its dominant reliance on investments from German manufacturers.

In this context, however, many of the former neoliberal policies have remained intact but have combined with selected industrial policies and a more centralized form of governance. In finance, for instance, the government and the central bank achieved sufficient regulatory capacity to change market relations between foreign and domestic banks, and to transform the market from a competitive stance to an oligopolistic structure under direct state supervision. Unlike the domestic services sectors (e.g., utilities, retail and telecommunication), this required no hostile takeovers. Rather, a win-win situation was created between international and domestic capital by Hungary's financial bailout scheme, where the government paid a relatively high price for foreign banks' insolvent assets (Mihályi 2015).[12] The post-crisis reorganization of banking was important from a political perspective, owing to the promises made to save the hundreds of thousands of households who were then in arrears after suffering a surge in installments. This constituted a main point of Fidesz' election campaign in 2010. In line with its general gestures of inclusion towards popular right-wing anti-neoliberalism, Fidesz borrowed the discourse of debtors' advocacy groups, and spoke of the forex mortgage crisis as an injustice imposed by Western banks on the Hungarian people. However, its actual measures to tackle the crisis prioritized the restabilization and nationalization of the financial sector. Among debtors, the reorganization of debt only served the better-off (Dancsik et al. 2015), and when debtors in worse financial positions started to mobilize against these measures, their movements were sidelined, and possibility of litigation cut short by successive rulings of the Supreme Court (Curia). On the other hand, the central bank launched a new mortgage loan program in the Hungarian currency that targeted new middle-classes (supported by state redistribution policies). This new loan scheme was conditioned upon demographic criteria (e.g. number of children in the family), underpinned by a pro-natalist moral discourse of "family deservedness" (Gregor 2017). This new scheme helped government-associated financial institutions overtake the private lending market which used to be under the control of foreign banks prior to the world economic crisis in 2008. Combined with further tax exemptions and other support for local construction industries, this created a protected circuit of capital accumulation, dominated by national financial capital. In addition to changing property

---

12   Mihályi (2015) argues that this was a win-win situation for both international and national financial capital because foreign banks were particularly hit during the financial crisis in 2008; they reported massive losses on mortgage debt.

relations, the private lending market experienced a massive concentration of capital. Through government assistance, newly acquired financial assets were integrated into a new giant bank with hopes that it would dominate the oligopolistic market. In short, the financial bailout scheme was designed to help domestic capital to renegotiate its relations with international finance capital, whilst subsidizing upper middle-classes and co-opting lower middle-classes through ideological and material means. In sum, banking serves as an example for the top-down political alliance that Fidesz was able to build for the sake of forming a new power block.

In other sectors of the economy, the state created various selective criteria for protecting domestic capital. First, the government needed a trade surplus to alleviate financial dependence and the influence of lenders on economic policies. For this purpose, economic policies were designed in a particular mercantile fashion to encourage large foreign exporters to increase their capacity and produce sufficient foreign currency for the reserves held by the central bank (Becker 2016). This particular kind of trade and industrial policy went as far as to provide the largest state subsidies of any country in the region to foreign companies with manufacturing plants in Hungary in order to help them export in the world market. However, state subsidies were also allocated to Hungarian companies on an increased level if they were shown to be associated with Fidesz-related businessmen (Figure 3.2).

Secondly, international capital in the domestic service economy was targeted by discriminatory and protectionist practices. While these protectionist policies were designed to appear compliant with European competition law, a wide range of market interventions, price regulations and specifically targeted sectoral surtaxes that were introduced at this time, have since been ruled in need of revision by the European Court of Justice. On top of those policies, hostile takeovers and disputed nationalizations took place. In addition to municipal utilities, targeted areas typically included retail, media, telecommunications and energy. Local infrastructure and services are other areas where the state has gained regulatory capacity in order to intervene and change market relations for the benefit of regime-allied domestic capital.

Lastly, banking and international finance is a specific area in which world-economic integration intersected with the capitalization of domestic groups through different sources of funding. As we have already highlighted, contestation among the various factions of foreign and domestic finance capital was relatively low due to the win-win situation created by the bailout scheme. What changed is the balance of international forces in the broader regional geopolitical space. Russian and Chinese capital, for example, has been favored by the Hungarian central bank to help diversify away from the dependence on

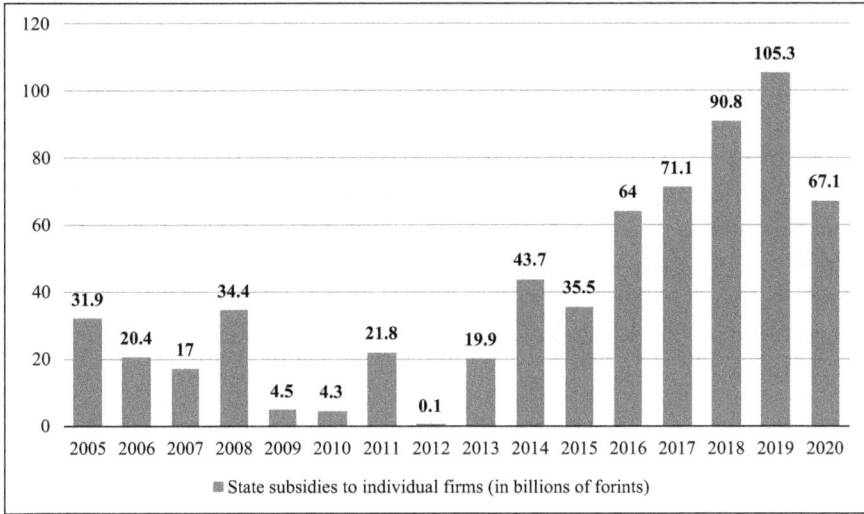

FIGURE 3.2   State subsidies allocated to individual companies by arbitrary decision 2005–2020
(billion HUF)
SOURCE: HIPA

European funds and German foreign investment. This shift has led to a new
geopolitics of indebtedness (Gagyi and Gerőcs 2019).

7   FDI-Based Export-Oriented Manufacturing and a New Labor Regime

As mentioned previously, industrial policies in Hungary encourage foreign
export-manufacturers to invest in the country (Gerőcs and Pinkasz 2019). This
set of policies was largely modeled after Germany's neomercantilist model. It
is notable that some of these industrial policies were co-drafted by Hungarian
government officials from the Ministry of Innovation and Technology and
agents of German lobby organizations, such as the German-Hungarian
Chamber of Industry and Commerce.[13] Labor regulation, education and taxation have been the main legislative areas in which the peripheral version of
Germany's neomercantilist model has been implemented.

---

13   Interesting to note for example that the co-president of the National Council on Scientific
Policy which oversights government spending on science and education is former
European Commissioner for Budget and Human Resources, Günther Oettinger.

7.1   Labor Reforms

As early as 2010, the newly elected Fidesz-government made radical amendments to the trade union laws, resulting in the sudden drop of strike activities after 2010. Moreover, a new labor code was enacted in 2012. With these
reforms, the national bourgeoisie's interests coalesced with those of foreign
capital; hence, overall dependence on Germany intensified. Upon further
requests from German industrial capital, amendments to the labor code were
added in 2018. Trade unions dubbed these reforms "Slave Law" because they
severely restricted their negotiating power vis-á-vis companies, while manufacturers' right to demand overtime work was greatly extended (Gagyi and
Gerőcs 2019).[14]

7.2   Public Workfare

Another important piece of legislation is the public workfare initiative (Hann
2016). The initiative was first introduced by the socialist-liberal government
as part of their crisis-management effort and extended by Fidesz in 2011. In
the meantime, Fidesz fulfilled a popular demand made by the rural middle-
classes to replace universal social transfers (such as family allowances and
unemployment benefits)[15] that the rural poor were eligible for, with public
work organized by local governments. Between 2011 and 2015, approximately
5% of the Hungarian workforce was employed by the workfare initiative, most
of which were in rural areas where high unemployment rates have been a
long-term phenomenon resulting from the post-socialist transition period.[16]
Local governments dominated by Fidesz were given full discretionary power
over managing rural employment through the initiative. This helped to obtain
the passive consent of the rural unemployed, many of whom were members
of the ethnic Roma community. In many parts of the country, mayors became
the sole legal employers of the local population. As a result, the initiative
has played a massive role in the tightening of patron-client relationships in
the areas most affected by rampant unemployment, thus producing significant consequences for local political mobilization.[17] On the other hand, local

---

14   From 250 hours to 400 hours per year and payment delays can also be extended up to
      3 years.
15   E.g. unemployment benefit was reduced from 9 to 3-month period in 2012.
16   Some of the rhetoric around social benefits was openly racist as it targeted the most vul-
      nerable Roma population which suffered greatly during the post-socialist transition.
17   In subsequent elections, the poorest regions with highest numbers of unemployment
      provided the highest numbers of pro-government votes, indicating the workfare pro-
      gram's function in the electoral machine.

mayors' dependence on the central budget has also increased, producing a nation-wide hierarchical system of clientelism where the central government reigns on top.

7.3   *Education*

The second area targeted by reforms was education. Here, Hungarian policy-makers introduced a blueprint based on the German vocational training system, combined with lowering the compulsory minimum schooling age from 18 to 16 years. Designed by the German industrial lobby and its Hungarian counterparts, the vocational training system aimed to provide companies with cheap flexible labor that is as young as legally viable. Beyond the low level of qualifications, trainees are formally supervised by their school programs, therefore avoiding any obligation on behalf of the companies to pay them equal wages or offer them secured contracts (Gagyi and Gerőcs 2019).

7.4   *Taxation*

Finally, Hungary introduced the lowest corporate tax rates in the European Union. The official corporate flat-tax rate is set at 9%, but the effective tax after specific allowances which companies pay across the board is only 4.7%, as of 2020, according to OECD database.[18] The Hungarian personal income tax system is similarly flat, with a universal rate of 15%. In contrast, Hungary introduced the highest sales tax that is possible within the tax-harmonization framework of the European Union with a rate of 27%, the burden of which is disproportionately borne by lower wage-earners, thus pushing the growing cost of labor's reproduction onto working class households.

8   The Diversification of Financing: New Alliances with Russian and Chinese Capital

To loosen its financial dependence on Western capital and, thereby, enable a larger maneuvering space for domestic capital, the government has sought alternative funding channels made available by geopolitical changes. This need for enhanced capital accumulation was filled by Russian and Chinese entry into the European market prior to Russia's attack on Ukraine in 2022. The Hungarian regime has successfully positioned itself as a 'gateway' for newly emerging transnational capital seeking entry to the EU. This positioning

---

18   https://www.compareyourcountry.org/corporate-tax-statistics/en/o/all/default.

resembles the framework of the bridge model in Hungary's international trade of the 1960s and 1970s.

In the case of Russia, capital export took the form of a well-defined investment package that included energy-sector investments involving concession agreements with oil companies, deliveries of technical equipment for nuclear capacity, infrastructural development related to energy extraction or transportation, and the renewal of credit lines offered by state-owned banks.

In total, three important investment packages were agreed upon between 2010 and 2018. The first agreement included the Hungarian government's repurchase of a majority stake in the Hungarian Oil and Gas Company (MOL Group) from Russia's Surgutneftegaz. National capitalist groups hoped to use this to acquire stakes in other regional energy networks in order to expand their influence in Central-East Europe.

The second important agreement involved the extension of the country's nuclear capacity in the Hungarian city of Paks by an international consortium led by Russia's Rosatom. Even though the tender did not comply with the European competition law, the European Council approved it in exchange for Western suppliers' access to the project which could provide with a framework for further renegotiations if EU sanctions against Russia after the invasion of Ukraine put the whole project on hold. In principle, the so called Paks-II nuclear capacity extension fits well into the peripheral neomercantilist model because it serves the needs of the eastwardly expanding German industrial complex by supplying it with cheap energy and labor. It was also hoped to serve domestic capital's needs as the agreement included inviting Hungarian companies to participate in the construction of the new block (up to 40% of the plan). The investment package was expected to create a new large pool of funds for domestic capital without having to comply with European Union competition law standards, however these conditions might be subject to change. The costs of this massive infrastructural investment were also hoped to be covered by a credit line agreement worth 10 billion USD between Russia's state-owned Vnesheconombank – now sanctioned by the EU – and the Hungarian government. According to the third agreement, the new regional headquarters of Russia's International Investment Bank (IIB) will be set up in Budapest. As part of the agreement, the Hungarian state raised the joint stock of the bank's capital by 10 billion EUR, making Hungary the second largest stakeholder in IIB.[19] New geopolitical tensions and Western sanctions against

---

19   Since this means that IIB staff would gain diplomatic immunity in the European Union, political quarrels have already emerged between senior EU officials and Hungary.

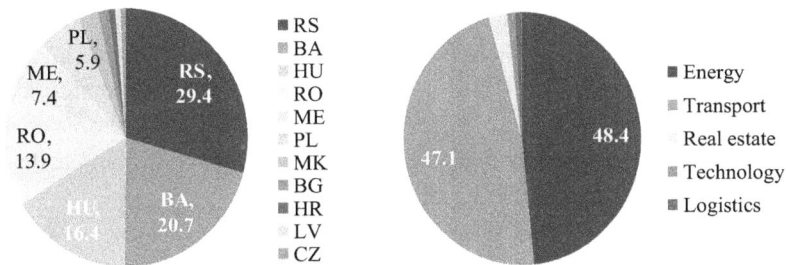

FIGURE 3.3   Chinese OFDI in EEU countries and sector breakdown, 2013–2017
SOURCE: GRÜBLER ET AL. (2018)

Russia could jeopardize Russian collaborations; it is however not clear at the time of closing the manuscript how exactly these sanctions will affect Russian investments in Hungary.

In the case of China, capital export is combined with China's urgent need to spread industrial overcapacity, for which it uses extensive capital investments in the multilateral investment framework of the Belt and Road Initiative (BRI). Western observers describe the BRI as a potential alternative to the IMF in the long run, although the size of its funds is still minuscule compared to those of major international donor agencies. China has set up a special credit facility for the Central-East and South-East European regions worth 10 billion USD to finance infrastructure projects in 17 countries (grouped into the category of CEEC-17 in the BRI framework).[20] They are eligible to apply for preferential loans that can be used for infrastructure projects mostly in transportation and energy within the scope of the broader BRI framework.

Figure 3.3 shows that Chinese investments are highly concentrated in both the sectors and regions identified above. The reason for this concentration is China had already launched two major infrastructure projects in these regions. In 2016 the Chinese shipping company (COSCO) acquired a 67% stake in the largest Greek harbor in Piraeus as part of its European-wide purchases in various harbor logistics.[21] In order to connect its harbors to European infrastructure, China is building a high-speed cargo-rail that will connect it to core markets in Europe. Agreements have already been signed in Serbia and

20   CEEC countries include: Albania, Bosnia-Herzegovina, Croatia, Macedonia, Montenegro, Serbia, Slovenia, Bulgaria, Romania, the Czech Republic, Hungary, Poland and Slovakia, Latvia, Lithuania and Estonia.
21   It is important to mention that the Greek government was pushed by the European Council and the IMF to privatize the harbor as part of the austerity program which the country had to make in exchange for the international bailout.

Hungary that would allow for the construction of a 336 km-long railway connection between Budapest and Belgrade that will be built by a consortium led by China Communication Construction Co., with 85% of the estimated 3.8 billion USD costs to be covered by China's Eximbank. Similar to the Paks-II model, but unlike other Chinese investments, local entrepreneurs can participate in up to 50% of the construction of the rail line.

Another important initiative was launched by the People's Bank of China (PBOC) in 2013 to promote the internationalization of its own currency, the renminbi (RMB). The Hungarian central bank was among the first to sign a bilateral foreign exchange swap agreement with the PBOC in the amount of 1.6 billion USD, permitting the Hungarian central bank to use the currency as a reserve.[22] In 2016 Hungary launched its own 'Budapest RMB Initiative' which was aimed at attracting Chinese financial institutions, mostly from Hong Kong, to use Budapest as an offshore location for regional RMB transactions.[23] Hungary and Poland were also among the first countries in the EU to issue foreign sovereign bonds in RMB (Gerőcs 2017: 180).

Hungary's attraction to Chinese investment is not unique within the broader region. One of the most tangible effects of the geopolitical shifts on the development of regional economies is the funding schemes of the CEEC-17 countries. Most of these countries must rely on external funding to service their debt and their diplomatic and geopolitical ties largely affect the type of external funding they can secure. Figure 3.4 shows a comparative overview of the types of external funding as part of the broader BRI scheme: European Union eastern member states, for instance, often have better access to European funds compared to their South-East European neighbors who are not in the EU. The latter group must rely on other funding resources, such as Chinese loans. Figure 3.4 also reflect the shift in Hungary's external funding dependence: it has eliminated European loans all together, and its share of EU funds is the lowest among all EU member states. This is related to Hungarian authorities' decision to seek out alternative, non-European funding to increase geopolitical space for maneuvering. Chinese loans in particular, but also Russian credit, has come to comprise a significant proportion of Hungary's external funding, transforming the regime's position into a new geopolitics of indebtedness.

---

22   We do not know the exact share of RMB in the Hungarian reserves because it is not fully convertible yet therefore it is not accounted as an official reserve currency according to the IMF standards.

23   Since 2015 three of the four largest Chinese banks by total assets, China Construction Bank, Bank of China and Agricultural Bank of China opened regional offices in Budapest.

100%
90% 210 100 36.7 130 900 51 400
80% 0 66.7 55 110 970.5 441.7
272.3 2110
70% 81.6
60% 2490 3150 1120 4470
118
50% 1213.7 1219.6
40% 1239.6 11963.2 594.7
1216.2 305.5 0 408.3 1334.9 795.6
30% 502.9 3369.0 2167.3
20% 1411.3 458.5 2774.4
10% 111.3 177.9
0% 202.1 37.9 162.8

BG CZ EE HR HU LT LV PL RO SI SK AL BA ME MK RS

■ EU transfers ■ EU loans ▪ Chinese loans

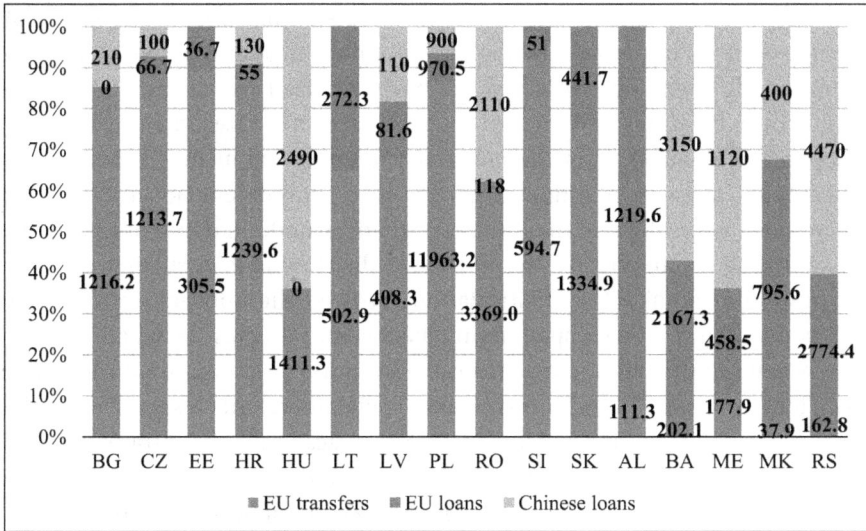

FIGURE 3.4 External funding in BRI infrastructure projects (in million EUR and percentage), 2007–2017
SOURCE: GRÜBLER (EDS.) 2018:17

9 Muted Resistance under Ongoing Capitalist Struggles

In recent years, Hungarian opposition parties were working to set up a unified coalition in order to create a chance to defeat Fidesz' super-majority in the national elections. This cross-party collaboration involved all parties from the liberals to the extreme right. At the 2019 local elections, all-opposition candidates, supported by metropolitan and urban middle-classes disgruntled with the regime's monopolization of power and mounting corruption scandals, secured several victories, including the Municipality of Budapest. These victories were interpreted as a sign that an all-opposition win at the 2022 parliamentary elections could be possible. Fidesz reacted to this possibility with moves to constitutionalize and/or privatize state companies to the benefit of allied national capitalists in the fear of a possible change of government. The conversion of political power to economic wealth alludes to the period of the late 1980s when state socialist bureaucrats and company managers privatized publicly owned assets in order to accumulate wealth in the anticipation of the regime change. As we have seen, the political and economic impacts of that conversion lasted as late as the 2000s, when neoliberal governments were dismantled, subsequently contributing to the rise of Fidesz' own national bourgeois agenda.

Throughout successive post-2010 Fidesz government cycles, a series of demonstrations dominated by the urban middle-class and by political coalitions among liberal opposition parties have criticized the regime's rollback of democratic freedoms and its turn towards Eastern – Russian and Chinese – geopolitical alliances. These demonstrations somewhat included social grievances (such as issues of ethnic discrimination, xenophobia, housing, poverty, or union struggles), yet framed these grievances under a dominant narrative of returning to pre-2010 Western-oriented development. A smaller segment of post-2010 middle-class politicization involved the appearance of a new left constituency who stepped up in alliance with liberals' social critiques of the system. In the buildup towards the opposition's 2022 electoral campaign, new left groups organized together with social liberal-green segments of the opposition, led by Budapest Mayor Gergely Karácsony. In the intra-opposition contest for all-opposition candidates for the national elections, Karácsony withdrew from the final contest, allowing Péter Márki-Zay, a conservative mayor of a rural city with a former marketing career in North America, to take the lead over the social-democratic candidate Klára Dobrev (the wife of former prime minister Ferenc Gyurcsány). Márki-Zay was portrayed by local and international liberal circles as the ethical opposition candidate to Orbán, and enjoyed the support of neoliberal experts and capitalists (like former neoliberal minister of economy, Gordon Bajnai) who have supported attempts at liberal restoration since 2010. Jobbik, the extreme right party who earlier benefited politically from voicing social grievances under the Orbán regimes, has been contained and fragmented by Fidesz splitting into a deradicalizing Jobbik that became an unhappy supporter of Márki-Zay within the opposition alliance, and into the Our Homeland party, which carried radical right messages further without their social aspect, outside of the opposition coalition. In this process, previous oppositional collaborations with groups expressing social claims have been largely canceled or reduced to lip service.

In the last months of the 2022 election campaign, in an increasingly tense context of post-pandemic crisis and the sudden outbreak of the war in Ukraine, the liberal opposition supported Euroatlantic integration and free markets, with social elements toned down. Fidesz' penetration of the popular classes remained the only significant political outreach felt among those who suffer most from social polarization; this effect has been enhanced by strong messages emphasizing the country's energy security and keeping the country outside of the Western efforts for military help for Ukraine. Election results, featuring a stronger super-majority of Fidesz than in 2018, suggest that support for Fidesz' security messaging goes beyond the numbers achievable through

Fidesz' monopolization of the communicational channels and its use of electoral techniques.

In the context of sanctions against Russia, the subsequent intensification of the geopolitical tensions, and a generic crisis following the pandemic, the post-2010 pro-capital recovery that constituted the operating ground of the Orbán regime can be expected to be significantly modified. With its strong grip over domestic economic and political infrastructures, Fidesz is well placed to attempt to control some of the crisis dynamics – without being able to contain the crisis itself. Yet as the conditions of accumulation are shattered, this control might shift towards mainly oppressive and disciplinary mechanisms.

10   Conclusion

Instead of approaching post-2010 Hungarian illiberalism as a case of democratic backsliding after postsocialist democratization, this chapter looked at the present Hungarian regime in the context of reconfigurations in internal and external political, economic and geopolitical relations. In order to understand these relations, we have emphasized the importance of Hungary's position as a semi-peripheral country and how it integrates into the world economy given post-WWII hegemonic cycles. We showed that after the 1956 Revolution, Hungarian state socialism was reconfigured through a class compromise built on a "bridge model" mediating between Western and Comecon trade. Once the balance of this model was overturned in the 1970s, Hungary shifted towards taking on external debt and economic liberalization. The alliance that formed in this period between socialist managers, reform socialists, liberal experts and regime dissidents, international donors and Western capitalist lobbies, defined Hungary's post-1989 neoliberal integration model, and remained dominant until the late 2000s. The contender postsocialist power bloc, favoring national capital, remained subjugated to a subordinated economic position. Despite their differences, both the bloc that favored Western integration as well as the bloc that favored national capital shared the interest to weaken and divide workers' self-organization within the process of democratization. By the time the neoliberal model had been exhausted in the late 2000s, popular discontent was successfully tapped into by the conservative bloc's nationalist anti-neoliberalism and was channeled towards supporting a super-majority victory for Viktor Orbán's Fidesz party. After 2010, the new conservative regime used its parliamentary super-majority to both reorganize and stabilize capitalist extraction. It boosted a new state-backed oligarchy in domestic services, maintained and subsidized export-oriented FDI by (mostly German automotive) multinationals. This allowed the regime to compensate for its crisis-driven losses through an aggressive mercantilist industrial policy-mix (cheap labor, tax allowances and a new educational model), while at the same time diversifying external financing through new Russian and Chinese investments. Instead of a change of direction between democratic/authoritarian or East/West poles, the illiberal regime represents an adaptation to and state-driven reorganization of internal and external capitalist alliances, within a context of geopolitical reconfiguration under shifting hegemonic cycles. Having mobilized popular discontent with the neoliberal model of postsocialist integration to solidify its state power in its early phase, the present regime has since stepped up and diversified the degree and ways that foreign and domestic capital can exploit local labor. This has already posed challenges from far-right organizations to the regime's political legitimation. In a response to the challenges the regime has attempted to contain its own delegitimization through stepping up political tactics of ideological propaganda, interest-based support by the new middle-class benefiting from Fidesz policies, and electoral techniques targeting poor and expatriate electorates.[24] The formation of an all-opposition coalition prior to the 2022 elections had raised hopes for breaking Fidesz's super-majority, or even achieving electoral victory in the national elections. With these hopes proved futile, Fidesz is embarking on a super-majority government in the context of deteriorating conditions of accumulation, external systemic instability and growing tensions in the geopolitical sphere, which will significantly narrow down the maneuvering space for Fidesz, despite its internal hegemony based on its super-majority rule.

References

Arrighi G (1990) The Developmentalist Illusion: A Reconceptualization of the Semiperiphery. *Semiperipheral States in the World-Economy.* Greenwood Press: 11–42.

Becker J (2016) Europe's Other Periphery. *New Left Review,* 57(99): 39–64.

Bello W (2019) *Counterrevolutions: The Global Rise of the Far Right.* Agrarian Change & Peasant Studies.

---

24   The Fidesz regime made it possible for Hungarians outside the border to get Hungarian citizenship, and then used intensive electoral techniques to use their votes to its benefit.

Berend T I (1996) *Central and Eastern Europe, 1944–1993: Detour from the Periphery to the Periphery*. Cambridge University Press.

Bideleux R (1996) The Comecon experiment. *European Integration and Disintegration: East and West*. Routledge: 174–204.

Boatcă M (2006) Semiperipheries in the World-System: Reflecting Eastern European and Latin American Experiences. *Journal of World-Systems Research*, 12(2): 321–346.

Bohle D and Greskovits B (2012) *Capitalist Diversity on Europe's Periphery*. Cornell University Press.

Böröcz J (1999) From Comprador State to Auctioneer State: Property Change, Realignment and Peripheralization in Post-State-Socialist Central and Eastern Europe. *States and Sovereignty in the Global Economy*. Routledge: 193–209.

Brenner R (2006) *The Economics of Global Turbulence: The Advanced Capitalist Economies from Long Boom to Long Downturn, 1945–2005*. Verso.

Burawoy M and Lukács J (1994) *The Radiant Past. Ideology and Reality in Hungary's Road to Capitalism*. University of Chicago Press.

Cardoso F H (1972) Dependency and Development in Latin America. *New Left Review*, 1(74): 83–95.

Chase-Dunn C (1980) Socialist State in the Capitalist World Economy. *Social Problems*, 27(5): 505–525.

Dancsik B, Fábián G, Fellner Z, Horváth G, Lang P, Nagy G and Winkler S (2015) *Comprehensive analysis of the nonperforming household mortgage portfolio using micro-level data* (No. Special Issue 2015). MNB Occasional Papers.

Fábry Á (2019) *The Political Economy of Hungary: From State Capitalism to Authoritarian Neoliberalism*. Palgrave MacMillan.

Frank A G (1977) Long Live Transideological Enterprise! Socialist Economies in the Capitalist International Division of Labor. *Review*, 1(1): 91–140.

Galasi P and Kertesi G (1985) Second economy, competition, inflation. *Acta Oeconomica*: 269–293.

Gagyi Á (2015) Reform Economics at the Financial Research Institute in Late Socialist Hungary: A Case of Globally Embedded Knowledge Production. *Intersections: East European Journal of Society and Politics*, 1(2): 59–79.

Gagyi Á (2016) Coloniality of Power in East Central Europe: External Penetration as Internal Force in Post-Socialist Hungarian Politics. *Journal of World-Systems Research*, 22(2): 349–372.

Gagyi Á and Gerőcs T (2019) The Political Economy of Hungary's New 'Slave Law. *criticatac.ro*, 2019. January 1. Available at: http://www.criticatac.ro/lefteast/the-politi cal-economy-of-hungarys-new-slave-law/.

Gagyi Á and Gerőcs T (2022 forthcoming) Dependent development under geopolitical reconfiguration: Hungary's new geopolitics of indebtedness. *Globalizations*.

Gates L (2018) Populism: A puzzle without (and for) World-Systems Analysis. *Journal of World-Systems Research,* 24(2): 325–336.

Gereffi G and Evans P (1981) Transnational Corporations, Dependent Development, and State Policy in the Semiperiphery: A Comparison of Brazil and Mexico. *Latin American Research Review 16*: 31–64.

Gerőcs T (2017) Challenges of Internationalisation from the Perspective of the Chinese Currency. *Financial and Economic Review,* 16(1): 170–185.

Gerőcs T (2022) The Structural Dilemma of Value-Chain Upgrading: Hungarian Suppliers' Integration into the World Economy. *Society and Economy,* 44(1): 159–181.

Gerőcs T and Pinkasz A (2018a) Conflicting Interests in the Comecon Integration: State Socialist Debates on East-West-South Relations. *East Central Europe,* 45(2–3): 336–365.

Gerőcs T and Pinkasz A (2018b) Debt-Ridden Development on Europe's Eastern Periphery. *Global Inequalities in World-Systems Perspective: Theoretical Debates and Methodological Innovations.* Routledge: 131–153.

Gerőcs T and Pinkasz A (2019) Relocation, Standardization and Vertical Specialization: Core-Periphery Relations in the European Automotive Value Chain. *Society and Economy,* 41(2): 1–22.

Gille Z (2010) Is there a Global Postsocialist Condition? *Global Society,* 24(1): 9–30.

Gregor A (2017) Who is for sale? *The Future of the European Union: Feminist Perspectives from East-Central Europe.* Friedrich Ebert Stiftung: 9–20.

Greskovits B (2020) Rebuilding the Hungarian right through conquering civil society: The Civic Circles Movement. *East European Politics,* 36(2): 247–266.

Haney L (2002) *Inventing the Needy. Gender and the Politics of Welfare in Hungary.* University of California Press.

Hann C (2016) Cucumbers and courgettes: Rural workfare and the new double movement in Hungary. *Intersections: East European Journal of Society and Politics* 2: 38–56.

Krausz T (eds). (1998) *Rendszerváltás és társadalomkritika: Tanulmányok a kelet-európai átalakulás történetéből.* Budapest: Napvilág.

Kumral Ş and Karatasli S (2020) Capitalism, labour and the global populist radical right. *Global Labour Journal,* 11(2): 152–155.

Lóránt K (2010) *Magyarország külső eladósodása és annak következményei.* Manuscript.

Melegh A (2018) Counter Hegemony and the Rise of a New Historical Political Block. *tranfrom! Europe.* Available at: https://www.transform-network.net/blog/article/counter-hegemony-and-the-rise-of-a-new-historical-political-block/.

Mihályi P (2015) A privatizált vagyon visszaállamosítása Magyarországon 2010–2014. *Műhelytanulmányok 7.* MTA Közgazdaság- és Regionális Tudományi Kutatóközpont Közgazdaságtudományi Intézet.

Pellandini-Simányi L and Vargha Z (2018) Spatializing the future: financial expectations, EU convergence and the Eastern European Forex mortgage crisis. *Economy and Society*, 47(2): 280–312.

Poulantzas N (1974) *Fascism and Dictatorship. The Third International and the problem of fascism*. NLB.

Pósfai Z (2018) Reproducing Uneven Development on the Hungarian Housing Market. *Doctoral Dissertation*, University of Szeged. Available at: http://doktori.bibl.u-sze ged.hu/9753/1/p%C3%B3sfai%20zs_phd%20final_2018.04.05..pdf.

Scheiring G (2020) *The Retreat of Liberal Democracy: Authoritarian Capitalism and the Accumulative State in Hungary*. Palgrave.

Scheiring G and Szombati K (2020) From neoliberal disembedding to authoritarian re-embedding: The making of illiberal hegemony in Hungary. *International Sociology*, 35(6): 721–738.

Stark D (1996) Recombinant Property in East European Capitalism. *American Journal of Sociology*, 101(4): 993–1027.

Szabó A and Mikecz D (2015) After the Orbán-revolution: the awakening of civil society in Hungary. *Social Movements in Central and Eastern Europe: A Renewal of Protests and Democracy*. Bucharest: University of Bucharest: 34–43.

Szelényi I (1988) Socialist Entrepreneurs: Embourgeoisement in Rural Hungary. In collaboration with Manchin R and Juhász P and Magyar B and Martin B. Madison: University of Wisconsin Press.

Szombati K (2018) *The Revolt of the Provinces: Anti-Gypsyism and Right-Wing Politics in Hungary*. Berghahn Books.

Thoma L (1998) *A rendszerváltás és a szakszervezetek: 1988-1992: szociológiai-politológiai vázlatok*. Villányi úti Konferenciaközpont és Szabadegyetem Alapítvány.

Vigvári A and Gerőcs T (2018) The Concept of 'Peasant Embourgeoisement' in the Perspective of Different Historical Conjunctures. *Studia UBB Sociologia*, 62(1): 65–84.

Voszka E (1994) An Attempt at Crisis Management and the Failure of the Spontaneous Privatization. *Industrial & Environmental Crisis Quaterly*, 8(1): 23–40.

Wallerstein I (1976) Semi-Peripheral Countries and the Contemporary World Crisis. *Theory and Society*, 3(4): 461–483.

Webber J (2021) The Crisis of the Capitalist State and the Democratic Socialist Response – Latin-American left populist regimes. Paper delivered at the conference *Democratic Socialism in Global Perspective*, La Universidad Abierta de Recoleta – Wright-Havens Center. Available at: https://www.youtube.com/watch?v=j3Kbd-qq 9so&list=PLz0-Rs6r4XDWuFWsgj1vdFEiu_SkYoL3V&index=6.

Wilkin P (2016) *Hungary's Crisis of Democracy: The Road to Serfdom*. Lexington Books.

CHAPTER 4

Modi's New India

Hatred, Dispossession, Desperation

Aparna Sundar

1   Introduction

During a recent Hindu festival to celebrate the birth of the God Rama, several parts of the country saw large mobs of Hindu men wearing saffron bandanas, armed with sticks and swords, marching aggressively through Muslim neighborhoods chanting anti-Muslim songs and slogans; Muslims were beaten up, and property destroyed. The police stood by and watched; in one BJP (Bharatiya Janata Party)-ruled state, Muslims defending themselves had their shops and properties razed to the ground by the municipal government on grounds of 'illegal construction.'[1] This is but the latest, if the most widely organized, instance of the anti-Muslim violence inaugurated when Narendra Modi and the BJP came to power in 2014 that has seen a frightening escalation of late, with complete silence on the part of the Prime Minister. As extremist Hindu religious leaders declare the killing of Muslims and the rape of Muslim women a religious duty, knowledgeable observers have issued warnings of an impending genocide (Joshua, 2022).This hatred politics has combined with neoliberal policies of rampant extraction and accumulation to create multiple forms of dispossession across the country. The images of migrant workers trudging hundreds of miles back to their villages after the summarily-declared pandemic lockdown in March 2020, or of Covid patients dying outside hospitals and corpses floating down the holy Ganges river in April-May 2021 indicate a growing mass desperation, confirmed by data on rising unemployment, malnutrition, deprivation, and inequality, and regression on virtually all global economic and political rankings (Patel, 2021). Only a decade ago, it was assumed that such desperation had been left behind as India's high growth rates led to its being hailed as a 'rising power.'

---

1   I am grateful to Fabio Luis Barbosa dos Santos for his support and extraordinary patience and Nandini Sundar for her timely assistance, and to both and Gayatri Menon for thoughtful comments that have greatly helped to improve this chapter.

Despite this regression, Modi and his BJP continue to be popular, as the BJP's wins in four out of five of the state elections concluded in March 2022 demonstrate. Part of their popularity rests, of course, on the success of the project of *Hindutva*, or Hindu nationalism, whose longevity and ideological and organizational strength distinguish the Indian case from the others in this volume. The project's hatred and violence against Muslims and other religious minorities has become easily normalized within the already violent upper-caste and patriarchal social order it seeks to uphold. It is Modi's ability to secure the support of capital, however, and to bind the public through a canny combination of personal appeal, populist welfare measures, institutional capture, and straightforward repression that has enabled the *Hindutva* project to become politically hegemonic.

In order to highlight the continuities and breaks represented by the Modi regime, I begin by introducing the central political-economic structures and fault lines, as well as the distinctive tropes of Indian politics as they originated in the immediate postcolonial context, sketching briefly the social compacts of the four decades between independence from Britain in 1947 and the liberalization of the economy in 1991. In subsequent sections, I outline the nature of India's economic liberalization and describe how neoliberal economic conditions; long term ideological penetration by the *Rashtriya Swayamsevak Sangh* (RSS), the BJP's mother organization; policy and political developments under the Congress-led government in 2004–2014; and Modi's own mass-mediated charisma brought the BJP to power in 2014. A substantial core of the chapter examines the BJP's strategies of domination and legitimation since 2014 that ensured its re-election in 2019 and its continuing hegemony, as well as the kinds of resistance it has generated. I conclude by assessing the extent to which Modi and the BJP's success in crafting a 'new India' will set the terms of Indian politics in the foreseeable future, regardless of the outcomes of the national elections in 2024.

2   The Post-independence Decades (1947–1991)

India's postcolonial development, from the largest colony in the British empire to an independent republic, set in place a series of oppositions and contradictions, many of which have come to a head under the BJP.

The post-independence response to colonial extractivism and 'drain of wealth,' coupled with the influence of Fabian socialism and Soviet planning on the first Prime Minister, Jawaharlal Nehru, resulted in the adoption of the goals of autarky and 'self-reliance.' This was to be achieved through a mixed economy, with a central role for the state in planning, import-substituting industrialization, state ownership of the 'commanding heights of the economy,' and the restriction of foreign capital to a handful of consumer goods in joint ventures with domestic capital (Frankel, 2005). Known as the 'Bombay Plan,' this program had the support of India's handful of capitalist houses, for it provided them protection while also ensuring public investment in necessary infrastructure (Chibber, 2003). However, investment in agriculture, where the bulk of the population was employed, was limited. While officially mandated land ceilings broke up the largest holdings, actual land reform was uneven, with adverse consequences for both redistribution and agricultural productivity.[2] The protection of domestic capital, limited land reform, and the central role of the state produced a dominant class coalition consisting of industrial capitalists, rich farmers, and bureaucrats (Bardhan, 1998). Although the success of India's nationalist movement was attributed to Gandhi's mass mobilization, this has been described as a 'passive revolution' whereby peasants and other popular classes were rallied to effect an essentially bourgeois revolution (Chatterjee, 1986; Kaviraj, 1988). The persistence of feudal power structures and social relations in the countryside, albeit no longer legally sanctioned, and the general absence of a more deep-rooted social upsurge, also meant that the Hindu caste system, a ritually-sanctioned occupational and social hierarchy that determines the distribution of wealth and power, remained largely intact; the dominant classes were almost entirely drawn from the upper castes.[3] In practice, distinct sub-castes (*jatis*) exist in a "graded inequality" (Ambedkar, 1989) that is regionally specific; along with religious and ethno-linguistic identity, and the presence of significant indigenous communities (Adivasis), this makes for a complex social calculus where class as an abstract category in itself has very little political resonance.While introducing reform, postcolonial India also retained elements of the colonial administrative apparatus, including repressive 'emergency' laws and the 1860 Indian Penal Code. New ideals of nation-state sovereignty and territorial integrity led to the incorporation of various princely kingdoms in 1947; although India was established as a federation of states, there remained a centralizing impulse that justified the military occupation of several states in the north-east of the country, and of Kashmir from the early 1990s. A strong nation-state was seen everywhere as desirable

---

2   Since land reforms were a state subject, it was only in the Communist ruled states of Kerala and West Bengal and in Kashmir that there was significant land distribution to the actual tiller.

3   Despite the lack of scriptural sanction, caste and class overlap even among Muslim, Christian, and Sikh communities in India.

in the era of anti-imperialism, decolonization, development, and modernization. In its relationship to its people, however, the developmental state played
a more ambivalent role, casting people as 'populations' and objects of policy,
to be mapped, measured, and tutored into modernity, and legitimating the dis-
placements of development in the name of nationalism (Ludden, 1992).

At the same time, the new constitution adopted in 1950 contained a different conception of the people (and one at some odds with that of the developmental state): as citizens of a republic. The Constitution put in place the tenets
of a liberal democracy, with civil rights and 'directive principles' aimed at
achieving a more equal society, including: prohibition against caste and other
forms of discrimination; affirmative action for historically oppressed castes
and marginalized tribes;[4] 'secularism' as a principle of equal respect for all religions; and the recognition of some 15 official languages. As Dr. B.R. Ambedkar,
principal architect of the constitution and leader of the Dalits, warned in his
speech to the Constituent Assembly, the tensions and contradictions put in
place by the constitutional principles of legal and political equality in a deeply
unequal society could ultimately only be resolved through the achievement of
'social democracy' (Ambedkar, 1949). Although social democracy has remained
distant, over the decades the Constitution has created the conditions for a
popular attachment to the idea of rights and democracy as the bases for the
transformation of an unequal society (De, 2018).The Indian National Congress
(Congress), which had led the anti-colonial nationalist movement, was a broad
tent, containing liberals, socialists of diverse shades, Gandhians, and right-
leaning nationalists; outside it were Hindu supremacists to its right, and the
Communist Party to its left. After Nehru's death in 1964, the Congress consensus began to fray, with regional challengers arising from the late 1960s onward,
as well as factions from both the left and right moving out to form new parties
and alliances. Nehru's daughter, Indira Gandhi, came to power in 1967. Aside
from a two-year period of opposition rule in 1977–80, she remained in power as
leader of the Congress until her assassination in 1984. She led the country to the
left, nationalizing banks and ejecting several multinationals, passing constitutional amendments to include the words 'socialist' and 'secular' to characterize
the Indian Republic, and enacting populist policies addressing the poor. But
she also became increasingly authoritarian, declaring a constitutional 'emergency' with the suspension of civil liberties and democratic rights between
1975 and 1977, and putting in place several of the tendencies of centralization,

4 These are listed in separate schedules of the Constitution and thus described as 'Scheduled
   Castes' (SCS) – the most oppressed castes, including those deemed 'untouchables' who now
   identify as 'Dalits,' and 'Scheduled Tribes' (STS) – indigenous peoples, or Adivasis.

personalization of power, and deinstitutionalization that have been brought to a head under Modi (Guha, 2017). Aside from three incomplete terms of government by opposition coalitions, and one BJP term in 1999–2004, the Congress remained in power nationally until 2014. Its electoral strength varied over this period, however, sometimes necessitating reliance on other parties for support; in several states it had been completely replaced by strong regional parties. While it retained its brand of centrist, pragmatic politics and remained socially liberal and largely faithful, at least discursively, to the constitutional vision of India as a plural society, its politics on the ground – the use of money and muscle power, the populist instrumentalization of social identities as 'vote banks,' and the opportunistic recourse to majoritarian violence – left it with little of the moral hegemony of the Nehru era.

3   Liberalizing the Economy

By the 1980s, the public sector occupied a significant share of organized industry, banking, paid-up share capital, and sales (Frankel, 2005). But, several problems had become apparent with this model: the slowdown of industrial growth caused by inefficiencies in the public sector and the decline in real investment, frequent shortages of key infrastructural goods like power, coal, and cement, and lagging consumer demand. The latter was tied to the failure of widespread growth, employment, and purchasing power in the agricultural sector, although a Green Revolution policy adopted in 1969 had seen the emergence of a class of more affluent large farmers who had benefitted from the subsidized provision of agricultural inputs (Frankel, 2005).

Attempts to remedy this through a 'pro-business' approach were made throughout the 1980s, first under Indira Gandhi in 1980–84 and then under her son Rajiv Gandhi in 1985–1989, with the loosening of license controls, opening up of several sectors for private investment, and investment in telecommunications technology development (Kohli, 2006). However, throughout the 1980s, Indian capital remained wary of opening up to international competition, as did the left of the Congress party still attached to Nehruvian self-reliance and Indira Gandhi's pro-poor programs (Frankel 2005: 586). Opposition to these policies from across the political spectrum led the Congress to be voted out in 1989 and a short-lived coalition government (that included the BJP, then opposed to the entry of foreign capital) to take its place. By the time the Congress was returned to power in 1991, the increased cost of debt servicing, declining foreign exchange, and high debt to GDP figures forced them to turn to a large IMF loan, but the political unpopularity of this won the case for the 'pro-market' reformers who sought to bring in foreign investment as the solution. By then, several domestic capitalists were keen to expand globally and seek out export opportunities. The beneficiaries of the Green Revolution, too, had emerged into what Balagopal (2011) termed the "Provincial Propertied Class," seeking out new investment opportunities in small town real estate, food processing, and retail.

India's official liberalization dates to 1991, when Finance Minister Manmohan Singh and his team put in place a set of polices cutting back the number of industries reserved for the public sector, relaxing the licensing requirements for the private sector, devaluing the rupee, removing export quotas, reducing tariffs on imports, removing FDI limits, and permitting foreign financial institutions to make direct portfolio investments in India's two stock markets (see Corbridge et al., 2011; Frankel, 2005). But, a second round of pro-market reforms met with resistance from public sector unions, farmers, and middle classes worried about losing subsidies on utilities, and bureaucrats who had thrived in the *'license raj'.*[5] This contributed to impeding the Congress's return to power in the 1996 elections. Two rounds of elections led to unstable coalitions, until the BJP came to power in 1999 at the head of a coalition, and continued several of these reforms.Growth rates had already begun to rise in the 1980s, reaching 6.3% on average from 1991/92 to 2000s, according to World Bank statistics. Along with the growth of foreign capital inflows, internal savings were successfully mobilized. By the mid-1990s, a consumer class for white goods and vehicles had begun to emerge, including in the rural areas. However, the urban-rural income and wealth gap as a whole widened, and a vast rural majority remained poorly integrated into consumer goods markets. Thus, while there was a fall in overall poverty figures in the first two decades of liberalization, there was little public investment in human development and no growth in agrarian employment (Frankel, 2005).

4 The Rise of the BJP

The project of Hindu nationalism or *Hindutva* has a long history. The BJP is the political front of a larger and far older organization, the *Rashtriya Swayamsevak Sangh* or RSS, founded in 1925 with the long-term political project of establishing a Hindu nation. Its ideologues were inspired by the racialist ideologies and practices of Nazi Germany, with "a religio-cultural definition of nationhood function[ing] very much the way theories of race used to function in the Nazi

---

5   Rule by licenses and permits, used to refer to the period of state control of the economy.

ideology" (Ahmad 2015: 171). The RSS grew out of a longer effort at uniting and 'modernizing' what were a diverse set of beliefs and practices into a Hindu religion along the lines of Islam and Christianity – seen as more politically powerful – with a set of core tenets, foundational texts, and central institutions (see Sharma, 2011). It was also a project of upper-caste (Brahminical) patriarchy, aiming to shore up the caste hierarchy.

As important as its ideology is *Hindutva*'s extensive and sophisticated organizational apparatus (known collectively as the '*Sangh Parivar*' or Sangh family), aimed at building broad-based cultural consent for its doctrines. The RSS has thousands of fronts across the country, catering to different social groups – children, youth, women, university students, workers, soldiers, Adivasis, different caste groups; it is multi-layered, multi-faceted but highly centralized, with the exact extent of its organizational reach still unknown to outsiders. In 1964, the *Vishva Hindu Parishad* (VHP) or World Hindu Organization was founded with the aim of building the Hindu community worldwide (Agarwala, 2015; Jaffrelot and Therwath, 2007) and has been enormously successful in attaching the Hindu diaspora to the project of *Hindutva*. The VHP and RSS have built bases through systematic service work, as in the schools they run for Adivasis (Sundar, 2019) and low-income communities, and the relief work they have carried out during major natural disasters (Bhattacharjee, 2019; Thachil, 2014). The RSS was never part of the nationalist movement and was banned for a few years after independence because Gandhi's assassin was a member. Given this history, the hold of Nehruvian secularism into the mid-70s prevented RSS ideology from gaining much political traction. It was during the Emergency of 1975–77 declared by Indira Gandhi that the forerunner of the BJP, the *Jan Sangh*, gained legitimacy as part of the democratic opposition to the Emergency. The BJP was formed in its modern incarnation in 1984.

The BJP's ascent over the next three decades must be understood in the context of significant social transformations that had become visible by the late 1980s, and their intensification as an outcome of liberalization since 1991. The social and economic transformations, aided by the notable, if still inadequate, impact of affirmative action policies, had begun to change the caste-class structure in rural areas, with many Dalits and lower castes refusing menial work and ritual hierarchy and moving away to the city to work (see, for instance, Jodhka, 2014). Likewise, over this period, there had been a "silent revolution" (Jaffrelot, 2003) of increased assertiveness and political mobilization of the Other Backward Castes (OBCs).[6] In 1990, a short-lived non-Congress coalition

---

6   These lie between the Dalits and the upper castes, and are politically important, making up some 40% of India's population, and especially its farming communities.

government, of which the BJP was part, extended reservations in public sector jobs and higher education to a broad range of OBCs in addition to those already granted to the Scheduled Castes and Tribes. This provoked angry anti-reservation protests across the country by upper-caste youth, setting the stage for the revanchist caste politics of subsequent decades. The BJP withdrew from the coalition government, causing the latter to fall (Guha, 2017).Later that same year, in a counter-project of Hindu consolidation, the BJP launched a massive campaign to build a temple to Ram at his putative birthplace by destroying the 500-year-old Babri Mosque on the same spot. The campaign contained all the elements that were to become the hallmarks of the BJP's modus operandi: massive spectacle in the form of a garishly decorated chariot that travelled the country; the distribution of audio-tapes with the leaders' speeches (a precursor to its present use of social media); the collection of funds and of bricks consecrated for the temple from supporters across the country and the world; and the fomentation of violence along its route. The Babri Mosque was finally destroyed in 1992, marking a historic break in the public ethos of 'secularism' (Jaffrelot, 2021).

With liberalization arose new class formations. The 'provincial propertied classes' that had emerged with the Green Revolution and risen under liberalization to become the dominant regional capitalists had begun to form regional parties. These parties splintered Congress dominance, and became increasingly important to any coalition at the Center. In recent years, many of these parties have come to support the BJP, or in some states, these classes themselves have entered the BJP (see Desai, 2014). Other beneficiaries of liberalization included: a growing consumerist middle class whose interests were tied to employment in large private enterprise and who experienced a growing continuity with the affluent sections of the diaspora; and a layer of the less affluent middle class (dubbed the 'aspirational' or 'neo' middle class) that also became able to enter the consumer goods market. These emerging classes, along with the BJP's traditional class base of urban traders, were increasingly drawn to its brand of politics that sought simultaneously to embrace globalization and to assert an 'authentic' Indian (read: upper-caste Hindu) identity, as against the westernized English-speaking elites of the Nehruvian era.

Liberalization led to other transformations in the public sphere. As commentators (Jain, 2016; Madan, 2010) have pointed out, the Indian public sphere was never evacuated of religious practice and symbolism; in fact, credit for the revival of Hindu mythology in the public sphere is often given to the inauguration of a national audience for the serialization of the Hindu epic, the *Ramayana*, by what was still a state-run TV in the late 1980s, in the Congress era (Roy, 2010). Nevertheless, the new century has seen a heightened and more insistent desecularization of social life: the building of new shrines and temples; the merging of commerce and religiosity with new occasions for gift-giving tied to the increasingly ostentatious celebration of festivals, including several previously minor ones (Nanda, 2011); and the rise of new forms of "entrepreneurial spiritualism" (Gooptu, 2013). The intensification of this embrace by the 'modern' middle class of 'traditional' rituals, and the elective affinities between the commercial and the philanthropic interests of the "vernacular capitalists" who are leading patrons of many of the new temples, statues, and other religious iconography marking the visual sphere (Jain 2016) has had the effect of anchoring the *Hindutva* project in the textures of everyday life, giving it its quality of 'common sense.'

The rise of the BJP must also be seen within the current geopolitical moment, as a kind of Global South 'rising-power' populism (Arat-Koc and Sundar, 2020). With economic growth, and given its demographic power, India even prior to Modi had begun to seek a greater global role for itself (Kaur and Blom Hansen, 2016) within global re-alignments. But, this has been a double-edged sword. On the one hand, it has sought to assert its non-aligned and Global South status in global negotiations around climate change and trade, or through formations like the BRICS. On the other, it has sought to realign itself closely with the US, projecting itself, like Israel, as a democracy in a troubled region. Both postures originated with the Congress, but the embrace of America's 'war on terror' with the Islamophobia central to it has particularly benefitted the BJP. This 'rising-power' populism speaks to the "extravagant middle-class fantasy of private and national greatness" (Mishra and Waheed, 2020), shared by the Hindu diaspora in the West, now able to boast of the essential compatibility of *Hindutva* and liberal democracy (Agarwala, 2015; Jaffrelot and Therwath, 2007).

In its first time at the head of the national government, albeit at the head of a coalition, the BJP embraced this assertive nationalism, carrying out a nuclear test in 1998 (India's second, the first being in 1978 under Indira Gandhi) and offering a version of dual citizenship to the diaspora located in the West. However, the inability of the government to address the now visible harms of liberalization – increased inequality, joblessness, and agrarian distress – while adopting a slogan of 'India Shining' led to its defeat in 2004 and the return to power of the Congress.

In its first term (2004–2009), the Congress-led coalition – the United Progressive Alliance (UPA) – pursued 'growth with a human face' or what Nilsen (2019) calls "inclusive neo-liberalism." Even as one of its first pieces of legislation was the Special Economic Zones Act 2005 involving the acquisition of huge tracts of agricultural land, significant tax concessions to corporate houses, and loosening of labor regulations, under the pressure of social movements and the communist parties that were its electoral allies, it also implemented a number of landmark laws like the Right to Information Act 2005, the National Rural Employment Guarantee Act 2005, the Scheduled Tribes and other Traditional Forest Dwellers (Recognition of Forest Rights) Act 2006, and the Right to Education Act 2009 (Ruparelia 2013). In its second term (2009–2014), however, especially after the communists broke with the Congress over India's nuclear deal with the US, the government progressively became more isolated. Despite high levels of growth, corporate India raised accusations of policy paralysis and not moving fast enough with public sector divestment. Persisting unemployment, inflation, a series of violent clashes over land acquisition, and above all, allegations of corruption successfully highlighted by its political opponents resulted in significant public disaffection. The RSS was one of the forces behind the anti-corruption movement that arose in 2011–12, resulting in massive electoral gains for the BJP in 2014 (Gatade, 2021).

As corporate India grew increasingly nervous about the Congress, it turned to an actor known to have delivered reliably. In his 15 years as Chief Minister of the western state of Gujarat, Modi had been successful in creating a government that combined corporate-friendly and *Hindutva* policies, making it a precursor for what was to follow in India as a whole (Jaffrelot, 2019). Modi is the first leader to rise from the ranks of the RSS. Soon after being appointed mid-term as Chief Minister, he presided over a pogrom in 2002 where nearly 2000 Muslims were killed, women raped, and houses and businesses destroyed in the space of three days (Varadarajan, 2002). Modi's assertion of Hindu Gujarati pride in the wake of the pogroms established him as the 'King of Hindu Hearts.'

In the lead-up to the 2014 elections, it was Gujarati capitalists who helped swing the Indian industry body, the Confederation of Indian Industry (CII), behind Modi despite its initial nervousness given his record of presiding over the pogrom (Desai, 2014). The BJP PR machine, which he had had a big hand in putting in place, played him up as a 'Man of Development' and the solution to the problems with the UPA. The corporate-owned mainstream media ran with this, making no attempt to examine the 'Gujarat model' (Sud, 2022); in fact, Gujarat was well behind other states in its human development indices (Jose, 2012).

In the 2014 elections, big capital put its weight entirely behind the BJP, giving Modi's campaign a budget as large as Obama's in 2012 (Desai, 2014). The BJP came to power in 2014, at the head of a coalition of parties dubbed the National Democratic Alliance (NDA). The success of the BJP's project of Hindu consolidation can be seen in their winning votes across the caste spectrum in

2014 – they were able to draw in OBC votes in large numbers while not losing upper caste votes. They also did well among Dalits and Adivasis (Palshikar and Suri, 2014).

In the lead-up to the 2019 elections, as the BJP's popularity appeared to be waning, Pakistan-based Islamic militants carried out a timely attack on an Indian army convoy. The Prime Minister's muscular response to this 'threat to the nation' in the form of a bombing raid on Pakistan's border areas returned the BJP to power with more seats and a larger vote share than before. Analyses of the 2019 election show that the BJP's base had widened since 2014:[7] it received votes from rural as well as urban voters, from several Dalit and OBC castes, from poorer voters as well as the middle and upper classes, and its share among Adivasis had grown. There has been greater Hindu consolidation behind the party, with only Muslims voting consistently against it (Kumar and Gupta, 2019).[8]

5   The BJP in Power

The BJP came to power promising development and good governance. Yet, these have largely been steadily subverted. Instead, three chief imperatives have defined the BJP's nearly eight years in power: the transformation of India into a Hindu nation ('New India'); accelerated accumulation for Modi's crony capitalists and, more broadly, for capital as a class; and the consolidation of power for Modi and the party by any means possible. These goals have been pursued using an extraordinary array of techniques and strategies, with no area of life left untouched.

5.1   *Constructing the Hindu Nation*
Modi's 'New India' is imagined as a Hindu nation, recognized and respected as such on the world stage. To construct this new India, war needs to be waged on what was considered the old India – a multi-ethnic, multi-denominational nation – both in terms of its social fabric and in terms of its constitutional

---

7   The BJP alone has 303 seats in the current Parliament (272 constitutes a majority), and increased its vote share to 37% from 31% in 2014; the NDA as a whole received 45% of the popular vote, and 350 seats out of 543. The main opposition alliance, of the Congress and some allies, stands at a weak 90 seats; other unaffiliated parties have another 101.

8   The BJP's vote share among Muslims remained at 8% from 2014 to 2019, but its share among Dalits went up from 24% to 33%; among Adivasis it was a massive 44%; among lower OBCs 48%.; the BJP captured 61% of the upper caste vote (Kumar and Gupta, 2019).

guarantees of secularism, equality, and non-discrimination. The people of the new nation need to be re-defined, as well as those no longer part of it.

The Hindu nationalist movement in its current incarnation gained political saliency from its 1990 campaign of opposition to the extension of affirmative action provisions to Other Backward Castes (OBCs). Its success lies in incorporating these very backward castes, along with others low in the hierarchical order such as Dalits (16.6% of the population) and Adivasis (8.6%),[9] into the idea of a Hindu people, while continuing effectively to maintain and even intensify their socio-economic exclusion. This is largely through symbolic appeals, for example the December 2021 announcement of ten museums dedicated to tribal freedom fighters (Times of India, 2021), as well as complex electoral alliances with Dalit and OBC groups in different regions in order to obtain its majority (B. Narayan, 2009; Sarkar, 2019).

The attempt to incorporate the Adivasi communities that have traditionally stood apart and independent of the Hindu caste order (not ritually incorporated at its bottom in relations of servitude and exploitation like the Dalits) into the Hindu fold has an old genealogy. The religious and spiritual practices of these communities vary, from animism, to forms more closely affiliated to the recognizably Hindu, to Christian. The RSS / VHP have a long history of 'social work,' among them, running schools and other welfare activities to counter the presence of the Catholic Church, and more recently of evangelical Protestant sects (Sundar, 2019; Thachil, 2014). In recent years, the VHP has organized a series of large-scale *'ghar wapsis'* or homecomings, where Adivasis are purified and brought back into the fold of Hinduism to which they had supposedly belonged before animism or Christianity led them astray. This, and a series of anti-conversion laws passed by several BJP-controlled states which seek to criminalize any conversion activity have become tools to simultaneously exclude and intimidate Christians and include Adivasis and Dalits, two communities seen as particularly vulnerable to the 'allurement' to convert (Parthasarathy, 2022).

Given the strong overlay of caste and class, conditions for both caste-oppressed groups and Adivasis have worsened on every front under Modi. For Adivasis, statistics show continued socioeconomic exclusion, poor representation in higher education and government, and disproportionately high representation among those displaced by mining, large dam construction, and other such development projects who make up a large portion of the migrant workers seeking seasonal employment across the country. As inhabitants of forests

---

9   Figures from 2011 census.

and mineral-rich areas, Adivasis have also been on the frontlines of resistance to accumulation by dispossession, intensified under the Modi regime by the weakening of environmental protection laws (Dutta and Nielson, 2021), and victims of the crossfire between armed Maoist guerillas acting to protect these areas and the armed forces of the state (Sundar, 2016).

Dalits have been subject to increased humiliation, violence, and atrocities including the rising number of rapes of Dalit women (Teltumbde, 2019; Thorat, 2019). Constitutional provisions of affirmative action in education and jobs have been rendered increasingly empty as the public sector shrinks in favor of the private sector (including in universities) where these provisions do not apply (Thorat, 2019). It is only in contrast to the costs of exclusion from the nation – the stigmatization, violence, and legislative disenfranchisement meted out to Muslims, other religious minorities, and those deemed 'anti-national' (see The Wire Staff, 2021a) – that the value of the 'wages of Hinduness' (Arat-Koc and Sundar, 2020) in the form of symbolic inclusion, becomes clear.

The nature of the continuous attacks on India's 160 million Muslims, 14.2% of its population (2011 census), illustrate most vividly the kinds of 'othering' involved in this work of nation-building. In addition to the rewriting of histories and the changing of place names, this othering takes more abusive forms in the media and social media and sets the context for the almost daily incidents of violent attacks against Muslims. These began in 2014, with a growing number of lynchings of Muslim men by vigilante groups for eating or trading in beef, or for 'luring' Hindu women into marriage in order to convert them to Islam ('love jihad'). They progressed in 2020 to attacks on Muslims for supposedly spreading the coronavirus directly in a 'corona jihad.' Impoverished Muslim men have been particular targets, set upon and beaten up by vigilante mobs and asked to recite *Jai Sri Ram*' ('Long live Lord Ram') (Jaffrelot, 2021; Patel, 2021). The stigmatization has also taken the form of calls for the economic boycott of Muslim businesses, deepening the economic and social marginalization that was already a pervasive fact of Muslim life in many parts of the country, with Muslims unable to find homes for rent in many cities, for instance (Sachar Committee, 2006). Muslim women have been targets of another kind, with apps listing prominent Muslim women 'for sale' and young hijab-wearing women in the BJP-ruled state of Karnataka being prevented from attending college (Jafri and Ather, 2022).[10]

---

10   As anti-caste activists have argued, the vocabulary of the attacks on Muslims is derived from the language of caste – prohibitions against 'polluting' foods, the insistence on faith-based endogamy, and the violent erasure of the offending presence from public space (Menon, 2007).

Modi and other BJP leaders have made dog-whistle references to provoke this violence, and have sought to intensify the polarization for electoral purposes (Fatima, Barton and Jafri, 2022). Almost none of those who have carried out the lynchings and other attacks have been arrested, in sharp contrast to the routine arrests of critics and civil society actors. In February 2020, in a reprise of the violence in Gujarat, Muslims in Northeast Delhi were attacked in what was described as a 'riot' but was well-known to be retaliation for the protests against the Citizenship Amendment Act (CAA);[11] the police stood idly by as people were hurt or killed and homes and businesses destroyed. Two years later, perpetrators were yet to be named or charged, while perversely, 18 young Muslim student leaders who were active in the anti-CAA protests were arrested for their alleged role in the 'riots' (Karwan e Mohabbat, 2020–22; Singh, 2020).

A final move is the legislative disenfranchisement of Muslims through what Nielson and Nilsen (2021) and have called "Hindu nationalist statecraft." Several BJP-ruled states have passed cow protection laws and laws forbidding inter-faith marriages for purposes of conversion, adding the force of the police and courts to legitimize the vigilante violence, which can now portray itself as aimed at 'upholding the law.'

At the start of its second term, the BJP government introduced three major legislative and legal changes: the Kashmir Reorganization Bill, the Citizenship Amendment Act (CAA) and National Register of Citizens (NRC). In 2019, the government passed the Kashmir Reorganization Bill, which stripped Jammu and Kashmir of its status as a state, the right to its own constitution and flag, and autonomy to legislate in most areas. It also divided the former state into two federally administered union territories and reversed a constitutional prohibition on the sale of land to non-Kashmiris. Simultaneously, and supposedly to enable the Bill's passage without armed opposition, a state of emergency was declared in Kashmir, increasing the already massive military presence, shutting down the internet, closing schools, and carrying out large-scale arrests. Although the emergency has since been lifted, random arrests continue to be carried out, especially of journalists and human rights activists, and the armed forces continue to carry out violence against women, disappearances, and 'encounter killings' with the impunity they have been granted under the Armed Forces Special Powers Act, in force in Kashmir for over three decades now (Forum for Human Rights in Jammu and Kashmir, 2021; Kaul, 2021).

---

11   The CAA provides a fast track for Indian citizenship to non-Muslim migrants from Afghanistan, Bangladesh, and Pakistan.

The second piece of legislation, the CAA 2019, fast-tracks citizenship to non-Muslim (Hindu, Sikh, Christian, Jain, Buddhist, Parsi) refugees from Muslim-majority neighboring countries; Muslim refugees are not eligible. This legislation, coupled with an earlier National Register of Citizens set up to ascertain contested citizenship in the northeastern state of Assam, and intended to be extended to all of India, makes faith-based identity a criterion of citizenship as never before (Chatterjee and Raheja, 2020).

The final move was a Supreme Court judgement on the Babri Mosque. As noted in an earlier section, the Ram-temple / Babri Mosque issue brought the BJP to national prominence in 1989. While the mosque was demolished in 1992, the site had remained a matter of legal dispute. A Supreme Court judgement in November 2019 (passed by a pliant bench) gave the land to the Hindu parties to build a temple, while Muslims were given five acres of land elsewhere to build a mosque. On August 5, 2020, marking a year since Kashmir's occupation was made official, and even as Covid restrictions remained in place, Modi conducted the religious ceremony laying the foundation stone for the new Ram temple (The Wire Staff, 2020), thus symbolically ending Muslim claims for equal treatment by the law.

While Muslims have been the subject of the greatest hostility and disenfranchisement, Christians have also been subject to violent attacks for allegedly carrying out conversion activities; likewise, the leading role played by Sikh farmers in the protest against three farm laws led to the protests being dismissed as the work of 'separatists,' 'terrorists' and 'anti-nationals.' Others that too have been cast as 'anti-nationals' include left and liberal intellectuals and activists, journalists, university faculty and students, artists, and members of civil society organizations, all portrayed as members of an established, anglicized, 'pseudo-secularist' elite, against whom the BJP portrays itself as the representative of the authentic nation. These groups have faced arrests under national security laws, vilification, and both vigilante and state violence.

5.2   *Accelerating Accumulation*

Modi was crucial to the rise of the BJP to power because of his proven success in combining *Hindutva* politics with strong state support for corporate growth. Since 2014, he has also attempted a series of quick fixes and spectacular schemes to address (unsuccessfully) the slowdown in India's economic growth as a result of the 2008 global recession, the downturn in 2011 of the commodities supercycle, and the limits of the model of debt-led investment that had fueled the rapid growth of the previous decade. Patel (2021) suggests that while Modi's economic policies often seem erratic and incompetent, there is a method to the madness, aimed at concentrating capital in the hands of a few large players at the expense not only of the poor and working classes, but also of small and middle capital.

One of the biggest economic policy spectacles devised by Modi in his first term was demonetization. On 8 November 2016, he suddenly announced the overnight withdrawal of currency notes of the two highest denominations, amounting to some 87% of the cash in circulation. This was done against the advice of India's central bankers, and even the concerned ministries were not given advance notice. The result was chaos, as people scrambled to get into line at the banks to exchange their now worthless currency for new notes that the banks and ATMs were unprepared to issue (Reddy, 2017). The aims of the policy were declared as flushing out 'black money,' weeding out corruption, and targeting 'terrorists' who were supposedly paid in counterfeit notes printed in Pakistan. Within a year of the policy, it became clear that it had not met any of these goals since most undeclared wealth is held in the form of land, real estate, gold, or in Swiss bank accounts, not cash. The main impact was felt by the large proportion of Indians employed in medium and small-scale enterprises, in the informal sector, and in farm work, all of which operate primarily in cash. Some 1.5 million jobs in the informal and small-scale sector were estimated to have been lost right away; the policy's effects continue to be seen in shrinking investment in medium and small-scale enterprises, increasing unemployment, and worsening human development indicators (Patel, 2021).

Modi's government has failed spectacularly to address India's biggest economic challenges – increasing investment in manufacturing, attracting foreign investment, job creation, and export growth. Modi began by continuing, if repackaging and announcing as new, earlier UPA policies, chief among these being 'Make in India,' aimed at attracting FDI in manufacturing, and 'Skill India,' aimed at addressing the lack of employable skills among India's workforce. Six years after Make in India was launched, data showed that industry's share of GDP in India was at a two-decade low (Patel, 2021). Likewise, Modi's policies have not succeeded in stalling or reversing the declines in private investment and in fixed capital formation ongoing since 2011, in large part because these were also due to the massive growth in bad loans in public banks due to stalled projects (Jha, 2019). Almost half of the 20 billion USD of FDI that came into the country in 2016–2017 was for the purchase of distressed assets by international speculators (Jha, 2019: 97–98). Exports have also declined (Patel, 2021).

A fleet of neoliberal laws have been passed to further privatization (Ram Mohan, 2021) and improve 'ease of doing business' in India. The Land Acquisition law passed by the UPA in 2013 to ensure a modicum of fair compensation to landholders was amended in 2015 to enable the state to acquire land at lower cost. BJP-run states such as Uttar Pradesh first passed labor reforms decimating labor regulation and industrial relations standards; the BJP government at the center used the cover of COVID-19 to introduce such reforms nationally. Changes to the Environmental Impact Assessment (EIA) legislation now allow for EIAs to be carried out after the project has begun, with many sectors granted relaxations from requiring EIAs at all. The Forest Rights Act 2006, passed to make historical reparations to Adivasis deprived of their lands by the forest laws, has been diluted to allow officials to bypass elected village governments in order to launch commercial operations on forest lands (Dutta and Nielson, 2021).

As noted earlier, Modi had built a close relationship with leading Gujarati corporate actors, who bankrolled his campaign in 2014. These cronies have been richly rewarded since 2014, assisted in acquiring land cheaply and given licenses to build everything from ports to universities (see Thakurta et al, 2017; Thakurta, Palepu, and Jain, 2017; Patel, 2021).

The rich have also grown richer through policies such as the shift to indirect taxes like the goods and services tax and cuts in corporate tax rates. While India has always depended heavily on indirect taxes, these changes in tax policy have further contributed to a lopsided reliance on indirect taxes and to an increase in India's fiscal deficit (Oxfam, 2022). Oxfam reports that India's richest 1% now hold more than four-times the wealth held by the bottom 70% of the population. During the pandemic, (from March 2020 to November 2021), as the wealth of billionaires increased from USD 313 billion to USD 719 billion, over 46 million Indians are estimated to have fallen into extreme poverty (nearly half of the global new poor according to the United Nations.) Meanwhile, India's social welfare expenditure is among the lowest in the world: health spending remains at 1.2 to 1.6% of GDP and actually declined in 2021, and likewise education spending has averaged 3% of GDP for the past two decades (Oxfam, 2022).

Reports show that unemployment by the end of 2018 was the highest it had been in four decades and that labor force participation (LFP) also dropped, especially for women whose participation had declined to 10% by the end of 2020. A report from the Center for Monitoring the Indian Economy (CMIE) cited by Patel (2021) showed that almost 19 million salaried jobs (22% of all salaried jobs in India) were lost between 2019 and July 2020. The report showed a corresponding increase of some 8 million jobs in the non-salaried or informal labor market. There has been an appreciable rise in household debt, and a fall in consumption for the first time in half a century, including middle class consumption of such things as automobiles.

5.3   *Consolidating Power*

Despite the economic crisis, the swindles, and the failure to deliver on the promised 'good days,' the BJP has retained its hegemony. Cooptation into the hatred politics of *Hindutva* is a large part of the explanation; the remainder rests on populist measures, including the deployment of what Anand, Dimble, and Subramanian (2020) have termed the "new welfarism." Undergirding these forms of legitimation is an extensive authoritarianism.

Modi, as Arvind Rajagopal (2014: 13) notes, is "a man of many masks." He is simultaneously monarchical – issuing policies as decrees and raising monumental projects to mark his reign – and a man of the people, belonging to a humble OBC family, not a dynasty like the Gandhi family of the Congress. And while he wears a new outfit a day and designer accessories, he is described by fawning journalists as a *fakir* (ascetic); after the 2019 elections, he withdrew to the Himalayas to meditate, in a 'cave' outfitted with a camera that would broadcast to the nation this act of solitary spirituality. The decision to make worthless 87% of India's currency with a few hours' notice, or likewise to impose a national lockdown overnight, were hailed as 'masterstrokes' (Karthik, 2021) and evidence of the decisionism required of a strong leader. His projects and schemes demonstrate a technocratic imagination – the plan to create a hundred 'Smart Cities,' Digital India, aimed at extending internet access across the country (and indeed, digitization has been initiated in several areas, raising concerns around data privacy); and a bullet train to be built by Japan between Gujarat's premier commercial city, Surat, and Mumbai. None has been completed, and many have not even been started, but the image created is one of action and modernization.

The public's support for demonetization, despite the devastation it wreaked, illustrates Modi's skillful ability to combine personalistic appeal with Hindu and nationalist images and tropes. He announced demonetization as a purifying ritual requiring the "total mobilization of society" (Mehta, 2016) that would rid the economy and the nation of the corrupted elements seen to be undermining India's inherent potential as an economic superpower.

If Modi's populism relies heavily on discourse, it also has a material element. Modi describes his approach to welfare as one of 'empowerment' as opposed to the Congress-led UPA's approach of 'entitlement' (Aiyar, 2019). Empowerment is to be delivered through financial inclusion, by means of the *Jan Dhan Yojana* (bank accounts for the poor) and through Direct Benefits Transfers (DBTs). In addition to targeted cash transfers (of ultimately quite small amounts), these DBTs have included schemes for the distribution of toilets (*Swachh Bharat*), gas cylinders (the *Ujjwala* scheme), housing, electricity, and water connections; women have been particularly targeted as beneficiaries. This "new welfarism," is in contrast to welfare understood in terms of nutrition, health, or education, all of which require long-term investment and may not produce immediate benefits that can be associated with the benefactor. The "new welfarism" has two other important elements – it is personalized, with Modi's picture on the gas cylinders, food parcels, and billboards promoting the schemes. And it is centralized, its quantum and mode of distribution determined centrally rather than in response to local needs (Anand, Dimble, and Subramanian, 2020).

Modi's PR successes are aided by his effective capture of the public sphere. Already in 2014, the corporate-owned media had built him up even before he was elected. Since then, this media has been kept in line by threats to with-draw government advertising revenue that constitutes a large proportion of its income, or raids for income tax violations. Meanwhile, new sources of pro-government media have been created. Modi does not hold press confer-ences and has done only one interview in eight years. Instead, the public is treated periodically to his '*Mann ki Baat*' (Thoughts) on radio. Social media play another important role in disseminating the BJP's messages.[12] Paralleling the control and construction of what counts as news is the non-collection, suppression, or fudging of data, combined with the systematic undermining of universities and research institutes. For instance, no data seem to have been collected on various aspects of the pandemic. This made it possible for the government to declare in Parliament that there were no deaths due to shortage of oxygen in April-May 2021. It later tried to delay a WHO report showing over 4 million Covid-related deaths in India, eight times the official figure (Nolen and Singh, 2022).

Enabling the control of information is the centralization of India's other-wise federal structure. The slow penetration and capture of state and related institutions that was part of the longer game of the RSS accelerated once Modi gained power. This is particularly concerning in the case of the judiciary: a growing list of challenges to the government's actions have not been heard.

The state is at war against civil society. NGOs have been threatened with police action or the cancellation of their licenses to receive foreign funding. Among the countries found to have deployed the Pegasus surveillance soft-ware, India's target group was among the largest and included opposition leaders, journalists, and a range of civil society actors (The Wire Staff, 2021b). Dissenters and truth-tellers – anti-CAA protestors, opposition party leaders, farmers, journalists – have been criminalized under the colonial-era sedition

---

12   The BJP learned the uses of social media early on, and has a large and active social media team and has paid millions for ads on Facebook that disseminated pro-BJP messages (Sambhav and Ranganathan, 2022).

law and the anti-terror Unlawful Activities Prevention Act (UAPA). The extraordinary case of 16 Bhima Koregaon arrestees is emblematic of many of these tendencies: among India's leading human rights lawyers, journalists, academics, and activists who work closely with Dalit and Adivasi communities, the 16 were arrested supposedly for fomenting violence at a large Dalit celebration and charged under the UAPA for being part of a banned Maoist party. They have been held without bail for close to four years now, despite compelling analysis showing that the documentary evidence used to charge them was planted remotely on their computers using digital malware (see Bag, 2022).

In its March 2021 report on the status of democracy, the Swedish V-Dem Institute downgraded India to an 'electoral autocracy.' This formulation captures the increasingly performative role of democratic rituals and the continued use of elections to demonstrate legitimacy even as much of the process of governance is removed from public accountability. This is possible because of two things: the political pressure on the Election Commission, historically respected for its neutrality (Chishti, 2022); and the availability of vast amounts of funds to the BJP, which has more money than all other parties combined, raised, among other routes, through opaque financial instruments called electoral bonds that draw massive corporate donations made anonymously from India and abroad.[13] The BJP is constantly in election mode and the funds are necessary to maintain its formidable election machine; if another party wins the election, the funds are used to bribe opposition legislators to switch sides and cause the government to fall.

6   Resistance

In Modi's first term, there were several protests against the growing instances of anti-minority violence, with one in particular, #NotinMyName, against the lynching of a young Muslim man, leading to national and global demonstrations. Writers and artists returned their national awards in a campaign of protest against the growing intolerance of the regime. Students in central universities mounted a spirited campaign against *Hindutva* and consequently, were among the first to be charged with anti-nationalism (Hariharan and

---

13   Ahead of the recent polls in five states, electoral bonds worth Rs 1,213 crore were sold, making this amount the highest so far in state elections, and second only to the Rs 3,622 crore bonds sold ahead of the general elections in 2019. At least three-fourths of the amount sold in the financial year 2019–2020 has been revealed to have gone to the BJP (Chishti, 2022) and this latest round is unlikely to be an exception.

Yusufji, 2019). In Gujarat, attacks on a group of Dalit men led to a widespread
and militant Dalit movement of protest. However, it is two legislative moves
in Modi's second term that provoked widespread movements: the Citizenship
Amendment Act and a set of three farm laws. The scale of these movements
was unseen at least since the nationalist movement.

The first of the widespread movements began in November 2019 against
the Citizenship Amendment Act, with students from the Jamia Millia Islamia
University in Delhi initiating it. The movement spread across the country, with
protests and demonstrations held even in smaller towns, and bringing out
large numbers of previously apolitical Muslims as well as significant numbers
of non-Muslims. The emblematic protest of this movement was the neighborhood sit-in initiated by the women of Shaheen Bagh, a largely Muslim neighborhood in Northeast Delhi, in solidarity with the students of Jamia who had
been assaulted by the police. The Shaheen Bagh sit-in grew every day; women
spent entire days there with their children, and the men learned to feed them
and run the home. It became a focal point of the anti-CAA movement nationally. The protest was shut down when the pandemic lockdown was declared in
March 2020, and simultaneously, many of the anti-CAA activists were arrested
for supposedly having incited the previous month's violence in Northeast
Delhi (Mustafa, 2020).

The second movement was in response to the three farm laws aimed at
corporatizing agriculture (see S. Narayan, 2020). Starting in November 2020,
some 250,000 farmers from the northern states of Punjab, Haryana, and Uttar
Pradesh camped at three sites on the borders of Delhi for a year, with the singular demand of having the farm laws repealed. Farmers' organizations from
across the country sent contingents. The action was coordinated and run dem-
ocratically by a national coordination committee. Over the year of the movement, the resistance to the corporatization of agriculture grew to connect
issues of labor and agricultural distress, patriarchy and women's work, caste
and landlessness, and *Hindutva* and the repressive state (Singh, 2021). Modi
tried various tactics: ignoring them, unsuccessfully trying to divide the organizations and coopt some, the arrest and repression of allies, and active attempts
to counter the growing international support for the farmers' cause – before
finally agreeing to withdraw the laws a few weeks before elections in Punjab
and Uttar Pradesh.

These two large movements, the earlier protests, and the range of *Hindutva*'s
targets – Muslims, Dalits, liberals, artists, students, etc. – have created alliances
well beyond the left. In India, 'the Left' – referring mainly to the mainstream
parties of the left, the Communist Party of India (CPI) and the Communist Party
of India-Marxist (CPM) – was already facing a critique for its lack of inclusion

of caste and identity issues and historic attachment to industrial development. From 2014 onward, new Blue (caste-oppressed / Dalit movements)-Red
(Communist) and sometimes Green alliances have been forged on campuses
and more widely, joining hands with the national trade unions, the Gandhi-
inspired social movements against development-induced-displacement that
defend the rights of natural resource dependent communities, and the civil
and democratic rights organizations that have been a vital part of the democratic landscape since the Emergency of 1975–77. Their efforts are documented
and amplified by a small but influential section of the digital media, most of
it less than a decade old, that continues to speak truth to power despite court
cases and the surveillance and arrests of its journalists.

Recent years have also seen more spontaneous and localized expressions
of anger and frustration: by migrant workers demanding assistance and provisions during their long march back to their villages during the pandemic
lockdown; by families of Covid patients angered by the shortages of oxygen,
hospital beds, and space for cremations during the deadly second wave of the
Covid-19 pandemic in May 2021; by young men protesting the limited number
of government (specifically railway) jobs posted in February 2022. Yet these
protests, or even the more sustained ones by the farmers, have had limited
electoral impact.

In the electoral arena, the BJP rules supreme. The Congress is but a shadow
of its former self, though it is still the only party with a national presence
and essential to any coalition that might emerge. While the Congress, the
Communist parties, and some regionally strong parties speak out against the
BJP's hatred politics and centralizing moves, a soft *Hindutva* has become pervasive, and most parties are careful not to be seen as 'pandering to Muslims': the
only party that politically represents Muslims (the AIMIM) is treated almost
as a pariah despite its clearly constitutional and often progressive stands. On a
couple of occasions, opposition parties including the Congress have signed a
common statement of protest (PTI, 2022), but ongoing efforts to form a common electoral front have still to see fruition.

7   Conclusion

This chapter has traced the transition between two hegemonies (Vanaik,
2018): the Congress hegemony of the immediate post-independence decades,
resting on a dominant class coalition of large land owners, industrial capital,
and state bureaucrats cohering around a protectionist developmental state
with a commitment to 'secularism' and a degree of social reform; and the

hegemony of the BJP. Although the hegemony of the Congress had begun to weaken by the late 1970s, it was the processes set in motion by the economic liberalization it initiated in 1991 that eventually led to its eclipse. The new classes that emerged – of regionally influential agrarian capitalists, a globally-oriented and upwardly mobile middle class, as well as a new 'aspiring' middle class – were attracted by the BJP's challenge to the anglicized elites and established landed classes, and its promise of a 'clean,' technocratic alternative to the corruption of the Congress.

As the contradictions of (neo)liberalization deepened, the 'inclusive neo-liberalism' of the Congress was no longer adequate to hold them together. As elsewhere across the world, Modi's authoritarian-populism arose as the 'solution' for capital (see, for instance, Bruff, 2014). What distinguishes the BJP from other such formations, and gives it its enormous efficacy, is the deep and extensive organizational and ideological strength of the project of *Hindutva* or Hindu nationalism on which it is based (Sundar, 2021). As a project of upper-caste dominance that speaks in the name of national greatness and assertive authentic 'Indian-ness' (implicitly Hindu-ness), it appeals to the classes of capital as well as the middle classes and their diasporic counterparts, all largely drawn from these upper castes. This same language of nationalism and of Hindu unity also allows it to co-opt oppressed castes and indigenous communities against the non-Hindu and anti-national 'other' – Muslims and Christians, critics and dissenters.

There are contradictions. A look at the composition of the mobs involved in the anti-Muslim violence would suggest that these displays of power by essentially poor and unemployed young men represent the pitiful 'wages of Hinduness' that compensate for their growing precarity under the predatory neoliberalism put in place by Modi's economic policies. Some such form of psychological compensation and distraction from joblessness, inflation, and declining purchasing power might equally explain middle class consumption and circulation of media glorification of this violence. Yet surely, sooner or later, the declining material conditions will begin to seem intolerable. By then, the mobs that have been unleashed may not be easy to call back.

References

Agarwala R (2015) Divine Development: Transnational Indian Religious Organizations in the United States and India. *International Migration Review* (July).
Ahmad A (2015) India: Liberal Democracy and the Extreme Right. *Socialist Register* 52.

Aiyar Y (2019) Maximum Schemes, Minimum Welfare. *Majoritarian State: How Hindu Nationalism is Changing India*. Hurst and Company: 157–191.

Ambedkar B R (1949) Speech in the Constituent Assembly, CAD 25 November 1949, *Constituent Assembly Debates*, Vol IX. Delhi: Government of India Press.

Ambedkar B R (1989). *Untouchables or The Children of India's Ghettos*. In Babasaheb Ambedkar Writings and Speeches, Vol. 5. Mumbai: Government of Maharashtra.

Anand A, Dimble V and Subramanian A (2020) New Welfarism of Modi Govt Represents Distinctive Approach to Redistribution and Inclusion. *The Indian Express*, December 22, 2020. Available at: https://indianexpress.com/article/opinion/columns/national-family-health-survey-new-welfarism-of-indias-right-7114104/.

Arat-Koç S and Sundar A (2020) 'Rising Powers' and Authoritarian Populism: Beyond Northern Left Perspectives. *Challenging the Right, Augmenting the Left: Recasting the Leftist Imagination*. Halifax: Fernwood Publishing: 62–73.

Bag S (2022) The Security Playbook Used to Erode Democracy in Modi's India and How the Tide Might Turn. *Article 14*, 4 March 2022. Available at: https://article-14.com/post/the-security-playbook-used-to-erode-democracy-in-modi-s-india-how-the-tide-might-turn-62208c605b96a.

Balagopal K (2011) *Ear to the Ground: Selected Writings on Class and Caste*. Navayana Publications.

Bardhan P (1998) *The Political Economy of Development in India*. Oxford University Press.

Bhattacharjee M (2019) *Disaster Relief and the RSS: Resurrecting 'Religion' Through Humanitarianism*. Sage Publications.

Bruff I (2014) he Rise of Authoritarian Neoliberalism. *Rethinking Marxism*, 26, 1.

Chatterjee P (1986) *Nationalist Thought and the Colonial World: A Derivative Discourse*. Zed Books.

Chatterjee S and Raheja N (eds) (2020). India's Citizenship Amendment Act (CAA). *PoLAR Online* series. Available at: https://polarjournal.org/2020/09/07/indias-citizenship-amendment-act-caa/.

Chibber V (2003) *Locked in Place: State-building and Late Industrialization in India*. Princeton University Press.

Chishti S (2022) Funding, the Election Commission, the Media – our electoral institutional framework needs scrutiny. *The Caravan*, 26 March 2022. Available at: https://caravanmagazine.in/politics/funding-election-commission-media-electoral-framework-scrutiny?utm_source=mailer&utm_medium=email&utm_campaign=special_reads&utm_id=96.

Corbridge S, Harriss J, Ruparelia S and Reddy S (2011) Introduction: India's Transforming Political Economy. *Understanding India's New Political Economy; A Great Transformation?* Routledge: 1–15.

De R (2018) *A People's Constitution: The Everyday Life of Law in the Indian Republic.* Princeton University Press.

Desai R (2014) A Latter Day Fascism. *Economic and Political Weekly*, 49(35): 48–58.

Dutta A and Nielsen K N (2021) Autocratic Environmental Governance in India. *Routledge Handbook of Autocratization in South Asia.* Routledge.

Fatima M, Barton N and Jafri A (2022) 100 + Instances of Hate Speech, Religious Polarisation, *Hindutva* Supremacy in Adityanath's Poll Speeches. *The Wire*, 3 March 2022, Available at: https://thewire.in/communalism/100-instances-of-hate-speech-religious-polarisation-*Hindutva*-supremacy-in-adityanaths-poll-speeches.

Forum for Human Rights in Jammu and Kashmir (2021) Two years of lockdown: Human rights in Jammu and Kashmir, 2021, *India Cultural Forum.* Available at: https://indiaculturalforum.in/2021/08/04/two-years-of-lockdown-human-rights-in-jammu-and-kashmir-2021/.

Frankel F (2005) *India's Political Economy (1947–2004).* New Delhi: Oxford University Press.

Gatade S (2021) Anti-Corruption Movements and the Right. *NewsClick*, 17 October 2021. Available at: https://www.newsclick.in/anti-corruption-movements-and-right.

Gooptu N (2013) New Spiritualism and the Micro-Politics of Self-Making in India's Enteprise Culture. *Enterprise Culture in Neoliberal India: Studies in Youth, Class, Work and Media.* Routledge: 73–90.

Guha R (2017) *India After Gandhi.* New Delhi: Macmillan.

Hariharan G and Yusufji S (2019) *Battling for India: A Citizen's Reader.* New Delhi: Speaking Tiger.

Jaffrelot C (2003) *India's Silent Revolution: The Rise of the Lower Castes in North India.* Orient Blackswan.

Jaffrelot C (2019) Business-friendly Gujarat under Narendra Modi: The Implications of a New Political Economy. *Business and Politics in India.* Oxford University Press.

Jaffrelot C (2021) *Modi's India: Hindu Nationalism and the Rise of Ethnic Democracy.* Chennai: Context/Westland Publications.

Jaffrelot C and Therwath I (2007) The Sangh Parivar and the Hindu Diaspora in the West: What Kind of 'Long-Distance Nationalism'? *International Political Sociology,* 1(3): 278–295.

Jafri A and Ather S (2022) The Anti-Hijab Campaign Is A Form Of Cultural Cleansing Of Muslims That We Ignore At Our Peril. *The Wire*, 15 March 2022. Available at: https://thewire.in/communalism/the-anti-hijab-campaign-is-a-form-of-cultural-cleansing-of-muslims-that-we-ignore-at-our-peril.

Jain K (2016) Post-Reform India's Automotive-Iconic-Cement Assemblages: Uneven Globality, Territorial Spectacle and Iconic Exhibition Value. *Identities,* 23(3): 327–44.

Jha P S (2019) How India Has Missed the Bus: The Political Economy of India's Burgeoning Economic Crises. *Re-forming India: The Nation Today.* New Delhi: Penguin Viking: 95–116.

Jodhka S S (2014) Emergent Ruralities: Revisiting Village Life and Rural Change in Haryana. *Economic & Political Weekly,* 49(26): 5–17.

Jose V (2012). The Emperor Uncrowned: The rise of Narendra Modi. *The Caravan,* 29 February 2012. Available at: https://caravanmagazine.in/reportage/emperor -uncrowned-narendra-modi-profile.

Joshua A (2022) India at Risk: Genocide Warning. *The Telegraph,* 20 January 2022. Available at: https://www.genocidewatch.com/single-post/india-at-risk-rwanda -killings-predictor-sounds-genocide-warning.

Karthik M (2021) India's Covid-19 Response: Modi's Masterstrokes are a form of fascist shock therapy. *The Polis Project,* 14 February 2021. Available at: https://www.thepolis project.com/read-tag/modi/.

Karwan-e Mohabbat (2020–22) Reports and Videos on the Delhi Pogrom 2020. Available at: https://karwanemohabbat.in/delhi-pogrom-2020/.

Kaul N (2021) Coloniality and/as Development in Kashmir: Econonationalism. *Feminist Review* 128: 114–131.

Kaur R and Hansen T N (2016) Aesthetics of Arrival: Spectacle, Capital, Novelty in Post-Reform India. *Identities,* 23(3): 265–75.

Kaviraj S (1988) A Critique of the Passive Revolution. *Economic and Political Weekly,* 23(45/47): 2429–44.

Kohli A (2006) Politics of Economic Growth in India, 1980–2005: Part I: The 1980s. *Economic and Political Weekly,* April 1, 2006: 1251–1259.

Kumar S and Gupta P (2019) Where did the BJP get its votes from in 2019? *Livemint,* 3 June 2019. Available at: https://www.livemint.com/politics/news/where-did-the -bjp-get-its-votes-from-in-2019-1559547933995.html.

Ludden D (1992) India's Development Regime. *Colonialism and Culture.* University of Michigan Press.

Madan T N (2010) *Modern Myths, Locked Minds: Secularism and Fundamentalism in India.* Delhi: Oxford University Press.

Mehta P (2016) It's Permanent Revolution. *The Indian Express,* 26 November 2016. Available at: https://indianexpress.com/article/opinion/columns/demonetisation -currency-rs-5001000-notes-ban-demonetisation-effects-debate-its-permanent-rev olution-4395371/.

Menon D M (2007) An Inner Violence: Why Communalism in India is About Caste. *The Future of Secularism.* Oxford University Press: 60–82.

Mishra P and Waheed M (2020) On the Death of India's Liberal Self-Image. *The Wire,* 5 January 2020. Available at: https://thewire.in/rights/pankaj-mishra-mirza-waheed -kashmir-caa-india.

Mustafa S (2020) *Shaheen Bagh and the Idea of India.* New Delhi: Speaking Tiger.

Nanda M (2011) *The God Market: How Globalization is Making India More Hindu.* NYU Press.

Narayan B (2009) *Fascinating Hindutva: Saffron Politics and Dalit Mobilisation*. New Delhi: Sage Publications.

Narayan S (2020) The Three Farm Bills: Is this the market reform Indian agriculture needs? *The India Forum*, 27 November 2020. Available at: https://www.theindiaforum.in/article/three-farm-bills.

Nielsen K B and Nilsen A G (2021) Hindu Nationalist Statecraft and Modi's Authoritarian Populism. In *Routledge Handbook of Autocratization in South Asia*. Routledge, 92–100.

Nilsen A G (2019) From Inclusive Neoliberalism to Authoritarian Populism: Trajectories of Change in the World's Largest Democracy. *State of Democracy: Essays on the Life and Politics of Contemporary India*. Delhi: Primus Books.

Nolen S and Singh K D (2022) India Is Stalling the W.H.O.'s Efforts to Make Global Covid Death Toll Public. *The New York Times*, April 18, 2022. Available at: https://www.nytimes.com/2022/04/16/health/global-covid-deaths-who-india.html.

Oxfam India (2022) Inequality Kills. India Supplement 2022. Available at: https://www.oxfamindia.org/knowledgehub/workingpaper/inequality-kills-india-supplement-2022.

Palshikar S and Suri K C (2014) India's 2014 Lok Sabha Elections: Critical Shifts in the Long Term, Caution in the Short Term. *Economic and Political Weekly*, 49(39): 39–49.

Parthasarathy S (2022) India's Anti-Conversion Laws: The Death of Secularism. *The India Forum*, 4 January 2022. Available at: https://www.theindiaforum.in/article/india-s-anti-conversion-laws-death-secularism.

Patel A (2021) *Price of the Modi Years*. Chennai: Westland Non-Fiction.

PTI (2022) PM's Silence Shows Armed Mobs Enjoy Official Patronage': Opposition Leaders in Joint Statement. *The Wire* 16 April 2022. Available at: https://thewire.in/politics/pms-silence-shows-armed-mobs-enjoy-official-patronage-opposition-leaders-in-joint-statement.

Rajagopal A (2014) Two Tyrants in the Age of Television. *Economic and Political Weekly*, XLIX(8): 12–15.

Ram Mohan T T (2021) India's Privatisation Drive. *The India Forum*, 15 February 2021. Available at: https://www.theindiaforum.in/article/india-s-privatisation-drive?utm_source=website&utm_medium=organic&utm_campaign=category&utm_content=Economy#tif-fn1.

Reddy R (2017) *Demonetisation and Black Money*. Hyderabad: Orient Blackswan.

Roediger D (1999) *The Wages of Whiteness: Race and the Making of the American Working Class*. Verso.

Roy S (2010) Temple and Dam, Fez and Hat: The Secular Roots of Religious Politics in India and Turkey. *Commonwealth & Comparative Politics*, 48(2): 148–172.

Ruparelia S (2013) India's New Rights Agenda: Genesis, Promises, Risks. *Pacific Affairs*, 86(3): 569–590.

Sachar Committee (2016) Prime Minister's High Level Committee. The Social, Economic and Educational Status of the Muslim Community in India (Chaired by Justice R. Sachar). Government of India: Cabinet Secretariat.

Sambhav K and Ranganathan N (2022) How a Reliance-funded firm boosts BJP's campaigns on Facebook. *Al Jazeera* 14 March 2022. Available at: https://www.aljazeera .com/economy/2022/3/14/how-a-reliance-funded-company-boosts-bjps-campai gns-on-facebook.

Sachar Committee (2006) Prime Minister's High Level Committee. The Social, Economic and Educational Status of the Muslim Community in India (Chaired by Justice R. Sachar). Government of India: Cabinet Secretariat.

Sarkar T (2019) How the Sangh Parivar Writes and Teaches History. *Majoritarian State: How Hindu Nationalism is Changing India.* Hurst and Company: 151–176.

Sharma J (2011) *Hindutva: Exploring the Idea of Hindu Nationalism.* Penguin Books India.

Singh C U (2020) *The Delhi Riots of February 2020: Causes, Fallout and Aftermath.* Delhi: Citizens and Lawyers Initiative.

Singh N (2021) Agrarian Crisis and the Longest Farmers' Protest in Indian History. *New Labor Forum,* 30(3): 66–75.

Sud N (2022) The Actual Gujarat Model: Authoritarianism, Capitalism, Hindu Nationalism and Populism in the Time of Modi. *Journal of Contemporary Asia,* 52(1): 102–126.

Sundar N (2016) *The Burning Forest: India's War in Bastar.* New Delhi: Juggernaut Books.

Sundar N (2019) *Hindutva* Incorporation and Socio-Economic Exclusion: The Adivasi Dilemma. *Majoritarian State: How Hindu Nationalism is Changing India.* Hurst and Company: 249–258.

Sundar N (2021) India's Unofficial Emergency. *The Emergence of Illiberalism: Understanding a Global Phenomenon.* Routledge: 188–201.

Teltumbde A (2019) Onslaughts on Dalits in the Time of *Hindutva. Re-forming India: The Nation Today.* New Delhi: Penguin Viking: 363–382.

Thachil T (2014) Elite Parties and Poor Voters: Theory and Evidence from India. *American Political Science Review,* 108(2): 454–477.

Thakurta P G, Palepu A R, Jain S and Dasgupta A (2017) Modi Government's Rs 500–Crore Bonanza to the Adani Group. *The Wire,* 19 June 2017. Available at: https://thew ire.in/business/modi-government-adani-group.

Thakurta P G, Palepu A R and Jain S (2017) Did the Adani Group Evade Rs 1,000 Crore in Taxes? *The Wire,* 14 January 2017. Available at: https://thewire.in/business/adani -group-tax-evasion.

The Wire Staff (2020) Babri Masjid: The Timeline of a Demolition. *The Wire,* September 30 2020. Available at: https://thewire.in/communalism/babri-masjid-the-timeline -of-a-demolition.

The Wire Staff (2021a) The Updated List of India's 'Anti-Nationals' (According to the Modi Government), *The Wire*, 19 February 2021. Available at: https://thewire.in/rights/india-modi-anti-national-protest-arrest-sedition-authoritarianism.

The Wire Staff (2021b) Pegasus Project: 174 Individuals Revealed By The Wire On Snoop List So Far, *The Wire*, 04 August 2021. Available at: https://thewire.in/rights/project-pegasus-list-of-names-uncovered-spyware-surveillance.

Thorat S (2019) Dalits in Post-2014 India: Between Promise and Action. *Majoritarian State: How Hindu Nationalism is Changing India*. Hurst and Company: 217–236.

Times of India (2021) India will soon have Tribal Freedom Fighters' Museum to honour unsung tribal heroes, *Times of India*, 6 December 2021. Available at: https://timesofindia.indiatimes.com/travel/travel-news/india-will-soon-have-tribal-freedom-fighters-museum-to-honour-unsung-tribal-heroes/as88115284.cms#:~:text=Recently%2C%20Union%20Home%20Minister%20Amit,the%20Ministry%20of%20Tribal%20Affairs.

Vanaik A (2018) India's Two Hegemonies. *New Left Review* 112.

Varadarajan S (2002) *Gujarat, the Making of a Tragedy*. Penguin Books India.

CHAPTER 5

Can Democracies Die Democratically?

Rodrigo Duterte in the Philippines

Cecilia Lero

On May 9th, 2016, Rodrigo Duterte was elected president of the Philippines. Thirty years after becoming a worldwide exemplar of democracy through the People Power Revolution, in which a million people spent four days on the streets of Manila to topple the 21-year rule of dictator Ferdinand Marcos, a plurality of the Filipino electorate voted for a presidential candidate who referred to Marcos as *"pinaka* the best *na presidente na dumaan"* (the absolute best president we've experienced), said he would be willing to declare a revolutionary government, and that, if faced with impeachment, that he would merely close congress.

With Duterte's election, the Philippines joined the ranks of, among others, India, Turkey, and Hungary (Brazil would join later) as a democratic country once thought to be on an inevitable path towards better-quality democracy that now found itself on a dangerous path backwards. Yet, in May 2016, there was little talk of a global turn to the autocratic right among Filipino democracy activists and scholars. They appeared to be mostly hopeful that democratic institutions, as immature as they were, would be enough to prevent Duterte from implementing the brazenly autocratic and violent ideas he seemed to use as punchlines during his campaign. Over the next six years, however, Duterte would prove just how fragile Philippine democracy was as he systematically pulled apart controls on executive power and instituted a regime dominated by violence, fear, and hate. Moreover, he did this while maintaining genuine popularity, indicating a move towards authoritarianism both institutionally as well as in political culture.

Section 1 presents a history of the Philippines leading up to the Duterte campaign, highlighting key aspects of its political system. Section 2 describes the Duterte presidential campaign and its main appeals. Section 3 seeks to explain why this campaign was effective and how it channeled frustrations stemming from the nature of capitalist and liberal democratic development in the Philippines over the past half century. Section 4 describes how the Duterte administration has used a combination of legal and extralegal strategies to close democratic space. Section 5 describes the political opposition and addresses why they have been unable to make meaningful inroads into Duterte's popularity. Finally, the conclusion summarizes the chapter's main points and reflects on the legacies of Duterte's regime that Filipinos will have to deal with for generations to come.

1   History of the Philippines and Its Political System

In the 333 years that Spain ruled the Philippines as a colony, it was generally uninterested in establishing state infrastructure, bureaucratic capacity, or a collective identity among the diverse ethnicities present (Anderson 1983). The Philippines' main roles in the empire were to serve as a trading port between the American colonies and China, and secondarily, as a source for raw agricultural materials. As a result, the archipelago of over 7,100 islands never developed a single ethnolinguistic identity (over 80 languages are spoken) and the southern Mindanao region was never successfully colonized, setting the stage for clan-based and religious conflict that was later exacerbated by the Marcos dictatorship. The appointed colonial governor was a weak figure. Rather, the logic that dominated the political power structure was the *encomienda* system wherein conquering Spaniards were rewarded with the right to collect labor and tribute from indigenous people. As the Spaniards intermarried with Filipinas (the conquerors were almost exclusively male), this developed into the *hacienda* system wherein powerful landowning families dominated economic and political power in a region. At the same time, the absence of a strong crown presence left a void of influence that the Catholic Church readily filled.

Following Spain's defeat in the Spanish-American War, Spain ceded the Philippines to the United States in 1898. The Philippine independence movement, which had been exacting high costs on Spanish colonial forces, was defeated by the United States through a combination of military might and the co-optation of high-ranking officers. As the new colonial power, the United States introduced elections for a national assembly. But, as the same regional families still monopolized local social status and economic power, these elections merely provided a veneer of democratic legitimacy to the same system. Like Spain, the US attempted and failed to subdue and colonize the Mindanao region, killing at least tens of thousands of Muslim Mindanaoans in the process.

The Philippines gained independence following World War II. The politics of this period were characterized by competition between two parties: the Liberal and the Nacionalista Party. However, these parties were ideologically indistinguishable and little more than rotating fan clubs with fluid membership around elite personalities (Quimpo 2007). In 1965, Ferdinand Marcos was elected president under the Nacionalista banner. He was reelected in 1969 amidst widespread allegations of violence and fraud. After several years of gradually closing democratic space, Marcos declared martial law in 1972.

The Marcos dictatorship, not unlike other dictatorships during the Cold War period, attempted to present as itself as the answer to years of corrupt and inept government by a closed circle of landed elites in order to establish a 'new society'[1] based on discipline and national development. This rhetoric of 'discipline', however, was strongly related to classist and colonial tropes of the poor Philippine masses as savage, uncivilized, and unprepared for democracy. The notion of 'discipline' also provided justification for widespread human rights abuses, including over 3,500 state-sponsored murders, 35,000 people tortured, and 70,000 people arrested, as well as hundreds of cases of forced disappearance and rapes (McCoy 2009).

What was presented as national industrial development was characterized by crony capitalism and massive, gaudy public works projects that benefitted and glorified the dictator and his family, while basic infrastructure and social services were largely ignored. Despite two years of high GDP growth in the mid 1970s, the Marcos years stifled long-term economic development through massive corruption (Marcos is ranked number two on the Forbes' list of all time most corrupt leaders) and the diversion of money away from education and healthcare towards security forces and personal spending (Ansell 2008; Fineman 1987). Furthermore, the complicated web of crony capitalism and interlocking corporations that Marcos constructed for his corruption has made it painstakingly difficult for subsequent governments and citizens' groups to reclaim the stolen wealth or hold the Marcos family and its cronies accountable.

Following years of popular organizing, much of it clandestine, Marcos was toppled by a bloodless coup in the EDSA People Power Revolution of 1986.[2] Formal democracy was restored, and a new constitution adopted. However, the democratic Philippines has been far from stable or ideal. After Marcos's ouster, Corazon Aquino, the widow of a prominent opposition leader slain by the Marcos regime, assumed the presidency. Aquino, a member herself of the landed elite, followed a path of liberal reformism rather than radical democratic and economic restructuring. She quickly declared to foreign creditors that the Philippines would honor all Marcos-incurred sovereign debt (which

---

1 The party Marcos eventually established, the *Kilusang Bagong Lipunan*, literally means the new nation movement.
2 Named for Epifanio de los Santos Avenue, the main highway in Metro Manila that a million people occupied for four days demanding an end to the Marcos dictatorship.

had reached US$ 24 billion by 1984) and seemed more interested in finding and recovering the wealth stolen by Marcos than undoing the institutional damage and embedded corruption and ineptitude in various state agencies or address-ing systematic inequality and widespread misery. To be fair, however, Aquino was president at a time of immense instability, surviving no less than six coup attempts by Marcos loyalists and factions of the military. Coalitions with elite families, big business, and holdovers from the previous regime offered a way for the nascent democracy to survive.

The presidency peacefully transitioned to Fidel Ramos following the elec-tion of 1992. The Ramos years were a period of continued liberal reformism and aggressive privatization. Following Ramos, then vice-president[3] and for-mer movie star Joseph 'Erap' Estrada was elected. Although Estrada came from a wealthy family, his numerous movie roles as a hero of the masses formed the basis for his political image. While his poor and working-class supporters proudly repeated his slogan, *'Erap para sa mahirap'* ('Erap for the poor'), the perfumed upper middle and wealthy classes were offended by his image as a drinking, smoking, cursing womanizer. Estrada would serve less than three years of his six-year mandate. A corruption scandal led to his impeachment in 2001 and brought people to the streets in what was dubbed "EDSA II". The head of the Armed Forces of the Philippines declared his support for then-Vice President Gloria Macapagal Arroyo and Estrada resigned the next day. He would later be convicted of plunder.

It is worth noting that four months after EDSA II removed Estrada from the presidency, another mass mobilization, dubbed EDSA III, attempted to rein-state him. Whereas the bulk of the EDSA II protesters came from the ranks of students, the middle class, the Catholic church, and the organized left, EDSA III protesters came from charismatic Christian groups and the unorganized urban poor. Although unsuccessful, the uprising was a marker of class tensions as well as a shock to the organized left that questioned how connected to the masses it actually was.

Arroyo initially seemed like she might offer governance that was at least competent, even if based on neoliberal economics. Arroyo was the daughter of a pre-Marcos president, held a Ph.D. in economics, and appointed several respected reform-oriented technocrats to cabinet positions. However, her first term was plagued by a crisis of legitimacy as well as corruption charges. Although presidential reelection is disallowed under the 1987 Constitution,

---

3   In the Philippines, the president and vice president are elected separately and do not have to be from the same party. Estrada was not a party-mate of Ramos, but rather ran under a party he founded.

Arroyo ran for reelection in 2004. Arroyo eked out a narrow victory over Fernando Poe, Jr., Estrada's friend and fellow former movie star.

In 2005, however, audio tapes of a call between Arroyo and a Commission on Elections official were released, wherein Arroyo was heard ordering that the elections be rigged in her favor. The scandal ignited widespread protests, calls for Arroyo's impeachment and ouster, and dismal public approval ratings – all of which would last until the end of her term. In reaction, Arroyo clamped down on democratic space, including ordering the repression of mass protests and threatening opposition figures. As the uncharismatic Arroyo commanded little personal loyalty, the need to buy the loyalty of other political actors gave her further reason to expand corrupt practices, including a number of opaque government-to-government deals with China that encroached on Philippine sovereignty. Extreme military generals were also given a free hand to torture and kill their historic enemy, 'communists', in exchange for loyalty. While there was impressive GDP growth under Arroyo, this was largely fuelled by the continuing aggressive privatization of state assets, the embrace of extractive industries, and remittances sent by overseas Filipino workers.

The lead-up to the 2010 presidential election was especially tense because Arroyo's desire to remain in power, by extra constitutional means if necessary, was clear. Despite Arroyo's dismal popularity, there was no unifying opposition figure until former president Corazon Aquino died in 2009. The wave of sympathy led to calls for Corazon's son, Benigno III (popularly known as 'Noynoy') to run for the presidency. Noynoy was, at that time, a senator without a particularly impressive record or inspiring rhetorical style. However, his and his mother's reputations for not being corrupt, the parallels being made to the closing of democratic space and corruption under Marcos, and Noynoy's image as the most consistently anti-Arroyo presidential candidate (except, perhaps, for Estrada who had since been pardoned and was running once again), helped him win victory.

The second Aquino administration began with a wave of hope that real changes would be made. Although P-Noy (as he was called after the election) still embraced neoliberal economic policies that emphasized the attraction of foreign capital as the main driver of growth, he appointed some progressive officials to his cabinet and was genuinely interested in expanding anti-poverty programs and reducing corruption and clientelism. The economy averaged 6.2% GDP growth during his term, inflation remained below 3%, investments were made in social services like elementary education and healthcare, and corruption decreased.

However, there was the general sense that the P-Noy administration over-promised compared to what it was actually capable of (or willing) to deliver.

The P-Noy administration took a liberal, reformist approach, meaning that change was by-the-book and, thus, slow-going. This was, in part, a reaction to Arroyo's haphazard way of skirting or attacking institutions and, in part, a function of overconfidence that P-Noy's Liberal Party could translate his personal popularity into an easy win in the next presidential election, ensuring policy continuity. Poverty declined by 5% that, while an impressive accomplishment in only six years, appeared modest compared to the fortunes the rich were accumulating. Corruption declined, but was far from eradicated. Some avenues opened for the organized basic sectors (notably, urban poor, farmers, and fisherfolk) to participate in policy-making and program design. However, their actual gains were limited and often did not spill over to the unorganized. Importantly, the P-Noy administration and Liberal Party had no vision of building a mass-based, programmatic party in order to counter the logic of local elite clientelism. Politics remained a game for the rich where the masses could only hope to catch some of the crumbs.

To summarize, democracy in the post-Marcos period has continued to be turbulent and exclusionary for the vast majority of Filipinos. Ethnolinguistic regionalism and local politics controlled by landed elites continue to color capital-region dynamics. Personality-centered patronage and clientelism are the dominant logics that undergird most people's relationship with their government officials. Relatedly, mainstream political parties continue to be weak and fluid formations without mass membership bases and ideologically indistinct from each other. Family names continue to be the markers that voters most widely use when casting their ballots. Both political and criminal violence are quotidian parts of life. The crushing sovereign debt and Marcos cronies that continue to be embedded among the political and economic elite have proven obstacles to inclusive economic growth and a reckoning with the abuses of dictatorship. Nevertheless, the democratic period witnessed substantial improvements in terms of protections for human rights, civil liberties, and inclusive social services. As we will see in the following sections, these improvements were insufficient to match the great promise that came with formal democracy. The latent tensions that existed in politics and society would boil over in the 2016 elections.

2   The Campaign

The Duterte campaign was based on two main messages: 1) I am not like the rest of these corrupt, traditional politicians, and 2) There are good people and bad people. In order for the nation to progress and for people to experience safety and prosperity, we simply have to kill all the bad people. This first message is ironic because Duterte is, in fact, the scion of a political family[4] and has himself been mayor of the southern city of Davao for nearly three decades.[5] The second message is an obvious oversimplification of the country's political, social, and developmental ills. At the same time, it is emblematic of the populist strategy of creating an existential threat in order to distinguish the 'real' people and justify extreme actions, including the curtailing of democratic norms and human rights (*see* Werner-Müeller 2016; Canovan 1999). Furthermore, Duterte's ability to convincingly expound the second message was largely the result of fake news, a tactic that would become key in his electoral campaign, as well as part of his governing strategy. A few months before Duterte's official declaration of candidacy, the website Numbeo.com ranked Davao as the fourth safest city in the world. Various mainstream media outlets carried the story, neglecting to mention that the ranking was not based on credible research but rather by a user-generated voluntary internet survey.[6] The narrative of the mayor whose iron fist approach had successfully turned Davao from a backwater crime capital to one of the world's safest cities – and whose approach could do the same for the Philippines – became central to Duterte's image.[7] The main culprits branded as 'bad' people were drug users, addicts and traffickers (who compromise a singular category in Duterte's rhetoric). His rhetoric purposefully

---

4 Duterte's father, Vicente, had been mayor of Danao, Cebu, governor of Davao, and a Interior Secretary under the Marcos government until his death in 1968. Later in the Marcos' regime, Vicente's widow and Rodrigo's mother, Soledad, became a prominent activist against the Marcos government and martial law. When Corazon Aquino assumed the presidency after the People Power Revolution, she wanted to appoint Soledad as the officer-in-charge of Davao City, but the 70-year-old Soledad asked the new president to consider her son, Rodrigo, instead.

5 Due to constitutionally-mandated term limits, local officials cannot serve for more than three consecutive terms. The first time he reached this limit, Duterte served one term as the congressman representing Davao City – a position he said was 'boring' – while his daughter served as mayor. The second time, he served one term as vice-mayor while his daughter was mayor.

6 Official crime statistics, on the other hand, report that Davao had the highest murder rate and the second highest rape rate in the country from 2010 to 2015.

7 Around the same time that the story reporting Davao as the world's fourth safest city came out, Alexander Nix, then-board director of SCL Elections, a company that would later become Cambridge Analytica and retain Nix as CEO, visited the Philippines and gave a speech at the National Press Club. The SCL Elections website would later boast that they rebranded their Philippine client as a "as a strong, no-nonsense man of action." Although the Duterte camp has denied engaging Nix's services, photos were posted online of Nix dining with Duterte's campaign spokesperson, social media strategist, and the then-NPC president who would later be appointed Undersecretary of the Presidential Communications Office (Robles 2018).

invoked images of the poor urban *tambay:* the trope of a young, indolent and jobless man who just hangs around the neighborhood all day, as the scourge responsible for the destruction of the country. The drug he demonized was methamphetamine, known locally as *shabu*, which is associated with the poor. The narrative Duterte pushed drew on deep-seeded classism and stereotypes propagated by the global war on drugs wherein poverty is equated with drug use, which is in turn equated with violence and social unrest. The narrative is a familiar one: poor people take drugs which drives them to commit burglary, rape, and murder, making them a threat to society as a whole. As president, he would later state that it was natural that his drug policy targeted the poor because the children of the rich do not use illicit drugs. According to Duterte, when the rich do use drugs, they use the relatively harmless cocaine and heroin, whereas the methamphetamine favored by the poor turns them into non-humans (Ho 2016).

The brazen use of violent and misogynistic language became a feature of the campaign that was interpreted as evidence that Duterte speaks 'authentically'. Duterte would often insult his opponents and critics as *bayot* (gay). In one of his most famous and shocking campaign revelations, he recounted an Australian missionary who was raped and murdered during a jail riot while he was mayor:

> One of them was an Australian lay minister. Tsk, now this is a problem. They brought the body outside wrapped up. I looked at the face. Son of a whore, it was like ... she looked like a beautiful American actress. Son of a whore, what a waste. What came into my mind: they raped her, they lined up for her in there. Did I get mad because they raped her? Yes, that was part of it. But she was so beautiful, the mayor should have been the first. What a waste.

An often-heard line by Duterte supporters in response to these and other similar statements was, "At least he says what he thinks, unlike others who think the same things but pretend to be pure. That way, at least we trust that he's honest." Duterte's violent and crude language surely reflects the embedded misogyny and homophobia that continues to permeate Philippines society. It is also, however, a reaction against political and social elites who cultivated facetious images of 'decency' while extorting and deprecating the common Filipino (Garrido 2017).

While the primary national enemy that the Duterte campaign created were poor people involved with illegal drugs, a secondary target was the party of his predecessor, 'P-Noy' Aquino of the Liberal Party. There was a targeted effort to systematically demonize everything associated with the Liberal Party and blame it for all of society's ills. Referring to someone as yellow (*dilawan*), the color of the Liberal Party, became an all-encompassing insult that meant everything and nothing in particular. *Dilawan* or 'Liberal' also came to be associated with the entire post-Marcos democratic period. It is important to note that by 2016, the Liberal Party under the two Aquinos only held the presidency for twelve out of the thirty years since the Marcos dictatorship. Of the three other former presidents, two are Duterte allies. Arroyo came to be the Duterte-endorsed speaker of the House of Representatives as well as the architect of Duterte's economic ties with China. Estrada, meanwhile, has lent his steady support base and populist image to Duterte, many believe in exchange for presidential pressure to drop graft and plunder charges against his son. Nevertheless, the Duterte campaign successfully presented the democratic period in general as the Liberal Party period. As such, he called into question the desirability of democracy itself in contrast to the harsh, discipline-oriented nature of the dictatorship.

It is also important to note that by the 2016 campaign, Duterte had cemented an alliance with the Marcos family who were looking to rewrite the legacy of the Marcos dictatorship and come back to power. Central to the Marcos family's strategy is presenting history as if it were a personal fight between the Marcos and Aquino families. This allows them to draw false equivalencies between the abuses of the Marcos regime and the shortcomings and abuses that have continued during democratic period, as well as brush off any criticism as personally motivated. This false dichotomic presentation of history also conveniently puts all the blame for democracy's shortcomings on the Aquinos and their few loyal allies while ignoring the fact that, for the most part, the same political dynasties have exercised power under both the dictatorial and democratic periods. Duterte (and the Marcos comeback) have no desire to change this elite political structure, but rather need to coalesce with or co-opt these families to gain and maintain power.

3   Socio-political Structural Explanations for the Rise of Dutertismo

Why was a candidate with such extreme and violent messages able to win the presidency in a country where the quality of democracy and human rights, while far from perfect, had progressed? Beyond opportune contingencies and mistakes other candidates made in their campaigns, I argue that Duterte's electoral victory is the expression of deep-seeded social frustrations related to long-term political and economic development, as well as the failures of liberal democracy to deal with such frustrations. Duterte's strongman populist style successfully exacerbated social schisms and directed and weaponized social and political resentment. I focus on three socio-political structural explanations. First, I argue that rapid and unequal economic growth as a result of the landed elite's capture of the economy and a neoliberal development strategy led to a new aspirational and consumerist middle class that energized Duterte's base early on. Second, I look at the Philippines' party and electoral systems, focusing on the lack of meaningful political parties and the effects of the one-term limit for presidents. Third, I expound on the population's general frustration with liberal democracy's ability to deal with basic problems and deliver meaningful change.

3.1   *Historical Bases of the Philippine Economic Structure*

For much of the 20the century, the Philippine economy stagnated in comparison to its regional neighbors. The small cadre of landed elites that controlled the government also controlled the economy. They thus often bent government policy and regulations to fit their economic interests, entrenching an oligarchic, semi-feudal system. Rapid economic growth in the 2000s and 2010s, fueled in part by the privatization of government assets, the late growth of the manufacturing and industry sector, and the steady growth of the services sector benefited the elite more than any other class, but also resulted in the rise of a new middle class. While this new middle class is no longer in abject poverty, it is still in a situation of economic insecurity. It is also in a situation of insecurity in terms of social status, as class relations are less defined by profession and increasingly defined by consumerism. This combination of identity via consumption and insecurity has combined with the frustrations about government's ineptitude and elite capture to make the new middle class especially vulnerable to Duterte's message. The result has been a vociferous and energetic support base that has helped mobilize support from other classes and intimidate critics.

As described in previous sections, throughout the colonial period, the Philippine economy was based on large agricultural landholdings controlled by regional elite families. The first substantial push for industrialization began in the decades following World War II. Although there were some landless economic elites (who mostly gained their wealth by acquiring government concessions to deal in natural resources) and traders and merchants who became industrialists, landed elite families diversified their holdings to become the dominant players in the industrialization process. Accordingly, there was never a marked conflict between the feudal and bourgeoise classes as these were one in the same (Rivera 1994).

The dominance of landed elites over the industrial sector meant that the post-war push for industrialization was weak and short-lived. The state remained captured by the interests of the landed elite-cum industrialists. Protectionist trade policies and onerous regulations are designed to protect the private interests of the oligarchy much more than national patrimony, small businesses, or the consumer. Oftentimes, business regulations only apply to small and medium enterprises because of the corruption that pervades the regulatory and court systems. Even the Marcos regime, for all its bluster about challenging the elite and modernizing the economy, never meaningfully challenged land distribution, not even the landholdings of its most prominent political rivals.

3.2   *Economic Growth and the New Middle Class*
The 2000s were a period of rapid though incredibly unequal economic growth in the Philippines, fueled largely by the aggressive privatization of state assets. According to the World Bank, GDP grew by over 400% between 2001 and 2016, from US$76 billion to US$305 billion (Figure 5.1). Steady growth in the service sector since the 1970s and a bump in the manufacturing and industries sector in the 2000s and 2010s formed a substantial, if delayed, movement away from agricultural-based employment to better (though not necessarily good) paying jobs in urban areas. At the same time, there was a jump in remittances sent back to the country by overseas Filipino workers. Whereas remittances comprised less than three percent of the country's GDP in 1990, it has comprised between nine and eleven percent of GDP since 2001 to 2020. Better paying jobs and more remittances, more access to cheap consumer goods from China, and more access to cheap capital as the country's international credit rating improved increased consumerism. At the same time, the legacies of the Philippines' delayed economic modernization and oligarchic state capture continued: weak organized labor (made weaker by contractualization practices), poor social services, access to government and services based on patronage, and corrupt legal and oversight systems that largely excluded the rich from *de facto* regulations. As such, this economic growth was not accompanied by sweeping changes in wealth distribution or class restructuring. Rather, the biggest winners in this period have continued to be the landed elite.

The second Aquino presidency, beginning in 2010, generally continued the neoliberal macroeconomic approach of his predecessors, but with expanded anti-poverty programs and policies, including the expansion of the conditional cash transfer program, a participatory budgeting program for poverty-reduction programs, primary school facilities improvement and enrollment,

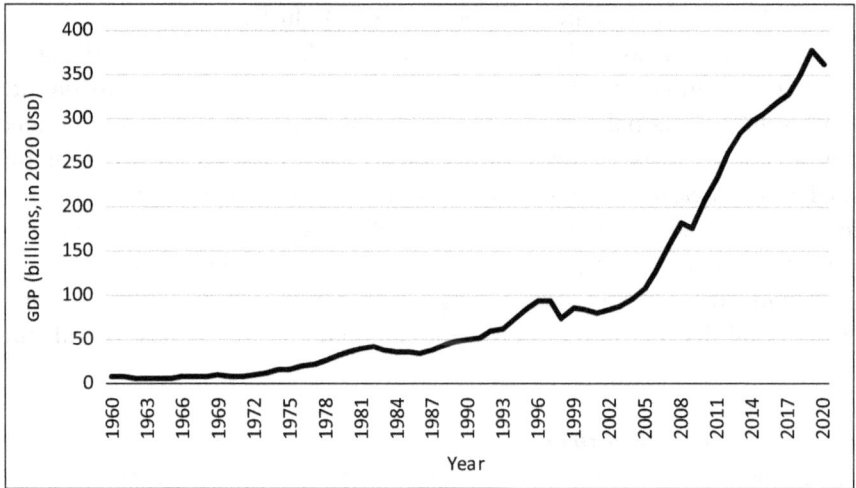

FIGURE 5.1   Philippine GDP 1960–2020

and an administration-backed family planning law (*see* Bayudan-Dacuycuy and Baje). GDP grew steadily at its highest average rate in the democratic period and poverty began to modestly decline from 28.6% in 2009 to 21% in 2018 (Philippine Statistics Authority).

A small, but influential new middle class developed. Albert et al. (2018) find that between 2006 and 2015, 5% of the population, that is, approximately five million people, moved from the poor to the lower middle class (Table 5.1). It is important to note that this is the only income mobility that occurred despite the period's high rate of economic growth.

Economic changes have cultural impacts. As Joseph Stiglitz (2019) writes, the style of capitalism adopted in the U.S. beginning in the 1970s, and that it pressured much of the developing world to adopt since the 1990s, has resulted in greed and selfishness at both social and individual levels. Similarly, the new middle class in the Philippines is one marked by consumption and aspiration that derives its identity from what it can buy. The sudden access to disposable income results not in savings or investment, but rather in more *stuff*, and that stuff in turn makes the new middle class feel increasingly distant from poorer classes while they psychologically identify more with the near rich and rich classes. At the same time, the new middle class is *not* rich. While they have the capacity to, for the first time, have a car or fancy cellphone, they do not have the capacity to replace such items in the case of robbery, nor can they afford private security or assistants to mind their things like the rich. This makes the new middle class especially sensitive to 'tough on crime'

TABLE 5.1   Changes in income distribution by class

Philippines		
	2006	2015
Upper middle class	4	4
Middle middle class	10	10
Lower middle class	57	63
Poor	27	22

appeals.[8] Furthermore, the emergence of the new middle class coincides with (and has in part been fueled by) an expansion in the number of Filipinos working abroad. The 1.9 million overseas Filipino workers in 2009 grew to 2.4 million in 2015 (Philippine Statistics Authority). The ability to travel abroad gave members of the new middle class a chance to see more developed states, and thus demand more from the Philippine government. It is also worth noting that the top regional destinations for both Filipino tourists and workers include Hong Kong and Singapore and that over 56% of overseas Filipinos in 2015 worked in the Middle East, meaning their experiences in more economically developed countries largely occurred in non-democratic states, possibly affecting perceptions that autocratic states are more efficient at delivering public services. The Duterte (and Marcos) online news machines have been especially adept at targeting Filipinos abroad with fake news and incendiary propaganda.

The new middle class also found themselves paying taxes for the first time. Payroll taxes were a surprise to many as they transitioned from informal to formal employment. Furthermore, while the Arroyo presidency's main project to increase government revenue was to institute an expanded value-added tax, Aquino's budget minister went after middle class income tax evaders, implementing a 'name and shame' campaign targeting professionals and the self-employed. This new relationship with taxes had two results. First, paying taxes for the first time made the new middle class especially sensitive to government ineptitude and corruption. Second, it reinforced their class identity and feelings of social and political exclusion. Gloria et al. (2014) found that 28% of

---

8   It should be noted that before the Duterte campaign made it a salient issue, crime was not one of the top voter issues. Furthermore, official data showed that crime had been declining in recent years. See Teehankee and Thompson 2016.

occupations, many of them middle class professions, paid the same marginal tax rates as millionaires. Albert et al. (2015) found that nearly seventy percent of all income taxes were paid by the middle class. While the rich greatly benefitted from the rapid economic growth of the 2000s and 2010s, and governments touted social programs that targeted the poor, the middle class left out and taken advantage of. An often-heard sentiment, especially during the later years of the second Aquino administration, was "We hear that the economy is doing great. But, the rich are getting richer and the poor are getting help. Meanwhile, we just work."

3.3   *The Philippines' Political Party and Electoral Systems*

Frustrations with the exclusive nature of the political system also fueled the appeal of an extreme, anti-system candidate. As described in previous sections, Philippine political parties are little more than rotating clubs of elites that form and reform around particular candidates every election (Quimpo 2007; Lero 2018). Candidates have little loyalty and turncoatism is rampant. Parties do not perform the function of identifying candidates for office. They certainly do not, as Levitsky and Ziblatt (2018) describe, perform the function of preventing demagogues from presenting themselves as candidates. Rather, candidates decide to run, and then later choose or found a party with which they can register. In addition to the non-functioning of political parties, the president serves a single six-year term while half of the senate and all other national and local positions are elected every three years. The Philippine constitution prohibits presidential re-election, meaning there is no incumbent advantage in presidential elections. Finally, presidential elections are determined by a simple plurality in a single round of elections. This discourages the formation of wide electoral coalitions and encourages many-candidate elections as winners can potentially be determined by a small percentage of the electorate.

As a result of these three institutional design factors, presidents generally enjoy positive approval ratings in the first half of their terms, and then sharp declines in the second half (Figure 5.2).[9] During the first half of a president's term, other politicians and political elites try to appear allied with the president in order to have executive support for their interests, as well as to try to gain access to state resources for midterm elections. After the midterm elections, politicians begin looking towards the next presidential elections.

---

9   The Estrada and Duterte regimes are slight exceptions from this pattern. Estrada was ousted shortly into his term on corruption charges. Duterte's approval ratings have remained high throughout his term.

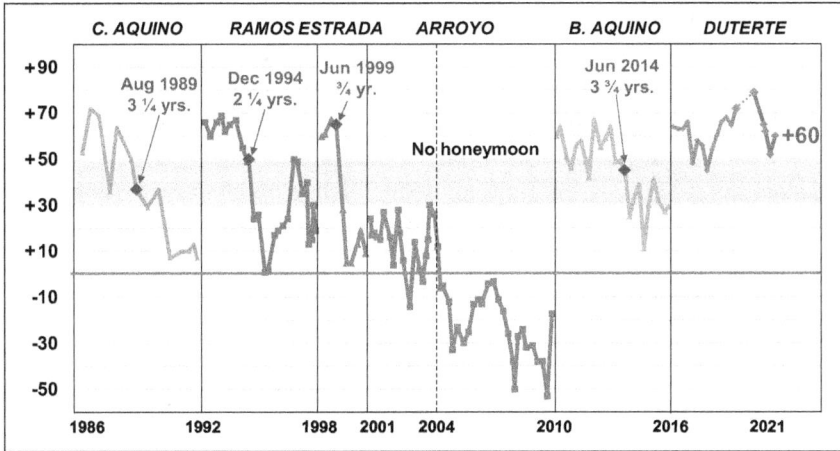

FIGURE 5.2   Net satisfaction ratings of presidents: Philippines, May 1986–Dec 2021
Note: % Satisfied minus % Dissatisfied correctly rounded. Ignores Don't Know
and Refused to Answer responses. Question. Please tell me how satisfied
or dissatisfied you are in the performance of [NAME] as President of the
Philippines. Are you Very satisfied, Somewhat satisfied, Undecided if satisfied
or dissatisfied, Somewhat dissatisfied, Very dissatisfied?
SOURCE: SOCIAL WEATHER STATIONS. FOURTH QUARTER 2021 SOCIAL
WEATHER REPORT, DECEMBER 12-16, 2021 NATIONAL SURVEY

Aspiring candidates who feel they will not be endorsed by the president, as
well as political actors that feel they may have a more advantageous position
with non-endorsed candidates, face incentives to not only distance themselves
from the president, but to actively undermine the president's popularity in
order to reduce the weight of his endorsement.

This pattern played out very clearly during the second Aquino administration. After nearly ten years of an extremely unpopular president, Aquino
began his term in an atmosphere of high optimism with the vast majority of
political elites scrambling to be perceived as close Aquino allies. Despite several missteps and politically costly actions early in Aquino's term, he continued to enjoy the vocal support of the vast majority of the political class. Nine
of the twelve senators who won during the midterm elections were part of the
administration slate.

In the second half of Aquino's term, however, political opponents vigorously
took advantage of national events and the administration's errors in order to
drum up discontent. In November 2013, Typhoon Haiyan hit the Philippines
with devastating effects. The storm killed at least 6,300 people, displaced
upwards of six million, and cost an estimated US$1.8 billion in damages. The

government response was widely criticized as slow and uncoordinated, high-lighting the state's lack of preparation and general ineptitude. Moreover, the political opposition to the Aquino regime took the opportunity to come down especially hard on Interior Secretary, Mar Roxas, who was put in charge of recovery efforts and generally assumed to be Aquino's chosen successor in the 2016 elections. In 2015, the Mamasapano incident, a botched police operation meant to capture an international terrorist in the southern island of Mindanao resulted in the death of 44 Special Action Force officers and 18 members of the Moro Islamic Liberation Front (MILF), an armed group with whom the Aquino government had recently signed a peace agreement. Opposition politicians took the incident as an opportunity to attack the administration as well as block the ratification of the peace deal with the MILF – a move intended to sway the loyalty of mostly Christian politicians in Mindanao opposed to the deal.

3.4 Frustration with Liberal Democracy's Ability to Deal with Basic Problems and Deliver Meaningful Change

The Philippine population had incredibly high hopes at the beginning of the second Aquino administration. As described in Section 1, the series of events leading up to the 2010 elections invoked strong parallels to the 1986 People Power Revolution. This, together with Aquino's slogan, *kung walang korap, walang mahirap* (if there is no corruption, there will be no poverty), made many Filipinos expect transformation with the new administration. However, the Aquino administration never approached governing with the intention to make radical transformations to how the government was structured, let alone to how political and economic power was structured in society. As Thompson (2016) and Teehankee and Thompson (2016) argue, the dominant discourse of governments after the EDSA revolution has been reformism towards 'good governance.' Leaders do not speak of fundamentally changing society or even undoing the bureaucratic authoritarian legacies inherited from the Marcos regime, and the negative legacies of the colonial regime before it, that systematize the reproduction of unresponsive and ineffective government. Rather, the overarching discourse of nearly all governments in the democratic period has been piecemeal reformism, macroeconomic development through a liberal paradigm, and reduced corruption.

A corruption scandal that began in 2013 is emblematic of this failure to pursue transformative change. This scandal resulted in widespread frustration with not only the Aquino administration, but with the political system in general. In July 2013, The Commission on Audit released a special report indicating that over US$ 190 million of so-called 'pork barrel' funds, a mechanism whereby individual legislators could identify projects to be funded outside of the normal budget process, had actually been diverted to fake NGOs and the money stolen. While the report only covered years before the Liberal Party held the presidency, the party and Aquino government faced immense public pressure to prosecute the erring congress people and abolish the practice of letting legislators allocate funding to their chosen projects. The government's actions were disappointing to many. Only three out of the 23 congress people named in the report were charged by the Justice Department and jailed. The pork barrel system was not totally abolished, but rather replaced with a similar mechanism with some reforms. At the same time, political opposition to the Aquino regime correctly pointed out the selective prosecution that took place, noting that no administration allies were prosecuted. The opposition furthermore took the opportunity to point to discretionary spending mechanisms within the executive and equate them to pork barrel. Thus, the message was that Aquino and his party were not the corruption-fighters they claimed to be. Rather, corruption and political vindictiveness were characteristics of all mainstream politicians. This finger-pointing fomented anger at the political system in general, opening the door for an anti-system candidate.

Just as P-Noy Aquino came to the presidency largely through the legacy of his mother as the democratic hope after the dictator, when he was perceived as unable or unwilling to deal with basic problems like systemic corruption, poverty, and underdeveloped infrastructure, it was a reminder of the high hopes and ensuing disappointment for Philippine liberal democracy in general. Thompson (2016) further observes that the perception that Aquino was personally not corrupt ironically helped Duterte's brand of radical anti-system politics, as frustrations were not directed towards Aquino personally, but rather towards the political system and liberal reformist democracy in general.[10] This frustration with the limits of liberal democracy to deliver meaningful change for what seemed like the second time helped prepare an opening for a presidential candidate who would take drastic actions to solve the Philippines long-standing problems based on the simplistic concept of 'political will.'

---

10   This channeling of frustration towards the system was exacerbated by the fact that President Benigno Aquino was the son of the country's first post-Marcos president, Corazon Aquino, and yellow had been the symbol of the EDSA People Power Revolution. The end of the second Aquino administration and Duterte's successful candidacy coincided with a concerted effort by the Marcos clan to recast history as a dyadic fight between the Marcos and the Aquino families, as if the entire experience of the country since Marcos's ouster had been dictated by the Aquinos and thus, all the shortcomings of the democratic experience should be seen as a failure of 'yellow politics.'

4   Duterte as President: Closing Democratic Space

The days when democratic regime breakdown came through dramatic armed coups are largely gone. Nowadays, gradual attacks on democracy from within are more common and authoritarians and authoritarian-sympathizers use a combination of legal and extralegal. As Levitsky and Ziblatt (2018) write, "Many government efforts to subvert democracy are 'legal', in the sense that they are approved by the legislature or accepted by the courts. They may even be portrayed as efforts to *improve* democracy" (5). This section will identify five ways the Duterte regime has used a combination of legal and extra-legal strategies in order to attack democracy and concentrate power in the executive: the use of literal and symbolic violence; attacks against vocal Duterte critics; the executive budget; the use of polarization, crisis, and the politics of distraction; and positioning his children in power. Finally, this section will also address how Duterte has positioned himself geopolitically, and in particular how his move away from the west and towards China is largely a reaction to western criticism of his human rights performance.

4.1   *Literal and Symbolic Violence*

As a candidate, Duterte said "I promise you blood. Manila Bay will be covered with corpses and the fish will grow fat" (Bonnet 2018). Prior to vying for the presidency, Duterte already had experience with the use of extermination squads to go after petty criminals as well as to frighten potential critics. During his tenure as mayor of Davao, over one thousand people had been killed by government-backed hitmen known as the 'Davao Death Squad' or DDS. The DDS was not only an open secret among both locals and in the national consciousness, but it had also been the subject of a report by the UN Special Rapporteur on extrajudicial, summary or arbitrary executions that pointed to Duterte's direct responsibility for the killings (Alston 2009, 2015).[11]

---

11   "The mayor is an authoritarian populist who has held office, aside from a brief stint as a congressman, since 1988. His program is simple: to reach a local peace with the CPP/NPA/ NDF and to 'strike hard' at criminals. When we spoke, he insisted that he controls the army and the police, saying, 'The buck stops here'. But, he added, more than once, I accept no criminal liability. While repeatedly acknowledging that it was his 'full responsibility' that hundreds of murders committed on his watch remained unsolved, he would perfunctorily deny the existence of a death squad and return to the theme that there are no drug laboratories in Davao. The mayor freely acknowledged that he had publicly stated that he would make Davao 'dangerous' and 'not a very safe place' for criminals, but he insisted that these statements were for public consumption and would have no effect on police conduct: 'Police know the law. Police get their training.' The mayor's positioning is frankly

The numbers of those killed in the government's 'War on Drugs' since Duterte assumed the presidency have been a point of contention with various government agencies reporting different figures, all of which vary starkly from the figures compiled by the media and civil society. As of June 2019, an academe-compiled database, which sources its information from media reports, has logged over seven thousand killings. Human rights groups, however, estimate the number at over twenty thousand.[12] The crackdown and killings began shortly after Duterte was elected, with some police officials declaring it was a message of goodwill to the new president. There was a dramatic spike, however, in killings once Duterte officially took office (David et al. 2018; Dahas, 2021).

The way the 'War on Drugs'" has been implemented combines legal and extra-legal tactics. Some killings have happened during police operations, wherein the state attempts to legally justify killings by saying that the police acted in self-defense – even in cases where victims were handcuffed or shot in the back. Other killings, however, have been committed by vigilante-style death squads. Early in the Duterte administration, these groups would leave bodies in visible areas, often with their heads wrapped in packing tape and with cardboard signs saying, "I'm a drug pusher, don't be like me," and other similar slogans. These bodies had the impact of both making it seem as if the government was taking decisive action against the social problem of illegal drugs, as well as establishing a climate of fear among those who would question the state (*see* Soriano et al. 2019; Reyes 2016). In an overt illustration of the combination of legal and extra-legal strategies, some police stations have also been known to employ mercenaries and police informants to participate in the killings. In some cities in the Metro Manila region, uniformed police and plain-clothed mercenaries have been seen patrolling together. Various surveys have demonstrated that while a consistent majority of Filipinos express support for the drug war, majorities also believe that there are many human rights violations that occur in the drug war, that the police are lying when they claim to only kill in self-defense, and that they fear that they or a loved one could

---

untenable: He dominates the city so thoroughly as to stamp out whole genres of crime, yet he remains powerless in the face of hundreds of murders committed by men without masks in view of witnesses." (Alston 2015).

12   The 20,000 figure comes from a combination of the number of killings the government has admitted are connected to the so-called War on Drugs as well as killings the government has classified as "under investigation." The government itself has been opaque about the number of killings. It has reported conflicting numbers and changed the way deaths are classified.

be a victim of the drug war (Social Weather Stations 2020). This violence has resulted in a climate of fear, especially in urban poor communities, that affects citizens' willingness to openly criticize the government or the security sector.

Furthermore, while the 'War on Drugs' has targeted and killed poor people almost exclusively, Duterte on several occasions has claimed to have a list of 'drug lords' and 'narco-politicians.' Local politicians also fear being placed on that list, irrespective of whether they are actually involved in drug trafficking or not. This fear was buttressed early on by the killing of Mayor Rolando Espinosa inside a Philippine National Police jail after Duterte claimed he was involved in drug trafficking, as well as the self-exile of Jed Mabilog, the popular mayor of one of the largest cities outside of Metro Manila, after Duterte named him as a narco-politician and relocated the chief of police from Espinosa's town to Mabilog's city.

The so-called 'War on Drugs' has been within the exclusive purview of the Philippine National Police while the Armed Forces of the Philippines, as a rule, has not been involved. Rather, the Armed Forces remains focused on its historic enemy: the Communist insurgency. Amidst the pandemic, the government rushed an expanded Anti-Terrorism Act though Congress at the behest of the military. The law greatly expands what kinds of groups can be labeled as official terrorists as well as the grounds for linking individuals to such groups. It also allows any law enforcement group to be detained without an arrest warrant for up to 24 days. The passage of the law has coincided with a spate of 'red-tagging' wherein labor leaders, lawyers, journalists, and students are labeled as communist insurgents and arrested or killed.

4.2   Attacks against the Political Opposition and Independent Media: Fake News and Social Media

The Duterte government has also used a combination of state and non-state entities to delegitimize opposition political figures and independent media. Their *modus operandi* is as follows: the Office of the Solicitor General, Justice Department, and private citizens or citizen groups controlled by the government file a series of manufactured legal cases against the chosen opponent. Allies in the legislature may open an ethics investigation. Meanwhile, the pro-government social media machine continually assails the character of the target with false claims and threats. This strategy has been successful at jailing two senators and removing the Chief Justice of the Supreme Court.

In addition to delegitimizing the political opposition, delegitimizing traditional and independent media has been another strategy key to maintaining Duterte's popularity and brushing off any criticism as a bad faith attack from a corrupt actor. Like other strongman regimes, the Duterte regime has used both official rhetoric and its considerable online machine to attack mainstream media as 'biased' and reporters as 'presstitutes' while establishing and funding its own circle of loyal bloggers and opinion columnists. In 2020, Duterte allies in Congress refused to renew the legislative franchise of the country's top broadcast network, ABS-CBN, after months of Duterte saying that he opposed the franchise renewal due to its airing of an anti-Duterte campaign ad in 2016 and supposedly biased media coverage of the drug war. One online magazine in particular, *Rappler*, has been the focus of Duterte's ire. Its leaders regularly receive death and rape threats from Duterte followers, and its reporters have been barred from covering presidential events. Over a dozen cases have been filed against the magazine, most having to do with back taxes, and its leadership have been arrested multiple times. In 2021, *Rappler* CEO Maria Ressa won the Nobel Peace Prize for defending press freedom amidst these threats and pressures.

In addition to assailing independent media, the Duterte regime has shrewdly used its own social media to spread fake news and sew social and political division. A 2017 Oxford working paper showed that Duterte spent US\$ 200,000 on an online troll army and prominent Facebook and Twitter personalities have been appointed to key communication positions under the Office of the President (Bradshaw and Howard). Notably, much of this online communication targets the over ten million overseas Filipino workers who spend copious amounts of time online to cope with their homesickness and communicate with their families. The social media messaging encourages supporters to trust no one but Duterte, as if an objective reality does not exist and only personal affinity with and loyalty to the Duterte 'tribe' matters.

4.3   *The Executive Budget*

Although the Philippine presidency has historically had overwhelming control of the national budget, Duterte has expanded discretionary executive control. In 2017, the first budget prepared by the Duterte regime, confidential and intelligence funds under the Office of the President jumped by five times their allocation in 2016. Confidential and intelligence funds are especially notable because their disbursement is not subject to congressional oversight. In Duterte's first years in office, government and police insiders conjectured that these funds were used to incentive police and contract assassins in the war on drugs (see Amnesty International 2017).

Additionally, Duterte limited the 'pork barrel' funds for legislators (described in section 2) to administration allies. Accordingly, in the 2016–2019 congress, the House minority declared itself allied with the president. Only seven members claimed to be an independent opposition.

4.4   The Use of Polarization, Crisis, and the Politics of Distraction

Müeller (2016) writes that one of the defining characteristics of modern populists is that they are anti-pluralist, dividing the population between 'the real people' and others, with others being a risk. As such, the populist leader is able to justify extreme action, including openly attacking democratic institutions and literally killing thousands of people, by presenting such actions as necessary to protect 'the real people' from an existential threat. Levitsky and Ziblatt (2018) echo this idea, writing that crisis is a factor that enables leaders to damage democracy. "Citizens become more likely to tolerate, and even endorse, authoritarian measures when they fear for their security" (192).

I have described above how the Duterte campaign demonized the 'yellow' label, pushing the idea that everything corrupt, inept, and morally hypocritical should be associated with the previous regime and, by extension, post-EDSA democracy. As president, this rhetoric has continued and expanded: the 'yellow' label has expanded to be attached to anyone who criticizes the Duterte regime, and its meaning has expanded to also mean drug addicts, drug lords, and their protectors. Therefore, anyone who is not totally loyal and uncritical towards Duterte is someone who advocates and likely participates in corruption, government failure, illegal drug use, and organized crime.

The creation of an enemy is followed by the creation of conspiracies and crises in order to consolidate and energize Duterte supporters around the idea that the country itself is under threat. Ironically, though Duterte cultivates the image of a 'strong father' who will care for the country, he also cultivates the image of being an underdog constantly under attack who needs the people to actively defend him. One of the ways the government reinforces this message is that every few months, the government declares there is a conspiracy of unsavory characters determined to unseat the president. For Duterte supporters, this is proof that 'yellows' and the 'presstitutes' are hell-bent on getting rid of Duterte. For Duterte critics, it demonstrates that at any time and with little to no evidence one may be labeled an enemy of the state.

The wide chance that one may be labeled an enemy of the state has been amplified since the second half of 2020 with the passage of the Anti-Terror Law. The law allows the government wide latitude to investigate potentially 'subversive' activities, and its passage has coincided with a spate of red-tagging, that is, accusations that citizens are dangerous members of the Communist Party of the Philippines. Not only have politically unaffiliated citizens been arrested for posting negative comments about Duterte on social media, but there has been a spate of murders of community organizers and lawyers associated with leftist groups. In 2021, as people faced hunger because of the lack of economic opportunity and support during the Covid crisis, ordinary citizens set up 'community pantries' around the country in order to collect and make available food donations. The government's initial response was to investigate these pantries' organizers for ties to the Communist Party and unleash a coordinated online attack.

4.5   *Positioning Duterte's Children in Power*

Family dynasties are among the defining characteristics of the Filipino state. While all presidents in the democratic period (except for Ramos) have helped place their relatives in public office, Duterte stands out for the powerful role his children took in his regime, as well as for positioning his children to take over national politics immediately after he leaves office. This is reminiscent of how he ran Davao, and is indicative of how he rose to power without the backing of a significant political party or party establishment. Rodrigo's daughter, 'Inday' Sara, served for many years as his vice mayor of Davao as well as the mayor of Davao when Rodrigo termed out. When Rodrigo ran for president, Sara again took over his position as mayor while another Duterte child, Paolo, took Sara's former position as vice mayor. In 2016, Sara ran unopposed for reelection as mayor and another son, Sebastian, who had no previous experience in government but was known for being a television host, model, and party boy, ran unopposed as her vice mayor. In 2019, Paolo ran and won the city's congressional seat and eventually became a *de facto* speaker of the House.

More interesting, however, is that in the 2019 elections Inday Sara was running for a local position. While the president's political party is technically PDP-Laban, Sara was the billeted as the head, spokesperson, and strategist of the administration slate of senate candidates, known as the *Hugpong ng Pagbabago* (HNP, Movement for Change) coalition, named after the Duterte family's local political machine. Although Sara was not running for national office, she was the key speaker at most campaign events and tarpaulins at rallies featured Sara's photo larger than any of the actual senatorial candidates.

Shortly thereafter, groups within the pro-Duterte coalition began pushing for a 'Sara 2022' presidential candidacy, cognizant that the first priority is to choose a future president that will not pursue criminal charges against the current president and key administration officials. In 2021, before any candidate had officially declared, "Run Sara Run" tarpaulins and motorcades appeared around the country, although both Sara and her father denied that she has presidential aspirations. Her father even once said that the presidency is no job for a woman when asked directly whether he would support her candidacy. This is similar to Duterte's tactic in the 2016 election wherein he, too, denied being interested in the presidency until supposedly pushed by a wave of popular support. How much of this support was truly spontaneous and how much was orchestrated is difficult to say, but it allowed the other candidates to concentrate on attacking each other as he gained in popularity as well as contributed to his image as a reluctant, unambitious politician. As of this writing, Sara is running for Vice-President with Ferdinand 'Bongbong' Marcos, Jr., the son of the former dictator, at the head of the ticket. This was a deal brokered by former President Arroyo, and there is widespread speculation that Duterte was unsatisfied that his daughter did not occupy the Presidential slot.

The positioning of his children reveals a characteristic of Duterte's style of leadership as well as society's relationship with politics. Duterte and similar leaders have often been referred to as some form of 'fascists'. However, Duterte substantially diverges from classical fascism in the sense that he is not at all interested in building an organization around his rule. In fact, there have been several attempts by allies to create an organized movement around Duterte whether in the guise of a civil society organization, a union of community organizations, or organized movement supporting constitutional change to federalism. The party under which Duterte ran for the presidency, PDP-Laban, which was largely inconsequential before his election, also tried earnestly to strengthen itself under his presidency more for the purposes of supporting his government than any other member politicians. In all cases, Duterte was uninterested in building any form of organization. All attempts to turn his personal following and momentum into a sustained political organization failed and PDP-Laban lost influence as well as the leadership positions in both houses of Congress.

Duterte is not interested building an organization. First, there is no program or ideology he is interested in furthering. It is more about personal power and influence. This is why his children are the best vehicle. Second, building an organization comes with the threat of that organization eventually asking for accountability from its leader, and Duterte does not want to be limited. Third, Duterte's style of rule thrives on people not being involved, but rather keeping their heads down and trusting the 'strict father' to address the nation's problems in any way he deems necessary. Continuing to work, consume, and remain uncritical of government are elements that facilitate personalistic authoritarianism.

4.6   *Duterte and the Philippines on the World Stage*

Due to its colonial legacy, the Philippines has long had a close relationship with the United States. This began to change under the Duterte regime as he has made a dramatic move towards China. Far from pursuing an independent foreign policy that plays two superpowers against each other, the Duterte government has kowtowed to Chinese influence. Duterte has treated the territorial dispute between the Philippines and China over the South China Sea with docility, claiming that the Philippines simply would not win a war with China. It is unclear if Duterte honestly does not understand diplomacy and only sees his choices as compliance or war, or if he believes that he needs to genuflect to China in order to obtain investment deals and electoral assistance.

It is also important to highlight that while Duterte has had longstanding disdain for the United States due to the latter's military involvement and historical abuses in Mindanao, his rejection of the west and move towards China is also predicated on the west's criticism of Duterte's human rights record. Western representatives to the Philippines, including the then American ambassador, had condemned some of Duterte's remarks on the campaign trail that endorsed rape and murder. Before then U.S. President Obama was scheduled to meet with Duterte for the first time in September 2016, Obama urged Duterte to conduct the war on drugs 'the right way' in an obvious reference to the spate of killings. Duterte responded by calling Obama a 'son of a whore' and giving a speech that recounted American atrocities in Mindanao during colonization. European and United Nations representatives became actively involved in lobbying and working with opposition legislators when Duterte included reinstating the death penalty and lowering the minimum age of criminal liability to 9 years old among his legislative priorities. Had these measures passed, the Philippines would have been the first nation to explicitly violate the International Covenant on Civil and Political Rights and the UN Convention on the Rights of the Child, thus setting a precedent for other nations and weakening the global system. Meanwhile, China was offering financial assistance (though it delivered much less than what was promised) and ego-boosting trips for Duterte and his entourage without any human rights prerequisites.

5   The Opposition

For those who were opposed to Duterte from the beginning of his candidacy, there was the feeling that his presidency would eventually fall under his own confusion and incompetence, and that it was impossible that the Filipino people would accept his authoritarian tendencies, and wanton murders. A wave of protests in November of 2016 erupted, catalyzed largely by non-affiliated young people, following the transfer of the dictator Marcos's remains to the National Heroes' Cemetery. The momentum quickly died off, however, as outrage did not translate into organization and experienced activists appeared to take a hands-off and put their hopes in spontaneous outrage by millennials. Many veterans of the human rights and pro-democracy movements found themselves off-guard and ill-prepared for the sudden attacks that came with the Duterte presidency.

Pro-Duterte candidates swept the 2019 midterm elections. The Liberal Party did not make a meaningful attempt to evolve from the usual non-programmatic club of elite politicians to a real party when it held the presidency. The vast majority of LP members switched to Duterte's PDP-Laban when he won, as has been the usual practice following previous presidential elections. Local LP politicians also faced powerful incentives to switch to a party allied with the president in the lead-up to the 2019 elections, for fear that a candidate with access to government resources would be assigned to run against them. Since the beginning of Duterte's term, the most prominent LP figure has been Vice President Leni Robredo (in the Philippines, the president and vice president are elected separately). Robredo has taken the approach of working quietly to build a base of support without inviting attacks from Duterte's machine of social media influencers and government-controlled NGOs. While this tactic has been successful at insulating her somewhat from the regime's extermination machine, it has left the opposition without a strong unifying personality.

The political left in the Philippines is divided into two major camps: the Communist Party of the Philippines (CPP), which follows a Maoist-Leninist ideology, and what is generally referred to as the 'Democratic Left,' which comprises a number of parties and political blocs that adhere to a range of communism, democratic socialism, and social democracy. The CPP had a longstanding relationship with Duterte when he was mayor of Davao. When the latter became president, the CPP entered into coalition with him and received cabinet appointments, including the Department of Social Welfare and Development, the Housing and Urban Development Council, and the Presidential Anti-Poverty Commission. By 2018, however, the relationship between the CPP and Duterte deteriorated. Groups within the CPP were unhappy with Duterte's policies, especially those pertaining to human rights and the 'war on drugs', mining, and labor unions. Additionally, CPP-allied organizations began making policy demands, especially in areas of housing, and Duterte did not like being tested or held to accountability. Finally, Duterte's relationship with the CPP was a sore spot for the military, who have historically seen the CPP as their main enemy. Having a good relationship with the military is of utmost importance for Duterte to remain in power – the withdrawal of military support has led to the ouster of two presidents in the last thirty-five years – and Duterte found it increasingly difficult to balance the CPP and the military, especially as he moves closer to China, another sore spot for the military.

The Democratic Left, on the other hand, did not take a clear or unified stance on Duterte at the beginning of his term. Many took a wait and see approach

hoping that Duterte would fulfill his campaign promises to institute a mining moratorium and controls on labor contractualization. They also hoped
that some of the progressive people that Duterte appointed as close advisors
and cabinet positions, particularly his first Cabinet Secretary, Leoncio 'Jun'
Evasco, would guide Duterte towards progressive. Additionally, many in the
Democratic Left were also very critical of the Liberal Party, and so did not know
how to position themselves in the manufactured dichotomy between Duterte
supporters and the 'yellow' forces. The delayed reaction to how to relate to the
Duterte regime made the already weak Democratic Left even weaker.

6   Conclusion

This chapter has argued that long-term social, economic, and political developments enabled the election of a violent, anti-system candidate as president
of the Philippines. In particular, the ascendency of an aspirational middle
class coupled with continued state capture by a small class of landed elite and
the failure of liberal democracy and to bring about transformational change
created a situation where voters were susceptible to radical, extreme appeals.
Candidate Duterte was able to take advantage of these frustrations and vul-
nerabilities by doubling down on a message of fear and hate targeted against
an already marginalized and ostracized group in society: young, poor urban
dwellers presumed to be illegal drug users.

Once in office, Duterte has followed no clear economic or political ideology, save an opportunistic and personalistic one to concentrate power in his
own position and family. He has systematically closed democratic space and
concentrated power through systematic violence, using state and nonstate
resources to attack and discredit the opposition and critics, increasing the
non-transparent budget allocated to the Office of the President, encouraging
polarization and outrage largely through a machinery of fake news and social
media operators, and placing his children in positions of power. Duterte's
move away from the U.S. and towards China reflects his desire to have access
to international funding without being limited by baseline human rights and
democracy requirements.

The mainstream opposition finds itself incredibly weak. The main opposition party, the Liberal Party, never developed a real infrastructure or wide
membership base, helping to make it vulnerable to rabid online attacks and
demonization. Much of the Left wavered on whether it would be outright pro-
or anti-Duterte until several years into his term, thus losing momentum and
legitimacy.

Duterte is constitutionally barred from running in the 2022 election. However, the very real possibility that his daughter, Sara, and the dictator Marcos's son, Bongbong, will win would signify the de facto continuation of the Duterte regime. The destruction of democratic institutions would continue, if not be exacerbated, there would be total impunity for the violence and corruption committed during the Duterte years, and the opposition would be decimated. Even if the Marcos-Duterte tandem were to lose, however, it is clear that the constituency for a radical, authoritarian, and violent leader exists and continues to be cultivated. The Philippines requires not just a change in the presidency, but an overhaul of the party system and the reinvigoration of social movements in order to build back what was lost during the Duterte years and expand democracy and inclusion moving forward.

References

Albert JR, Gaspar R and Raymundo MJ (2015) Who are the middle class? *Rappler*, July 8. Available at https://www.rappler.com/thought-leaders/98624-who-are-middle-class.

Albert JRG, Santos AGF and Vizmanos JFV (2018) Defining and profiling the middle class. Philippine Institute for Development Studies Policy Note 2018–18.

Alston P (2009) Follow-up Report Submitted by the Special Rapporteur on Extrajudicial, Summary or Arbitrary Executions, Philip Alston, Regarding his Visit to the Philippines. Report of the United Nations General Assembly Human Rights Council. Available at: https://www2.ohchr.org/english/bodies/hrcouncil/docs/11session/A.HRC.11.2.Add.8.pdf.

Alston P (2015) Report of the Special Rapporteur on extreme poverty and human rights, Philip Alston. Report of the United Nations General Assembly Human Rights Council. Available (Consulted 24 March 2022) at: https://digitallibrary.un.org/record/798707.

Amnesty International (2017) "If you are poor you are killed": Extrajudicial Executions in the Philippines' 'War on Drugs'. London. Available (Consulted 24 March 2022) at: https://www.amnestyusa.org/files/philippines_ejk_report_v19_final_0.pdf.

Anderson B (1983) *Imagined Communities*. London: Verso.

Ansell BW (2008) Traders, Teachers, and Tyrants: Democracy, Globalization, and Public Investment in Education. *International Organization*. 62(2): 289–322.

Baduyan-Dacuycuy C and Baje L (2017) Chronic and transient poverty and weather variability in the Philippines: Evidence using components approach. Philippine Institute for Development Studies Discussion Paper Series 2017–24.

Bonnet FX (2018) Portrait of Rodrigo Duterte – President of the Philippines. *Institut Montaigne,* 21 December. Available at https://www.institutmontaigne.org/en/blog/portrait-rodrigo-duterte-president-philippines.

Bradshaw S and Howard PN (2017) Troops, Trolls and Troublemakers: A Global Inventory of Organized Social Media Manipulation. University of Oxford Computational Propaganda Research Project Working Paper. Available at: https://demtech.oii.ox.ac.uk/wp-content/uploads/sites/89/2017/07/Troops-Trolls-and-Troublemakers.pdf.

Canovan M (1999) Trust the People! Populism and the Two Faces of Democracy. *Political Studies* 47(1): 2–16.

Dahas (2021) Timeline of Drug-Related Killings March 2011–February 2021. Available at: https://dahas.upd.edu.ph/database/timeline-of-drug-related-deaths/.

David C, Mendoza R, Atun JM, Cossid R and Soriano CR (2018) The Philippines' Anti-Drug Campaign: Building a Dataset of Publicly-Available Information on Killings Associated With the Anti-Drug Campaign. Ateneo School of Government Working paper 18–001.

Durdin T (1969) Charges of Fraud and Violence Follow Elections in Philippines. *The New York Times,* Nov. 16, p. 2.

Fineman M (1987) Neglected for Years: Health Care: Philippine Crisis Looms. *Los Angeles Times,* March 6.

Garrido M (2017) Why the Poor Support Populism: The Politics of Sincerity in Metro Manila. *American Journal of Sociology* 123 (3): 647–685.

Gloria E, Mendoza R and Pena-Reyes SP (2014) An Analysis of Philippine Income Tax Reforms. Asian Institute of Management Working Paper 14–018. Available (Consulted 16 October 2019) at https://papers.ssrn.com/sol3/papers.cfm?abstract_id=2466989.

Ho A (2016) Duterte explains: Why the rich are beyond reach of drug war. CNN *Philippines,* August 24. Available at: https://www.cnnphilippines.com/news/2016/08/24/Duterte-why-rich-beyond-reach-drug-war.html.

Lero C (2018) Specialization and Ownership: Social Movements in New Democracies. Doctoral dissertation. The University of Notre Dame, Notre Dame, IN.

Levitsky S and Daniel Z (2018) How Democracies Die. New York: Penguin Books.

McCoy AW (2009) *Policing America's Empire.* Madison: University of Wisconsin Press.

Müller J (2016) *What is Populism?* Philadelphia: University of Pennsylvania Press.

Philippine Statistics Authority. *OpenSTAT.* Available at: https://openstat.psa.gov.ph/Database.

Quimpo N (2007) The Philippines: Political Parties and Corruption. *Southeast Asian Affairs.* 277–294.

Reyes DA (2016) The Spectacle of Violence in Duterte's "War on Drugs". *Journal of Current Southeast Asian Affairs* 35(3): 111–137.

Rivera T (1994) *Landlords and capitalists: class, family, and state in Philippine manufacturing.* Quezon City: University of the Philippines Press.

Robles R (2018) Explainer: the connections between Philippine President Rodrigo Duterte and Cambridge Analytica. *South China Morning Post.* Available (Consulted 23 March 2022) at: https://www.scmp.com/news/asia/southeast-asia/article/2142 805/explainer-connections-between-philippine-president-rodrigo.

Social Weather Stations (2020) Fourth Quarter 2019 Social Weather Survey: 76% of Filipinos see many human rights abuses in the administration's war on illegal drugs, 24% see few. Available (Consulted 24 March 2022) at: https://www.sws.org .ph/swsmain/artcldisppage/?artcsyscode=ART-20200112221436&mc_cid=3dae64e 194&mc_eid=31b9d30a85.

Soriano CRR, David C and Atun JML (2019) Crystallizing the official narrative: News discourses about the killings from the Philippine government's campaign against illegal drugs. Ateneo School of Government Working Paper Series 19–001.

Stiglitz J (2019) *People, Power, and Profits: Progressive Capitalism for an Age of Discontent.* New York: W. W. Norton & Company.

Teehankee J and Thompson M (2016) Electing a Strongman. *Journal of Democracy* 27(4): 125–134.

Thompson MR (2016) Bloodied Democracy: Duterte and the Death of Liberal Reformism in the Philippines. *Journal of Current Southeast Asian Affairs* 3/2016: 39–68.

CHAPTER 6

Understanding the Myth

Bolsonaro's Brazil

Fabio Luis Barbosa dos Santos

When Luiz Inácio Lula da Silva's two terms as president of Brazil ended in 2010, the international prestige of the country and the Worker's Party (PT) he led, was at its peak. One year earlier, 'The Economist' had portrayed Rio de Janeiro's Christ the Redeemer statue rising like a rocket, with the caption: 'Brazil takes off', while Obama considered Lula the most popular politician on Earth.

Ten years later, Brazil was again making the headlines, but for a different reason. In 2018, Brazilians elected as president a former military man who personifies the most aggressive traits of both authoritarianism and neoliberalism. Jair Bolsonaro's election was preceded by a controversial impeachment that ousted President Rousseff in 2016 and by Lula's imprisonment two years later, preventing him from running for the presidency. Progressive expectations gave way to a reactionary offensive, which had been unthinkable years before.

This chapter analyzes this shift in Brazilian politics in light of the demise of the New Republic, as the times that followed the dictatorship (1964–1985) are known. In order to grasp a deeper sense of this shift, we will start with an overview of Brazilian history to set the context for the rise and decline of the PT, the first left wing party to have a mass base and reach the presidency in the country. Then, we will discuss Bolsonaro's election against the background of anti-PT feelings exploited during his campaign, before looking at his strategies of legitimation in the presidency, as well as resistances they raise. Across the chapter, we'll be looking at deeper historical trends and power rearrangements so as to understand what is going on in Brazil, beyond Bolsonaro himself.

1 Historical Background

As the only monarchy in the Americas and the last country to abolish slavery on the continent, Brazil was a conservative reference for the region throughout the 19th century – comparable to Czarist Russia in Europe. The main driver of abolition was British pressure. However, in the same year that the slave trade was forbidden (1850), the empire decreed state ownership of all undocumented land. In practice, the measure prevented blacks from owing land in anticipation of the abolition of slavery, creating the basis for the land concentration that would typify the country. In a phrase, the captivity of men gave way to the captivity of land (Martins, 2009).

When abolition was finally made official in 1888, the empire crumbled one year later, and the republic was decreed. Although popular agency was not absent, these were top-down processes, in tune with the design of the elites. At the beginning of the 20th century, the state of São Paulo was consolidated as the economic and financial center of the country, as the surplus from coffee exports stimulated an incipient industrialization process. However, like in all Latin American countries, the interwar depression had political and economic consequences. On the political front, the dominance of the paulistas (natives of São Paulo) was called into question by a brief civil war in 1930, which paved the way for the rise of Getúlio Vargas, the dominant figure in national politics in the following decades.

The legacy of the Vargas era (1930–1945) is controversial. Coinciding with a breakthrough in import substituting industrialization and a new level of labor organization, it was during this period that the rights of (urban) workers were consolidated, an arrangement that remained in force until the neoliberal inflection in the 1990s. However, the regime presented these achievements as fruits of Vargas' benevolence, who became known as the "father of the poor", while persecuting and imprisoning opponents. At the same time, Vargas embodied a development project where state interventionism fostered industrialization on a national basis, paving the way for a national bourgeoisie in the making, that is to say, a capitalist class grounded in the domestic market.

Although this did not imply any structural incompatibility between land owners and industrialists, whose business in practice often merged, capitalist development under Vargas did present the Brazilian upper class with a dilemma. According to sociologist Florestan Fernandes, in order to consolidate itself as a national bourgeoisie, it would be necessary to overcome the self-reinforcing relationship between export-dependence and social asymmetry bequeathed by the colonial past. This implied inverting the external orientation of production, making the domestic market the dynamic axis of the national economy. This reversal had economic as well as social implications, as the strengthening of an internal market required social reforms to alleviate the economic and political imbalances between those Fernandes described as "owners" and "non-owners". In other words, it required agrarian reform. In short, to consolidate itself as a national bourgeoisie, the new industrial class needed to confront the interests of foreign capital supported by an alliance with workers and sealed by social reforms aimed at mitigating inequality and privilege. However, such a path would turn upside down the nature of the Brazilian bourgeoisie's nexus both with international capital, never confronted, and with the workers, always oppressed. (Fernandes, 1975, 1982, 2015).

The military coup of 1964 resolved this historical impasse. According to Fernandes, the "bourgeois revolution" in Brazil was consolidated, paradoxically, as a permanent counter-revolution against its people. Since then, the country's ruling class has unified around a negative objective: to keep the people in a world of "political minimums", in order to assure for itself the monopoly of political power as a condition of its class domination (Fernandes, 1975). Once it gave up pursuing industrialization on a national basis, this bourgeoisie compensates for its economic impotence to compete in the world market with political omnipotence, aiming to assure the exploitation of labor and the devastation of natural resources, on which its privileges are based.

The ensuing association between national capital, the state and international capital that typified development under dictatorship was successful from the point of view of growth rates, to the extent that Brazil was among the fastest growing economies in the world, particularly in the early 1970s. However, this pattern sacrificed the national and social dimensions of development. The squeezing of salaries, made possible by the repression of workers and their organizations, was the other face of the multinationals' prosperity. As industries boomed and land concentration remained untouched, urbanization and internal migration accelerated. These trends are illustrated by Lula's trajectory, who himself left the poor hinterlands of northeastern Brazil to work in a multinational factory in the outskirts of São Paulo in the 1970s, where he blossomed as a union leader.

On the political front, the scale of state terrorism in Brazil was smaller when compared to neighboring dictatorships, such as Argentina and Chile. This observation helps to understand why vigorous social movements formed in Brazil in the late 1970s, still under dictatorship, with multiple manifestations: ecclesial communities, an offspring of the politicization of the poor carried out by Liberation theology; a diversity of urban and rural grassroot organizations nourished by Paulo Freire's pedagogy; a growing workers' movement that led memorable strikes, having as its dynamic axis the industrial belt around the city of São Paulo; and progressive intellectualism with organic bonds with this popular mobilization.

This was the political melting pot that gave rise to the Workers' Party (PT) in 1980. Conceived as a party of the masses and not of the vanguard, the PT aimed to overcome the main historical vehicles of popular politics in the country: on the one hand, the populist demagoguery associated with labor and Getúlio Vargas; on the other communism, plagued by dogmatism and fratricidal disputes, which hindered its rooting among workers. At the same time, the PT emerged in the shadow of guerrilla groups decimated under the dictatorship, while Eurocommunism was asserting itself in Europe. In this context, although socialism and anti-imperialism were not absent, strategic formulations asserting "democracy as a universal value" prevailed and crystallized in what became known as the "popular democratic project" (Coutinho, 1980).

Quickly, the new party agglutinated those identified with social change. The PT engaged in the last years of the struggle against the dictatorship and played an important role in broadening the debate around the transition, pushing for direct elections and social reforms. However, popular pressure was insufficient to break the class dikes that restricted the democratic opening, ensuring fundamental continuities. As planned by the regime, the transition was "slow, gradual and secure".

Despite the massive campaign for "Diretas Já" (Direct Elections Now), the military's departure was sealed by an indirect presidential election. In the vote held by the dictatorship's congress, the incumbent candidate was defeated by Tancredo Neves, a politician from the opposition, consented to by the regime, who died before taking office. Vice-president José Sarney took over, a man who made a career inside the dictatorship and only abandoned it at the last moment. It was a melancholic outcome, but also an eloquent representation of the nature of transition, in which economic and social continuity corresponded to political continuity. As was written later, "of the dictatorship, everything was left – except the dictatorship" (Ab'Saber, 2010).

As in other countries of the region, the 1980s in Brazil were marked by an external debt crisis, low economic growth and high inflation, a situation described as the "lost decade". The dictatorship's financial legacy limited the country's room for maneuver, which soon became entangled in the webs of the International Monetary Fund (IMF), which in turn aggravated the social dimension of the crisis, as social spending was cut. At the same time, popular struggles were on the rise in the cities and in the countryside. The formation of the Worker's Unified Central (CUT) in 1983 and of the Landless Workers Movement (MST) in 1984, signaled the intensification of social struggles, which found in the PT their main political vehicle. Their "popular democratic project" as a common reference corresponded to the "pincer strategy", according to which social movements would push for change in the streets, while the party would occupy positions in the state, generating a virtuous dynamic that would lead to social transformation and utlimately, to socialism. In the following years, this political convergence transformed into a relationship that oscillated between complementarity and symbiosis, important to assess the dilemmas of workers organizations after the party reached (and left) the presidency.

Despite the conservative nature of the transition, the PT embodied hopes for change in a context of rising popular pressure, which had a decisive impact in the constituent assembly established in 1988. This role was consolidated with the protagonism, disproportionate to its representation, of the party's parliamentarians in the drafting of the 1988 Constitution, known as the "Citizen Constitution", and still in effect today. Despite its limitations, the text consolidated a logic of social rights that translated, although imperfectly, social aspirations to a global periphery-version of the Welfare State. To give one example: the constitutional requirement that land fulfill a "social function" gave legal backing to the occupation of unproductive lands by the MST, opening the possibility for the State to expropriate land for social purposes.

The consolidation of the so-called "New Republic" culminated with direct elections held in 1989. By then, the PT had already achieved important local electoral successes, and the union leader Luiz Inácio "Lula" da Silva emerged as a strong presidential candidate. In a sordid campaign, in which conservatism united around a hitherto unimpressive politician marketed as a savior of the system, Lula was narrowly defeated in the second round of votes by Collor de Mello. At that time, the party nurtured organic bonds with a radical and diverse grassroots base and neoliberalism had not yet set foot in the country – quite different conditions from when he came to the presidency fifteen years later.

The defeat of Lula by Collor de Mello was a turning point, as the PT was faced with a dilemma. It became clear that in order to confront the establishment, it would have to put up a fight bigger than expected. On the other hand, if the goal was to achieve the presidency, adapting to conventional politics could offer a shortcut. The second path became evident in the following years and as the party accumulated electoral successes across the country, its political originality faded. Practices identified with the "*petista* way of governing", such as self-managed house building projects (*mutirão*) or participatory budgeting, gave way to the ideology of efficient management, which colonized the public sphere. In electoral campaigns, militant excitement was replaced by marketing and corporate donations. In short, the party converted to the means and ends of ordinary politics.

Meanwhile, Collor de Mello suffered an impeachment in 1992 amid massive protests motivated by corruption charges. Two years later, his successor, Itamar Franco, implemented a monetary stabilization plan in line with neoliberal orthodoxy, providing trade and financial liberalization, reduction of the state via privatization, tight monetary and fiscal policy, and high interest rates. As in other similar programs in Latin America, the "Real Plan" contained inflation, but aggravated structural imbalances in national accounts. However, its immediate political consequence was to project then Minister of Finance, Fernando

Henrique Cardoso (FHC), to the presidency in the elections that took place later that year.

Affiliated with the Brazilian Social Democratic Party (PSDB), a party formed in 1988 as a moderate alternative to the PT, Cardoso took advantage of low inflation and the overvaluation of the real (which was then equivalent to the dollar) to get reelected in 1998. That required two spurious maneuvers: the purchase of votes in Congress to change the constitution, allowing reelection; and a negotiation with the IMF that was key to delay the devaluation of the real, in exchange for the implementation of the fiscal responsibility law.[1] The devaluation that eventually took place in the first month of his second mandate announced that the fairy tale was coming to an end. Once the euphoria of import consumption and cheap holidays abroad had passed, neoliberalism showed its brutal face in the form of unemployment, impoverishment and state helplessness. All in all, the anti-popular character of the PSDB governments (1995–2002) had a deep impact on the Brazilian people, and although the party remained competitive in the decades to come, it never again won a presidential election.

In 2002, Lula ran for the presidency for the fourth time and won. His triumph took place in a regional context of political renewal, as conventional forces associated with neoliberalism were worn out. Hugo Chávez in Venezuela (elected in 1998), Néstor Kirchner in Argentina (in 2003), Tabaré Vázquez in Uruguay (in 2005), and Evo Morales in Bolivia (in 2006), were among those elected in this South American pink tide (Santos: 2020). Lula ran the country for two terms (2003–2010) before being succeeded by his party mate, Dilma Rousseff (2011–2016), who was also reelected, but had her second term cut short by an impeachment process. Altogether, the PT ran the country for thirteen years.

But, Brazil and the PT had changed since 1989. The adoption of the Real Plan in 1994 signaled the conversion of the country into a platform for the valorization of international financial capital. This means that, as the country became a destination for speculative capital, the flow of this capital became indispensable from the point of view of the implemented orthodoxy. Permanent fiscal adjustment, high interest rates, contractionary monetary policy, a floating exchange rate and free capital flows are the macroeconomic pillars to which Lula committed himself before setting foot in the presidency (Paulani, 2006).

---

1   The PT was against the law but didn't challenge it when it held the presidency. Ironically, this law provided the pretext to depose Rousseff in 2016.

Once in office, the PT government never challenged the austerity agenda it inherited. However, it never assumed itself as neoliberal. On the contrary, in Lula's second term, when there was a growth spurt driven by the rise in commodity prices in the face of Chinese expansion, the proposition that a "neo-developmentalist" project was underway gained ground among the government's followers. In broad lines, this approach supposed an alternative route between the financialization that typified neoliberalism and the nationalism linked to developmentalism which drove industrialisation after the Second World War. Renewed emphasis on production to the detriment of rentierism without incurring inflation, fiscal populism, nationalism, and other elements of national developmentalism was envisaged. The intention to reconcile "an external element, liberalism, with another internal element, Brazilian developmentalism" (Cervo, 2003), materialized in the support for the internationalization of large companies with national capital or headquartered in the country, understood as vectors of national capitalist development. This was the "national-champions" policy, whose main vehicles were the business diplomacy practiced by Itamaraty (Brazilian Foreign Affairs department), especially in South America, and the credit policy of the National Bank for Economic and Social Development (BNDES).

We have detailed the limits and contradictions of these policies elsewhere (Santos, 2018). What has to be underscored here is that the neo-developmentalist approach was incapable of reversing the deindustrialization trend that went back to the 1980s and was deepened by commercial liberalization in the 1990s, against the background of globalization (Esposito, 2017). On the contrary, the regime of financial accumulation supported by commodity exportation intensified. Nevertheless, a certain relief of social despair did take place as the PT's governments promoted conditional cash transfer policies (*Bolsa Família*), a discreet increase in the minimum wage and popularized credit. This real albeit modest improvement in well-being fostered a sense of social integration through consumption. At the same time, international conditions favored extraordinary profitability for the export, civil construction, and financial sectors, all of which benefited from high international commodity prices. This was the mainstay of the "Lulista mode of regulating social conflict," which ensured a relative pacification of the country for ten years (Braga and Santos, 2019).

However, structural constraints for expanded accumulation beyond commodity export-led growth and financialization meant this was doomed to be a short-lived cyclical process. Rather than the yearned-for nation-building, the influx of money under PT's inclusive neoliberalism unfolded in the competition of all against all, further dissolving class solidarity. Despite its anti-neoliberal rhetoric, social reproduction under the PT governments reinforced neoliberal reason, in which relations between individuals are reduced to mechanisms of monetary reward and punishment among increasingly atomized people, further compromising a social integration landscape (Dardot and Laval, 2010). Paradoxically, it can be argued that the popularity and legitimacy of PT's administrations were grounded on their ability to follow a neoliberal rationale in a more democratic and inclusive manner.[2] The contradictions of the PT's attempt to reconcile neoliberalism and inclusion policies surfaced in June 2013. Acknowledged as the largest cycle of popular mobilization in Brazilian history, the June days were a multifaceted movement that has generated varied interpretations. Albeit diffuse, mobilization demands orbited around three key issues: democratization of cities, universal public policies and disbelief in professional politics. In short, even though it did not target a particular government, the rebellion challenged the conservative modernization undertaken by the PT.

The following year, Rousseff managed to be reelected by a narrow margin. However, the conjunction of corruption scandals portrayed as spectacles by the corporate media, who converted trials into TV series and judges into popstars; and economic slowdown, which turned into recession by 2015, explained the waning popularity of the Lulista way of regulating social conflict. Against this background, there was a shift in the ruling classes' approach to governing social tensions. The times of inclusive neoliberalism gave place to an open assault on people's rights, while class conciliation was superseded by an authoritarian drive, which first became evident in the impeachment process. This is the backdrop for Rousseff's deposition in 2016, followed by Lula's arrest and Bolsonaro's victory in 2018.

This frame implies that while the deposition of Rousseff in 2016 should be seen as a *coup d'état* effectuated by the Congress in collusion with the judiciary and the mainstream press, this was not comparable in any meaningful way to its Cold War predecessors, such as Pinochet's coup against Allende in Chile in 1973. Rather than a dispute over the future of the country, the Brazilian coup was triggered by the loss of command over small politics that the PT had successfully handled for 13 years,[3] in a context of depletion of its social and political prestige. However, beyond the defenestration of the PT, this elite

---

2   This is very different from Perry Anderson's approach, which is heavily based on the writings of former Lula government spokesman André Singer (Anderson, 2019). For a critical review of his book, see Santos, 2021.

3   In a country where 84 parties contest elections since 1985, every president has to negotiate the support of different parties, a mode of government described as "coalition presidentialism".

shift indicates that the Citizen Constitution that underpins the New Republic is compromised. The utopia of a wage-earning citizenship supported by a peripheral Welfare State is gone, without ever having really arrived.

2   Strategies of Legitimation

This elite inflection was evident in the 2018 presidential dispute. Despite Lula's arrest in a markedly persecutory process and without any consistent evidence of corruption,[4] the candidate who replaced him, Fernando Haddad, reached the second round. Lula led the polls before being barred and the party tried to circumvent the legal trap by all means, and so Haddad's candidacy was not launched until one month before the election. His challenger was Jair Bolsonaro, a man who embodies a paradox: an ex-military captain who made a career going against the institutions and values through which he thrived. Bolsonaro graduated from the Military Academy in 1977 and eventually became a spokesman for the junior military who faced loss of prestige as the dictatorship was fading. In 1986, a leading magazine disclosed a plot to explode bombs to draw attention to their grievances. Brought to trial, Bolsonaro was acquitted but forced to retire in 1988. In the following year, he was elected to the city council of Rio de Janeiro and the introduction of the popular vote took him to the national parliament at the dawn of the New Republic in 1990. Since then, he was reelected six times, transiting through nine different political parties, before running for president in 2018.

In the 2018 election, the economy was not in dispute: either winner would face the problems brought about by neoliberalism with more neoliberalism, whether through the inclusive approach preached by the PT or through Bolsonaro's ultra-neoliberalism. The dispute revolved around the political form of governing the Brazilian crisis. What would be the face of the institutional, legal, and cultural arrangement that would replace the New Republic, which after the PT debacle, seems definitively doomed?

The institutional pillar of the New Republic is the Citizen Constitution, a landmark of the democratic transition. Since its promulgation in 1988, the Constitution has been frequently patched (Bercovici and Massoneto, 2006). The themes of universal social rights and the establishment of a welfare state in the global periphery that underpin the 1988 Constitution took root in Brazil

---

4   The judge who took Lula to prison, Sergio Moro, went on to became Bolsonaro's Minister of Justice.

at a time when the idea of wage citizenship was quickly receding worldwide. Nevertheless, these dual ideals, while far from being realized in practice, guided national aspirations from 1988 until recent times.

From this point of view, the brief Temer government (2016–2017) was a turning point, although the winds began blowing before he assumed office. In her second term, Rousseff implemented the very austerity program proposed by the candidate she defeated in the 2014 elections, leading her own constituency to accuse her of "electoral fraud". Rousseff was deposed without a fight in 2016, negotiating and giving in to those who overthrew her. For example, one of her last gestures was to sign an anti-terrorism law in a country where everyone knows there is no terrorism. Vice-President Temer who succeeded her, implemented a labor reform that paved the way to universalize outsourcing and intermittent work, dismantling the foundation of a wage citizenship that had not yet been achieved. Then, constitutional amendment 95 instituted a twenty-year cap on public social spending, though the same amendment does not limit debt service. Finally, Temer intended to reform social security, but the combination of street protests and accusations of corruption immobilized an illegitimate government that was largely rejected since its onset.

Leading towards the 2018 elections, there was a consensus among the ruling class that the next president should resume this anti-popular agenda where Temer left off, that is, the pension system reform. To this end, they put forward three names of their own. These three candidates combined, however, failed to garner even one-tenth of the valid votes in the first round.[5] It was only then that the elite fell in rank behind Bolsonaro.

The reasons for this alignment do not have to do with elite class interests, which neither candidate threatened, but rather with the shift in the approach to reconciling social tensions alluded to above. As the combination of the June Days, corruption scandals and economic recession weakened the Lulista form of social pacification, inclusive neoliberalism lost its ground and a different approach was required. The key issue is not whether or not a PT president would comply with an openly anti-popular agenda, but rather that the party had become unnecessary to advance it. An example illustrates the point. In the first year of the Lula government, the power of the ruling party's persuasion was tested in a push to reform the pensions of public employees. That was a telling moment, since the same reform had been stalled in the previous

---

5   Geraldo Alckmin was the candidate of the PSDB, the party that confronted the PT in the previous five presidential elections. Former head of the Central Bank under Lula, Henrique Meirelles, run under the PMDB (renamed as MDB), Michel Temer's party. João Amoedo is an entrepreneur, one of the founders of the "New Party".

government by the resistance of unions and the PT itself. In short, Lula's soft talk accomplished what Cardoso's confrontational approach did not (Santos, 2016). Fifteen years later, the context was very different. Working class organizations, social movements and the left as a whole were confused, divided and apathetic, while political momentum drifted to the right as the fall of Rousseff was preceded by street demonstrations mobilized by the far right from 2015 on. In this context, the Lulista mode of regulating social conflict not only lost effectiveness, but in fact, lost its *raison d'être*.

Bolsonaro, on the other hand, was in tune with the ruling class shift toward an economically more aggressive and socially more repressive mode of neoliberalism, a mode which itself corresponds to a global trend. Faced with the demise of the New Republic and in a world marked by the financialization of public policies and the precarization of labor relations, the dream for wage citizenship has become a relic of the past. In a context where the political momentum has shifted to the right, but none of its candidates have taken off; Bolsonaro emerged as a provisional response from a ruling class in the process of reordering itself. This reordering was expressed in the scattered distribution of votes among many presidential candidates in 2018. The last time this had happened was at the dawn of the New Republic in 1989, when Collor de Mello beat Lula. Since then, every presidential election has been a two-party fight between the PT and PSDB.

Inasmuch as Bolsonaro emerged as an outsider in the eyes of both the elites and his popular constituency, the strategies of legitimation he pursues do not stem from organic bonds with either those from above or those from below. They should rather be seen as contingent products of two sets of elective affinities. The first is between the authoritarian approach he stands for and the antipopular agenda of the Brazilian ruling class. The second is between the retrograde values he champions and conservative popular trends that have their prime constituency in a wide array of conservative Christian denominations.

The rationale of the ruling class was explained during the presidential campaign by Bolsonaro's future Minister of Economy, Paulo Guedes, a thoroughbred Chicago Boy who studied in Milton Friedman's university in the 1970s and worked in Pinochet's Chile in the 1980s: "A completely coarse, brute person emerged and attracted votes like Lula did," thus bringing to the Brazilian elite "an opportunity to change Brazilian politics for better," as long as it can "tame the animal." When Guedes was asked if this was possible, he said: "I think so, he (Bolsonaro) is already a different animal" (Gaspar, 2018). Taming the beast for the sake of its class interests was the ruling class's bet.

Financial capital, which Guedes personifies, views Bolsonaro as a means to their own ends. Once elected, the president's legitimacy with big capital rested

on a form of division of labor. Bolsonaro offered the framework for this authoritarian neoliberalism: a police state in a country where the militarization of the
police, intensified under the dictatorship, was never undone.[6] The economy,
he outsourced to Guedes, the forests to agribusiness, public health to the insurance companies, and so forth. A new ministry of Women, Family and Human
Rights was handed to the evangelicals while the Ministry of Labor, a hallmark
of the national industrialization days in the 1930s, was shut down.

Unlike the PT that had a blueprint of a national project, despite how flawed
it might have been, neither Bolsonaro nor his coalition allies appeared to have
a project. Not even the military, which associated their own power and prestige
with a vision of national industrialization that flourished between two periods
of dictatorship (1937–1946 and 1964–1985), offered a coherent project. In the
21st century, faced with industrial regression and social degradation, the bar-
racks gave up on a "powerful Brazil" (*Brasil Potência*). They assumed their role
as armed managers of social life, betting on a privileged relationship with the
United States. Bolsonaro's Minister of Foreign Affairs embodied this affinity
with the United State, writing: "Only a God could still save the West, a God
operating for the nation – including, and perhaps mainly the American nation."
And concluded: "Trump can still save the West" (Fraga Araújo, 2017: 356).[7]

In light of this shift, the PT governments can be seen as the last iteration of a
"powerful Brazil", the design once nurtured by the military itself. However, the
PT's downfall did not spark any solidarity from those summoned to the role of
a national bourgeoisie under the "national champions" policy. On the contrary,
this bourgeoise was quick to jump from the boat, denouncing real or invented
corruption schemes (as in the case that sent Lula to prison), in an effort to save
their own faces and resume business.

Business under Bolsonaro is financial accumulation supported by accumulation by dispossession. Although this is not a new approach, its elements having been present throughout the New Republic, the Bolsonaro government has
raised the drive to a new level. It has brushed off any social and environmental
concerns, while giving up on a national project of any sort. On top of that, "militias", or extortion rackets and other organized criminal operations manned by
retired and off-duty police officers and who have direct links with different
levels of the state apparatus, have been given a free hand. While militias and

---

6 In addition to a regular "civilian" police, every state of the Brazilian Federation has a "military
   police", which is officially a back-up force of the national Army. Both are staunch supporters
   of Bolsonarism.
7 Bolsonaro and the Bolsonarista movement identified itself not only with the US, but especially with the Trump-style right wing white nationalism.

their connection to the state are also not new, under Bolsonaro the boundaries between the two are further blurred. There is a connection between these socioeconomic dispossession trends. In the absence of a national project, the anti-popular agenda advanced by financial capital and export sectors further erodes the social fabric. This fosters the illicit economy and social violence which in turn, give political prominence to violent state actors,[8] while fueling private security businesses – where policemen and former military are also the main beneficiaries.

The rationale fueling Bolsonaro's support coming from violent state actors differs from his support coming from the bourgeoise. Similar to his evangelical support base, a blend of business interests and a crusade for civilization forms the basis of the police's support for Bolsonaro, as the institutions of security forces see themselves as the last bastion in defense of their vision of society (Feltran, 2021). Whereas the support coming from high finance can be characterized as cynical and opportunistic, the support Bolsonaro receives from security professionals, led by the police, and conservative Christians is ideological. This is not a marriage of convenience but rather a whole-hearted affair. These social actors are committed to the values Bolsonaro embodies, beyond personal allegiance to Bolsonaro as an individual. These values that high finance tolerates but dislikes, are key to forming the ideology that seals his popular support. In short, *Bolsonarism* as a social phenomenon equipped with popular appeal and guns, will not fade with an eventual electoral defeat.

While the ruling class does not share these values, they are also not a concern. From their perspective, neoliberal dispossession and authoritarianism converge on the horizon. Part of the impetus for the militarization of social life is an ambition to reshape Brazilian society in a comprehensive way, comparable to Chile under Pinochet.[9] The aim is to completely reorganize social relations in order to deplete any possibility of collective organization and, ultimately, resistance. Social disembedding produced by the commodification of life is the driving force of this assault, in which Guedes's neoliberal fundamentalism marries with Bolsonaro's authoritarianism, and conservative Christian values act as their ideological cover.

Seen from this angle, there is no mystery as to why the elite adhere to Bolsonaro. Although brutal and vulgar, the violence he embodies is first and foremost a class violence. His popular support is a different matter. In

---

8   Congressmen with a police or armed forces background raised from 12 to 28 in the 2018 elections.
9   Pinochet's Chile was a pioneer lab of radical neoliberal policies, as Naomi Klein analyzes (Klein, 2008).

Lula's absence, the sub-proletariat that supported Lulism has leaned toward Bolsonaro, except in the Northeast. Every Brazilian knows someone who once voted for Lula and then went on to elect the captain. Lula was in jail, but those who voted were not. What happened?

It is true that anti-PTism poisoned the debate, but several candidates waved this flag. What helped differentiate Bolsonaro is that he sold himself as a form of new politics, despite being part of the old system. His ability to do so has to do with form: the former army captain uses the language of brutality, which a brutalized people know and understand. In a perverse way, he speaks to the people, like Lula. But, unlike Lula, this language conveys a violent but real message: instead of the false promises of the usual politicians, who promise to relieve the crisis, Bolsonaro admits a social dynamic marked by the struggle of all against all. And, instead of containing the crisis, he promises to arm his voters to defend themselves by attacking – as he himself does. Hence, his perceived authenticity. This is the reverse of "Lulinha peace and love" – as the former president pictures himself. In a context where the rose-colored lenses with which Lulism used to portray reality have faded, Bolsonaro's aura of authenticity emanates from the unconventional way he does politics, as well as from the content of it.

As a consequence, if Lula was perceived as a messiah, Bolsonaro became a "myth", especially among the youth, where many call him simply as that: "the myth". Investigating young people from the urban peripheries' affinity towards Bolsonaro, Solano tells us how, to start conversations, she played a video with some of the candidate's statements – a macho, racist and homophobic character, who praises dictatorship, torture and violence. Atrocities are described in playful, colorful, and youthful language, unlike what the old serious and scowling right-wingers used to do. In response, the youth laugh and applaud. Why? "Because he is cool, because he is a myth, because he is funny, because he speaks his mind and doesn't give a damn." Solano concludes, "With more than five million followers on Facebook, the fact is that Bolsonaro represents a right that communicates with young people, a right that some young people identify as rebellious, as a counterpoint to the system, as a different proposal" (Solano, 2018: 22).

For this audience, Bolsonaro's notorious intellectual limitations, as he is unable to articulate cohesive reasoning in an interview, is cause for amusement rather than admonishment. His chaotic and fragmented style of communication, based on quick reversals, dry cuts, and slogans, is tailored for the short internet videos where he rules. His followers edit the best moments of his interventions in the mainstream media and circulate them in digital networks – from broadcast to multicast (Lago, 2018). That is why the first people he thanked in his inauguration speech were the internet users: the president does not rely on activists, but on followers.

These observations suggest a paradox: what the elites dislike about Bolsonaro (his vulgar style), is paramount to his popular constituency. The fact that Bolsonaro does not belong (to the elite) hinders his upper-class backing, at the same time that it draws him popular support. This leads to a second observation, which is that the Bolsonaro candidacy has perverted the concept of rebellion. Besides the admittedly many reactionary votes, many others were protest votes, especially among the youth, for whom the PT had been the establishment since 2003. The paradox is that the left was not part of the protest, but part of what was being protested against. Although the popular anti-Petism that has taken roots in recent years is a complex phenomenon, it is undeniable that it includes an enormous frustration with the expectation of change historically mobilized by the PT. While elite anti-Petism targets not what the party has become, but rather what it represents (autonomous organization of workers), popular anti-Petism resents the failure to fulfill the promise of change; the very change the party embodied in the past.

With the massive help of fake news networks, anti-Petism became a kind of empty signifier, filled with meanings ranging from "gender ideology" to "Bolivarianism", all serving as conduits for the politicization of social resentment operated by Bolsonaro and nourished by elements beyond anti-corruption. Contrary to what one might assume, surveys show that most of the protesters in support of Rousseff's impeachment in 2015 were opposed to a reduction in the social role of the state associated with neoliberalism, in the sense that they believed the state should provide adequate health care and education. Besides anti-Petism, they were united by punitivism, that is, the notion that it is necessary to increase punishment for lawbreakers. This is in line with what the police stands for. They were also united by the rejection of the *Bolsa Família* cash transfer program and quotas for blacks and indigenous people, which they interpreted as anti-meritocratic (Solano, 2018). Similarly, the rejection of racial and gender quotas, in turn, feeds on a conservative Christian reaction to the assertion of the rights of blacks, women, and the LGBTQIA + community. In short, Bolsonarism has embodied a moral crusade against corruption and privilege in defense of family and order. As this agenda successfully captured hearts and minds, public debate drifted to the field of moral values, hiding Bolsonaro's anti-popular agenda from his own base.

This ideological conjunction between competition and punishment, typical of neoliberalism, embedded in a devotion to family and order, typical of authoritarianism, is observed in different modalities of authoritarian neoliberalism across the contemporary world. It is as if values could bind the social bonds that economics dissolves. In the Brazilian case, this conjunction is fueled by conservative Christian voters. While many of these voters are conservative Catholics, its cornerstone is the universe of neo-Pentecostal churches, whose political influence has been growing since the 1980s. In the 1980s, 6.6% of the population identified as evangelical. Now, they account for about a third of Brazilians. Although there are various branches that compete among themselves, they merge in politics forming the so-called "evangelical bench". In 2018, the bench supported Bolsonaro *en masse,* electing 84 federal deputies (out of 513) and seven senators (out of 81).[10]

Just as the affinity between Bolsonarism and conservative Christianity goes beyond neo-Pentecostalism, its content is not limited to patriarchal authority. At close inspection, there is an elective affinity between the prosperity gospel and self-entrepreneurship, a cornerstone of neoliberal way of life. This affinity helps explain the low resistance and even a certain complacency among poor workers in the face of the ongoing assault on labor rights.

The political violence against organized labor precedes Temer's dismantling of labor protection in 2017. The hostility to unions has deeper roots, feeding on the exponential increase in precarious employment in the last three decades, as well as the increase in unemployment, under-employment, and informal work that resulted from the 2015–2017 economic crisis. Between 2015 and 2016, GDP decreased 7% and unemployment almost doubled, from 6.8% in 2015 to 12.8% in 2017.

With 42% of the economically active population engaged in informal employment, popular entrepreneurship has become, in practical terms, the only alternative for millions of poor workers. In the world of informality, labor rights are interpreted as privileges rather than rights to be achieved, preserved, and expanded, as they were seen during the decades of the country's industrialization process. On the contrary, in the era of widespread job insecurity, the resentment against the so-called "privileged" (those protected by labor rights) extends to institutions of organized labor (trade unions). At the same time, informality has further removed poor workers from unions, fragmenting and weakening their collective action, while strengthening their dependence on "small jobs" and assistance networks typically associated with evangelical churches.

In place of unions, the affections of informal workers are welcomed by evangelical churches. Their needs are then instrumentalized by the fundamentalist

---

10 Nearly 70% of evangelicals voted Bolsonaro. It should be noted that most evangelical leaders supported the PT in the past and their lobby was key to stall several proposals concerning gender and LGBTQ rights.

right which, through prosperity theology, offers them both spiritual support and labor volition (Birman, 2019). After all, to endure in an increasingly uncertain and violent economic environment, the entrepreneurship commonly found in the informal economy requires massive amounts of self-discipline. Popular religiosity claims to be capable of providing this discipline.

In short, contrary to what happened during the 1970s, when the flourishing of popular religiosity in communities fostered by Liberation theology added to the strengthening of union power, now a quite different theology has taken root in the popular terrain. This doctrine cultivates individualism, advocating that God will honor his contract with believers if they are sufficiently submissive to divine will. In this sense, the evangelical identity, while disciplining individual action within a community of faith, also values the satisfaction of material desires, reinvigorating the volition for work necessary for informal work (Almeida, 2017). Schematically, the expectation is that the more the believer offers to the church, the more God will repay him, in a spiral capable of satisfying both the particular desires of each believer and the collective needs of the "people of God" represented by the church.

At the same time, evangelical groups are generally guided by a conservative agenda with the clear domination of patriarchal authority. This brought them closer to Bolsonaro as he claimed to restore the power of the "father of the family" as an antidote to the supposed indoctrination of the "gender ideology" in force in the PT era. Popular conservatism is a phenomenon essentially anchored in the desire for stability and social protection. After all, when insecurity is the rule and one has no financial reserves of any kind, any disturbance of order, such as an assault, an early pregnancy, or losing one's job, imply an often irreversible deterioration of the reproductive conditions of working families. This is the background of Bolsonaro's successful politicization of social resentment in the name of order, albeit an oppressive one.

3   Cracks and Resistances

The contingent nature of upper-class support for Bolsonaro implies a relationship comparable to a marriage of convenience, not of love. The former captain emerged as a provisional response from a ruling class that is reorganizing itself in an anti-democratic and anti-popular direction. This relationship is grounded on a solid class foundation, as Bolsonaro fully committed to the elite's economic agenda. Nevertheless, the relationship is unsteady, not because of any incompatibility with the illiberal and retrograde values the president embraces, but rather because Bolsonaro's politics implies the constant production of conflict. This results in permanent instability which can be counterproductive from businesses' standpoint.

Bolsonarism's internal logic requires the fabrication of enemies to mobilize his base and divert attention. As a president, he follows an invariable script: he chooses enemies to attack, while portraying himself as the victim. Bolsonaro accuses people, but also institutions and the press, as obstacles to his (nonexistent) project. When the president accuses Congress of boycotting him, he shifts responsibility for his failures to those who "don't let him rule," while at the same time mobilizing popular support to face the institution that, in the eyes of citizenship, synthesizes rotten politics (Lago, 2020). When the Congress reacts, the president's narrative is legitimized, and therefore he raises the tone. When it shuts up, the president advances another square. In this game of inversions, Bolsonaro appears to be subversive, while the left brandishes the constitution in defense of order.

Bolsonaro's simple answers to complex problems in Brasilia corresponds to the narrative of a hero who faces successive villains, as in a video game. In this logic, the government's achievements do not matter, because the rule of political effectiveness is different: to inflame its supporters and make natural what was, until recently, intolerable. Bolsonaro rewrites what is normal, expanding the aspirational horizon of his base. It is a movement that cannot recede, but on the contrary, only accumulates mass, speed and violence in snowball fashion. In what was a potentially apex moment, the president summoned his base to demand the closure of the National Congress on March 2020. However, this was also when the Covid-19 pandemic reached Brazil, imposing new challenges and opportunities.

To be sure, Bolsonaro's snowball has a green light to roll because it is class oriented – capital's agenda is making headway. However, permanently contriving enemies and instigating conflicts draws instability, which can be counterproductive to business. For instance, the government had a hard time gaining Congressional support for reforms pledged to big capital.

Upper class malaise with Bolsonaro intensified during the pandemic. First of all, the president outright denied that Covid was a problem. This was a slap in the face of the wealthy and upper middle class who have the resources to travel abroad, brought the virus to Brazil, and were the first to feel its consequences. His denialism also caused international embarrassment for an elite that always fashions itself after developed countries, where more often than not extraordinary public health measures were quickly imposed. In any case, the rich confined themselves in social isolation on their own.

But the main issue is the unnecessary costs that Bolsonaro's confrontational style incurs: the devastation of the Amazon rainforest as state policy, hindering the ratification of the free trade agreement between Mercosur and the European Union; the delay of 38 days to recognize Joe Biden's electoral victory after supporting Trump's campaign; racist statements linking China to Covid-19 that harm the agribusiness sector. These are just a few international side effects of a larger problem: the political and managerial ineptitude of the government, which inhibits the accomplishment of any agenda.

However, upper class responses to Bolsonaro are limited to questioning his style, not his policies. Negative responses among the upper class can hardly be described as resistance, but more appropriately as cracks in his class support. The discontent within the ruling classes is publicly reflected in the emerging political disputes between different personalities who are willing to carry out the agenda of authoritarian neoliberalism without Bolsonaro's style. These personalities do not lack upper class support. Rather, they lack consolidated votes.

Meanwhile, Bolsonaro is attempting to consolidate his die-hard followers and nurture his own ideas for his political longevity. He appears to have dynastic ambitions, as he has three children in politics, and envisions state repressive forces as his party and conservative Christians as its organized base. From this point of view, his biggest challenge is to convert online support that elected him into real mobilization: to turn internet followers into street demonstrators.

In order to accomplish Bolsonaro's vision for longevity, social antagonisms need to be stoked. This may be a challenge in a country that has no external enemies and where the military only shoots its own people. Nor does the country have any significant religious or ethnic divisions, nor hostility towards immigrants. The main divide is racial, with blacks as the systematically oppressed race as well as the numeric majority. Divisions along class and gender lines, and their intersectionalities with race, have also been targets of social resentment. It is significant that the middle class that hit pots at their windows when Bolsonaro spoke at the beginning of the pandemic protesting against his negligence, fell silent when blacks took to the streets in the weeks following the assassination of George Floyd in the U.S. (and the police massacre of 29 people in a Rio favela) amid social distancing protocols that, in the majority black and working-class peripheral urban neighborhoods, were always hard to implement due to livelihood conditions.

The demonstrations deriving from the internationalization of "Black Lives Matter" in 2020 had a modest impact in Brazil, but they illustrate an important dynamic: the irreversible rise in mobilizations for the rights of black people, of the LGBTQ community, and especially, of women. One event illustrates this trend. A few weeks before the 2018 election, thousands of women took to the streets of many Brazilian cities under the slogan "#Not him", referring to

Bolsonaro. It was one of the most emotional demonstrations in the country since the end of the dictatorship, and those who participated were sure that "he," would not pass. However, in the following week, a wide network of fake news operating via WhatsApp circulated photos of women kissing each other or with their breasts out, claiming they represented the demonstration. These images had a negative impact, especially among evangelicals, who tend to see feminism and homosexuality as a threat to the traditional family.

I make this point to emphasize that in Brazil today, a reaction in defense of patriarchy coexists with the empowerment of thousands of black, white, Asian, and indigenous women who have reshaped norms of behavior in public spaces in recent years, making unacceptable acts and words considered normal a generation ago. In fact, it should be noted that men under thirty voted overwhelmingly for Bolsonaro (70–30) in the election, while among young women, PT's Haddad managed to edge out Bolsonaro (55–45) (Hochuli, 2020). It is possible to argue that this dimension of conservatism is a reaction to the blows suffered by the patriarchy, in a context in which the family structure based on a breadwinner father has been damaged by the decline of wage citizenship. Nevertheless, Bolsonaro's electoral victory with support from conservative Christianity does not diminish the rising strength of women, blacks and the LGBTQ population confronting him (Pinheiro-Machado, 2019).

Although diffuse, racial and gender tensions seem more disruptive than institutional opposition to the government, mainly embodied in the PT. Despite the setbacks it suffered, the party elected the largest parliamentary bench in 2018. Lula's release in 2019 reinforced hopes for electoral redemption in 2022, which, however, exists alongside a distaste for the party's way of doing politics and its cooling influence on social movements.

On one side, there are those who argue that the PT is the only party embedded in society, making it an unavoidable pillar of a front for democracy. Although it is commonplace among party members to admit that neo-Pentecostalism has thrived in the place once occupied by the grassroots organizing that has long ceased, the party still has a strong influence over CUT-affiliated unionism and the set of movements rooted in the popular-democratic project of the 1980s. The hope for a Lulista redemption is expressed in the words of the respected leader of the MST (Landless Workers' Movement), João Pedro Stédile: "Lula has to be our Moses, to convince the people to cross the Red Sea. There is no other character who can fulfill this role" (Stédile, 2019).

On the other hand, the Party's image has deteriorated beyond repair. This was a major hindrance to any kind of *Front Populaire* against Bolsonaro in the second round in 2018. On top of that, party logic prioritizes electoral considerations over opposing the government, resulting in ambiguities that lead to paralysis. While not a new phenomenon, it has been particularly conspicuous in recent years. After Rousseff was deposed, the party used its influence to calibrate the demonstrations against the brief Temer government (2016–18) so as to wear down the president, while avoiding a crisis that would bring him down. The calculation was that Lula would be reelected next, which was in fact likely at the time. The plan failed, however, because he was arrested in a persecutory maneuver, best seen as a political trial. According to the PT narrative, there was a coup in 2016, followed by a preemptive coup in 2018 – in other words, a coup within the coup.

In both cases, the party's response was to go along with the new situation. A month after the impeachment, the PT allied with parties that supported the coup in hundreds of municipal elections across the country. While the PT base denounced the deposition of Rousseff as a coup and the Bolsonaro government as the escalation of fascism, Lula in 2018 viewed the impeachment as something that "has already passed, is already part of history" (Lula, 2018), and two years later, opposed the impeachment of Bolsonaro. In an interview in March 2020, Lula said "I have warned the PT to be patient, because we have to wait four years. Unless he (Bolsonaro) commits an *act of insanity*, commits a *crime of responsibility*, then we can impeach him, but if he doesn't do it, we can't think that we can overthrow a president because we don't like him. We can't" (Lula, 2020, emphasis mine).

Shortly after that interview, the pandemic spread across Brazil. In light of Bolsonaro's calculated non-response to the health crisis costing thousands of lives (as will be discussed in a later chapter) we could ask Lula to define "act of insanity," and "crime of responsibility." In early April, while the country was plunged into Covid-19 and citizens beat their pots and pans with indignation at the president's every pronouncement, the PT leadership took a stand against impeachment. That month, more than twenty lawsuits were filed in the Chamber of Deputies, none of them by the PT. Weeks later, the party decided to join the public call for impeachment under pressure from its base, but this was only after any real chance for impeachment was impossible.

Impeachment became impossible because Bolsonaro bought off the "*centrão*" (large center), a cluster of small venal parties whose loyalty is bought with positions and money. While the PT insisted on being a responsible opposition, believing that Bolsonaro would dissipate like a bad dream and the party would redeem itself at the polls, the same professional politicians of the *centrão* who once negotiated with the PT now sell their loyalty to Bolsonaro. We may conclude that an escape from Bolsonarism led by Brasília is as unlikely as the feat of the Baron of Munchhausen, who pulled himself out of the swamp pulling on his own hair.

This deadlock could have been challenged by popular protest, but the people responded to the criminal management of the pandemic in other ways. Contrary to the indifference of the rich and the cynicism of Brasília, solidarity networks sprang up in peripheral communities. An iconic image is the photo of 425 "street presidents" who gathered on a soccer field in a favela in São Paulo, each two meters apart, to organize a solidarity campaign. While companies laid workers off, the MST donated tons of food. Altogether, it was possible to map thousands of popular solidarity initiatives, most completely disconnected from the state and the institutional left (Abers and Bulow, 2020).

On the labor front, there were two notable shutdowns of app delivery workers in 2020. The "#BrequeDosApps" (Apps breake) had wide repercussions, because the deliverers were a main artery in the political economy of the pandemic, providing those in home offices with everything they needed. Postal workers, another sector whose work intensified during the pandemic, participated in a long strike. All in all, the struggles of delivery workers, postal workers, and the numerous episodes of solidarity in the pandemic were silver linings of organized resistance in a bleak scenario. To a large extent, they appeared along the fringes of the institutional left and of mass mobilizations.

Despite the staggering death toll from Covid-19, the masses suffered with relative resignation. It will take time and research to understand why, but by the end of 2020 two things seemed clear. In the eyes of many, the president was not perceived to be even partially responsible for the deaths that were piling up. At the same time, an emergency financial aid program paid four times as much, to four times as many people as the lulista *Bolsa Familia*. This aid program compensated for his loss of popularity among the middle and upper classes by attracting loyalty of the poorest – just as had happened before with Lulism (Correio do Povo, 2020; Lichotti and Buono: 2020). Reconciling neoliberal fundamentalism with a universal minimum income was squaring the circle for a government that could not do without Paulo Guedes, seen as Bolsonaro's guarantor with finance and big capital.

However, the alchemy of an "inverted Lulism" did not last. In early 2021, the government cut the emergency aid while the country's economy plummeted. Between the first and second quarter of 2020, GDP shrank by 9.7%, gross capital formation fell by 15.4%, and household consumption by 13.5%. Unemployment exceeded 14% of the population, the highest rate ever recorded in the country. The deterioration of living conditions challenged Bolsonaro's ability to divert attention. By the end of 2021, the pandemic death toll surpassed 600,000. Still, the president was on a steady march towards completing his first mandate and running for a second. This steadiness was a form of normalizing his politics, although one year before the 2022 presidential elections, it was unclear whether they would take place under "normal" conditions.

Overall, Bolsonaro and his opponents seemed tied: if the president was unable to advance his authoritarian designs, those countering them were impotent to bring him down. So far, the most effective brake on Bolsonaro's authoritarian ambitions has been his own virulence in a context where the autonomy and reliability of institutions has been damaged, but they have not been captured. The president never concealed his distaste for the judiciary, the parliament and the media, and if these still operate relatively normally it is because he was unable to subdue them. It is hard to say whether this is because of the strength of the institutions or Bolsonaro's weaknesses in a context where the ruling class is not unified and is undergoing a crisis of direction.

In particular, relations with the Supreme Court (Supremo Tribunal Federal) have been tense. The president has had to backtrack his verbal attacks and threats more than once. It is thought that the multiple ongoing investigations concerning Bolsonaro and his sons, ranging from the criminal manipulation of fake news to direct links with the militiamen who murdered black, bisexual, left-wing Rio de Janeiro city councilor, Marielle Franco, in 2019[11] have been key to contain the president. Furthermore, in 2021, the Court annulled charges that suspended Lula's political rights (thus restoring his political rights, including the right to run in elections) in a decision that was not provoked by new legal facts nor by street pressure. Most likely, the judges responded to political pressures within the ruling class to produce an alternative to Bolsonaro for the 2022 elections. The same authorities who took Lula out of the dispute in 2018, three years later brought him back to the game.

On the congressional front, although the president was able to dodge impeachment by buying the loyalty of pliable congressmen, this has been an unstable relationship subject to permanent bargaining. A provisional measure allowing the president to nominate federal university deans during the pandemic was rebuffed, as was an attempt to change internet regulations aiming to relax boundaries for fake news. Perhaps the most significant defeat was the attempt to reinstate the printed vote in place of the electronic system in use since 1996. Behind the alleged concern for transparency, the proposal suited militia politics as it would facilitate territorial vote control.

Following Trump's steps, Bolsonaro feeds on a hostile relationship with journalists and sectors of corporate media, notably Rede Globo, the Brazilian TV empire nurtured under the dictatorship. However, the attacks on Rede Globo divert viewership to four other private nationwide channels, including the second-place TV Record, controlled by the owner of evangelical

---

11   Former policeman Ronnie Lessa who is accused of murdering Franco is Bolsonaro's condo neighbour in Rio.

Universal Church (Igreja Universal). Furthermore, smaller corporate groups openly aligned with Bolsonaro have received broadcast concessions. In print media, top Brazilian newspaper *Folha de São Paulo* has taken stands critical of Bolsonaro, while a myriad of independent online outlets counter the far-right online might.

All in all, Bolsonaro's march has not proceeded unchallenged. Institutional tensions arose with the judiciary, the congress and the media. Despite sporadic acts of violence and political persecution, civil liberties in 2021 were still widely preserved. Brazilians were not afraid to speak out their minds and trash the president in public venues, although far right activists would occasionally disrupt events. More tragic was the violence taking place in urban peripheries against poor black people and in remote areas of the country against indigenous people and peasant activists. Beyond state violence, the president's hatred politics entitled haters to act on their own.

Below the institutional battleground, the government has also been contested in the streets. Pot hitting in the first weeks of the pandemic was intense, allowing people a way to protest while social distancing. Although it was not enough to budge Brasilia, this momentum would contribute to mobilizations to come. One year later (2021), people took to the streets in massive numbers throughout the country on several occasions to protest, despite the pandemic. In some cities, demonstrators occasionally exceeded 100.000. On Independence Day (September 7th), Bolsonaro's supporters demonstrated in response. Even if these highly organized and financed demonstrations did not live up to the expectations of their leaders, they were all the same impressive. In addition to all that the president embodies, it must be recalled that over 500.000 Brazilians had passed away because of Covid-19 at that point. In that context, to see over 100.000 staunch Bolsonaro supporters taking to the streets in Brasilia and São Paulo, is not trivial. Occasional demonstrations against Bolsonaro were staged in the following months, but as the year came to a close, the political focus shifted to the presidential election, then perceived as the best shot to halt Bolsonaro even if bolsonarism was unlikely to subside in face of electoral defeat.

4 Concluding Remarks

Between the collapse of Lulism, which can be traced to the June 2013 rebellion, and a reliable way out of the New Republic, the Brazilian ruling class is reorganizing itself. This reorganization is in tune with a global trend in which the contradictions between capitalism and democracy are sharpening, breeding different shades of authoritarian neoliberalism. In the Brazilian case, the bourgeois support for Bolsonaro was a marriage of convenience, in which fundamentalist neoliberalism merged with Bolsonaro's authoritarianism against the backdrop of a cultural crusade that feeds on elective affinities between neoliberal subjectivity, the prosperity gospel and punitivism. Social disembedding is the driving force of the neoliberal assault. The twenty-year cap on public expenses, the labor reform and the pension system reform demonstrate that from the standpoint of the ruling class, the Citizen Constitution is a hindrance to be superseded and wage citizenship embedded in a peripheral welfare state is no longer to be aspired to.

Beyond the instrumental rationality of the ruling class, elective affinities between neoliberalism and conservatism are bred in different ways by Christian sects and security professionals (led by the police), who are wholeheartedly committed to the values the president embodies. These powerful institutions distill ideological tropes that garner wide mass appeal and blend them to produce Bolsonarism as a social phenomenon. Bolsonarism has deeper roots going far beyond allegiance to its present leader, and will not recoil or fade away in the face of his electoral defeat. Seen from this angle, upper class backing for Bolsonaro has been instrumental to lay the groundwork for an armed Christian order.

In the meantime, the president burns the thin layer of Brazilian civility, expands the authoritarian aspirations of his followers, and infests the government with military men. In this context, the fear of a *coup d'état* might be anachronistic: we should not look at 21st century politics with the grammar of the last century. At present, confronting Bolsonaro implies not only dealing with a family with notorious links to extortion rackets known as "militias", but also dealing with the armed forces and the police, who are more loyal to Brasília than to state governors. The president, who in 2021 was not affiliated with any political party, had three thousand military men in the government, more than the dictatorship ever had. If this is at all about a coup d'état, it likely has already taken place.

Regardless of the institutional framework, Bolsonaro's class mission, in form as in content, is to push the boundaries of what is acceptable. Much of the president's verbal violence does not become state policy, but people all over the country feel empowered to move from word to deed. The president makes the impossible possible – which, paradoxically, has always been a motto of the left. Hence, the upside-down world we live in: far-right politics intends to subvert the established order, while the left defends it.The political economy of Bolsonarism causes social reproduction to be ever more determined by capital reproduction. The cushions that social welfare policies and labor rights provided are being depleted. Neoliberal reason, the prosperity gospel, and punitivism combine to normalize social relationships based on the competition of all against all, which can also be described as naturalizing barbarism. This explains the president's engagement in a cultural battle on the level of values. This battle is not primarily about forbidding unions, parties or demonstrations (although these may eventually happen), but it aims to modify the conditions under which people consider it legitimate to demonstrate and rebel. In other words, the aim is to generate a new normal.

Even if Lula defeats Bolsonaro in the 2022 election, there will be no going back to the New Republic. Furthermore, the forces unleashed by Bolsonarism, will not subside. In their eyes, elections might be a lost battle, but the war is far from over. Regardless of the political future of Bolsonaro as an individual, the path he blazes necessarily implies violence, whether this violence will be to deepen barbarism or to prevent barbarism from becoming the new normal.

References

Ab'Saber T (2010) Brasil, a ausência significante política (uma comunicação). In: Safatle, Vladimir and Teles, Edson (eds.). *O que resta da ditadura?* São Paulo, Boitempo.

Abers R and Bulow M (2020) The struggle of civil Society groups in Brazil's urban peripheries (March–June 2020). Available at: https://resocie.org/wp-content/uplo ads/2020/07/Resocie-Research-Report-1.pdf.

Almeida R (2017). A onda quebrada – evangélicos e conservadorismo. *Cadernos Pagu*, no. 50, Campinas.

Anderson P (2019) *Brazil Apart (1964–2019)*. Verso: London.

Bercovici G and Massonetto L F (2006) A constituição dirigente invertida: a blindagem da constituição financeira e a agonia da constituição econômica. Coimbra: Boletim de Ciência Econômica, 49(1–23).

Birman P (2019) Narrativas seculares e religiosas sobre a violência: as fronteiras do humano no governo dos pobres. *Sociologia & Antropologia*, 9(1).

Braga R and Santos F L (2020) The political economy of Lulismo and its aftermath. *Latin American Perspectives*. 230, 47(1).

Cardoso F H and Faletto E (1974) *Dependência e desenvolvimento na América Latina*. Rio de Janeiro: Zahar.

Cervo A (2003) Política exterior e relações internacionais do Brasil: enfoque paradigmático *Revista Brasileira de Política Internacional*, 46(2).

Correio do P (2020) 'Auxílio emergencial injeta R$ 20 bilhões no comércio por pagamento digital'. Available at: https://www.correiodopovo.com.br/not%C3%ADc ias/economia/aux%C3%Adlio-emergencial-injeta-r-20-bilh%C3%B5es-no-com %C3%A9rcio-por-pagamento-digital-1.465709.

Coutinho C N (1980) *A democracia como um valor universal*. São Paulo: Livraria Editora Ciências Humanas.

Dardot P and Laval C (2010) *La nouvelle raison du monde. Essai sur la societé neoliberal*. Paris: La Découverte.

Esposito M (2017) Desindustrialização do Brasil: uma análise a partir da perspectiva da formação nacional. *Revista da Sociedade Brasileira de Economia Política*, n. 46.

Feltran G (2021) Polícia e política: o regime de poder hoje liderado por Bolsonaro, *Novos Estudos Cebrap*. Available at: http://novosestudos.com.br/policia-e-politica-o-regime-de-poder-hoje-liderado-por-bolsonaro/.

Fernandes F (1975) *A revolução burguesa no Brasil*. Rio de Janeiro: Zahar.

Fernandes F (1982) *A ditadura em questão*. São Paulo: Taq, 1982.

Fernandes F (2015) *Poder e contrapoder na América Latina*. São Paulo: Expressão Popular.

Fraga Araújo, E (2017). Trump e a história. *Cadernos de Política Exterior / Instituto de Pesquisa de Relações Internacionais*. – v. 3, n. 6. Brasília: FUNAG, 323–358.

Gaspar M (2018) O fiador *Revista Piauí*.

Hochuli A (2020) From antipolitics to authoritarian restoration in Brazil. *Jacobin* Available at: https://www.jacobinmag.com/2020/12/anti-politics-authoritarian-restoration-brazil-jair-bolsonaro.

Klein N (2008) *Shock doctrine. The rise of disaster capitalism*. New York: Picador.

Lago M (2020) Uma esfinge na presidência *Revista Piauí*. Available at: https://piaui.folha.uol.com.br/materia/uma-esfinge-na-presidencia/.

Lago M (2018) Bolsonaro fala outra língua. *Revista Piauí*, Available at: https://piaui.folha.uol.com.br/bolsonaro-fala-outra-lingua/.

Lichotti C and Buono R (2020). Esticando o auxílio *Revista Piauí*. Available at: https://piaui.folha.uol.com.br/esticando-o-auxilio/.

Lula L I (2020) Não podemos pedir impeachment de Bolsonaro só porque não gostamos dele IG, 2 mar 2020. Available at: https://ultimosegundo.ig.com.br/politica/2020-03-02/lula-nao-podemos-pedir-impeachment-de-bolsonaro-so-porque-nao-gostamos-dele.html.

Lula L I (2018) *A verdade vencerá*. São Paulo: Boitempo.

Martins J (2009) *O cativeiro da terra*. 9ª ed. São Paulo: Contexto.

Paulani L (2008) *Brazil Delivery* São Paulo: Boitempo.

Pinheiro M R (2019) *Amanhã vai ser maior*. São Paulo: Planeta.

Santos F L (2020) *Power and Impotence. A history of South America under progressivism (1998–2016)* Boston; Leiden: Brill.

Santos F L (2018) Neo-development of underdevelopment: Braziland the political economy of South American integration under PT. *Globalizations*, 16 (2): 216–231.

Santos F L (2016) *Além do PT*. São Paulo: Elefante.

Santos F L (2021) Book review. Perry Anderson, Brazil Apart, 1964–2019, Verso, *Socialist History*.

Solano E (2018) Crise da democracia e extremismos da direita, em *Análise*, n. 42.São
    Paulo: Friederich Ebert Stiftung.

Stédile J P (2019) Stédile: Lula foi escolhido pelo povo para explicar o que está aconte-
    cendo no país *Brasil 247* Available at: https://www.brasil247.com/brasil/stedile-lula
    -foi-escolhido-pelo-povo-para-explicar-o-que-esta-acontecendo-no-pais.

CHAPTER 7

Comparisons

Fabio Luis Barbosa dos Santos

As French Historian Marc Bloch once noted, every comparison entails similarities and differences. When similarities spring from very different historical contexts, it can be assumed that structural forces are at play. The countries analyzed in this volume have extremely different historical backgrounds. Yet, none of them belongs to the core of capitalist development. As such, dependency and social inequality have always been issues, albeit to different degrees. The historical differences are remarkable even among countries with colonial pasts (India, the Philippines and Brazil), as their colonial experiences have different roots, encompass different time spans, and involve different colonial powers. Their legacies are also distinct: there are no expansive railways nor cricket in Brazil and in the Philippines, as there are in India.

As we come across comparable shades of hatred politics in such diverse countries in the 21st century, we sense that structural forces are at play. However, this has to be qualified: to say that these regimes signal a crisis of capitalism would do little to enhance our understanding of either the crisis of capitalism or of these regimes, even if that assumption is correct. We must examine how global structural forces are mediated and how specific national dynamics play out; this is where comparisons can be fruitful.

With this in mind, the scale of comparison is decisive. Our analysis unfolds on at least two scales. When these governments are compared between themselves, their unique aspects are likely to be highlighted, illuminating particularities of each case. A Turkish citizen is likely to enhance his understanding of Erdogan's regime in contrast with the other cases presented in this book, while his grasp of these kin regimes would be eased having his own as a reference. Moreover, besides distinct historical backgrounds, we are looking at leaders who have been in power for different time ranges (Erdogan since 2002, Bolsonaro since 2019), and this is crucial to gauge comparisons. Not only does a lot happens in two decades of rule, but ruling approaches evolve as well. When Erdogan first came to power, the international community welcomed him as a soft form of an Islamist leader, similar to how Brazil's Lula was also welcomed as a soft left leader. Both built their legitimacy on inclusive social approaches. Ten years later, Brazil and Turkey experienced social unrest and economic slowdowns, which paved the way for an authoritarian slide. However, while in

Brazil Lula and the PT were brought down and Bolsonaro stepped in, a comparable shift took place in Turkey under the same man, as neoliberalism with an inclusive face transformed into authoritarianism with a popular face. It is as if Lula and Bolsonaro were to be found in the same regime. Altogether, as we scrutinize the differences and similarities between these regimes, framing them under a single concept becomes increasingly complex.

The second scale of comparison arises when these five regimes are considered together as a group and compared with other regimes. In that case, the similarities between the five are highlighted and analysis can be drawn across space and time. For example, as Dan Geary shows in another chapter, politics of hate seen from the margins can enrich reflections about this phenomenon in the Global North – and vice-versa. At the same time, it is worthwhile to contrast these regimes with what authoritarianism looked like during the Cold War, thus complexifying contemporary debates around the term.

This chapter will focus on this first scale of analysis, while occasionally referring to the second. It brings these regimes in contrast with each other to highlight convergences and particularities, contributing to lay the ground for evidence-based studies aiming to conceptualize this challenging global political phenomenon.

1   Roots of Popular Authoritarianism

As the country chapters show, not only are these regimes rooted in very different historical backgrounds and cultural landscapes, but they also embody distinct historical currents of varying depth and reach. Hindu nationalism as championed by the RSS dates back to the interwar years when India was still a colony, but it has consistently built up its political might from the 1980s on, as the hegemony of the Indian National Congress eroded. Compared to the family of Hindu organizations known as *Sangh Parivar*, leaders like Duterte and Bolsonaro, who hardly have any organized social base, look like newcomers.

Furthermore, these governments cover different time spans. Erdogan has been in power for two decades and Orbán for more than one, while Duterte and Bolsonaro have only been elected once so far.[1] If patterns can be traced, we can hypothesize that the most consolidated among these regimes (Erdogan and Orbán), indicate the direction in which others might evolve. At the same

---

1 The president cannot be re-elected in the Philippines but Bolsonaro will run for a second term.

time, we also observe that the 'newcomers' are the most contested. In any case, differences between these regimes and the resistances they face also have to do with how long they have been in power.

As the context-setting work places the ascent of these regimes within broader historical perspectives, it becomes visible that they all prospered amidst a crisis of the previous political hegemonies: Kemalism in Turkey, which dates back to the constitution of the modern Turkish nation state early in the 20th century; the dominance of liberal and socialist politics in Hungary following the demise of state socialism; the erosion of Congress Party hegemony rooted in its leadership in the struggle for independence in India; the liberal democracy framework that followed both the Marcos dictatorship (1965–1986) in the Philippines and the military dictatorship in Brazil (1964–1985), which in the latter case has been known as the New Republic.

In all cases, free elections featuring competing political parties have been in place at least since the 1990s, in tune with the consecration of political liberalism promoted by Western powers after the end of the Cold War and boosted by the 'end of history' ideology. At the same time, neoliberal structural adjustments were implemented. Their devastating social effects produced political consequences as well, as forces identified with this anti-people agenda lost prestige at the polls. As it became the norm for political parties to alternate in power, oppositions had a go in each of the five countries. In Brazil, the election of Lula in 2002 embodied an alternative to neoliberalism in the context of the South American Pink Tide. In hindsight, it is visible that as the expectations raised by political alternation framed by liberalism were not met, not only did ordinary political players lose prestige, but the very framework under which the game was played was undermined. It is not a coincidence that the regimes analyzed in this book have all been preceded by governments associated with neoliberalism with a human face, except in Turkey: a liberal and socialist coalition in Hungary, a Congress Party comeback in India, Benigno Aquino III in the Philippines and three and a half mandates of the PT in Brazil.

In the Turkish case, Erdogan ascended against the background of a major political and economic crisis, while Hungary is the only case where the impact of the 2008 global economic crisis was decisive. In these countries, which showcase the two longest and perhaps most consolidated of the governments discussed, it can be said that there was a crisis of the previous accumulation regime, which is detailed in their respective chapters. This was not the case in Brazil, although the country traversed a major political crisis in the context of economic recession, which unfolded with the impeachment of Rousseff in 2016 and Lula's arrest in 2018. As in India, there was mounting pressure towards accumulation by dispossession, intensifying aggressive trends that never subsided. However, the decline of the New Republic and of Congress Party hegemony did not correspond to major shifts in the accumulation regime.

Overall, the prevailing political forces lost legitimacy and alternatives arose from the right, but not from the left. In Turkey, the left had been crushed in the 1980s while in India and the Philippines, a solid left presence at the national level had always been a challenge. In Hungary, the left was identified with a discredited past and in Brazil, with a discredited present. Beyond national contingencies, neoliberalism had eroded the social fabric and undermined wage citizenship everywhere, implying that traditional left politics backed by trade unions and worker's parties, was losing its historical bearings.

At the turn of the century, as various shades of neoliberal governments alternated in power while social grievances aggravated, the end of history was no longer a promising landscape. However, the discrediting of the liberal democratic framework comprised the left, which in the distant past had denounced this very framework as a scam. When the doors of history opened again, the keys were not in their hands. New political forms were required, but change was captured by the right.

In this context, popular discontent targeted the political establishment while economic orthodoxy was hardly questioned. On the contrary, this book shows that structures of capital reproduction have been revamped and reinforced. As the establishment lost legitimacy but responses from the left did not capture this social malaise, popular discontent was channelled by a new political form, which is voted within political liberalism, to go against it. The peculiarity of this new form of authoritarianism, as opposed to authoritarianism during the Cold War, is that it is popular.

2   Nationalism under Neoliberalism

If this new political form embodies a rejection of political liberalism, economic liberalism remains unchecked (with the partial exception of the Hungarian case which will be detailed below). Privatizations, fiscal austerity, and further economic deregulation and de-industrialization go hand in hand with accumulation by dispossession, crony capitalism and corruption – the latter traits being raised to a new level by all these governments. Although none of these traits are new, they have been remarkably intensified under these regimes. At the same time, neither globalization nor neoliberalism has been meaningfully questioned – despite Orban's or Duterte's campaign rhetoric. Overall, it can be asserted that on the economic front, continuity prevails.

A similar rationale applies to labor. In all these cases, work conditions are being downgraded: labor precarity is on the rise and informal work is the norm for large swaths of their populations. The growth of the digital platform economy and the promotion of self-entrepreneurship are the flip side of comprehensive labor reforms (or a hands-off approach in the Philippines) and the dismantling of social rights. Again, these trends are not new, but they have been intensified in range and depth.

The acceleration of economic liberalization, labor precarization, and the dismantling of social rights has further compromised the tenuous bonds that link these populations together as nations. Although these countries have been marked since their inception by abysmal social disparities, making it debatable to speak of nations understood as cohesive societies (except Hungary), the articulation of national industrialization and wage citizenship provided a civilizational horizon that inspired the Global South throughout the 20th century. Furthermore, it provided the substance to anchor nationalism on the periphery of capitalism. Even if none of these countries ever 'caught-up' with the industrialized center, there was always hope they would do so. Furthermore, the dispute between different national development paths provided a distinguishing aspect of the political dispute between the left and the right.

In the 21st century, the twilight of the national development landscape implied that a social fabric woven by organized labor and social rights against the background of a national industrialization process, had lost its historical ground: it was no longer a realistic aspiration. As formal, stable employment and welfare state support became ever more unlikely, social reproduction as such faced a crisis. The neoliberal response was to enthrone competition as a core value presiding over social relations and individual subjectivities, thus raising the atomistic tendencies inherent to the ideologies of merit and self-entrepreneurship to new levels. These dynamics, in turn, further dissolved social bonds, aggravating the conditions of social reproduction, which is experienced more and more as a war of every man against every man. On another scale, grist to the mill of the clash of civilizations is provided. Under such conditions, the mere reproduction of life produces hate, fear and indifference in massive scale. Instead of countering these tendencies as ordinary politicians claim to do, the various shades of hatred politics analyzed in this book weaponize them.

These historical shifts in social reproduction and in the political landscape lay down a crucial challenge that hatred politicians face: how to conciliate nationalism and neoliberalism? This book makes it clear that the 'nation' is a key ideological artifact these regimes invoke, while neoliberalism is not consistently challenged. However, variations of nationalism and varieties of neoliberalism are to be found. For instance: Turkey and India conjure up a distant Ottoman or Hindu past which admits no parallels in the Philippines or in Brazil. At the same time, these countries are military players who display their repressive might both domestically (against Kurds, naxalites or in Kashmir) and in their respective regions (the Syrian conflict or episodic bombing of Pakistan), while nothing like that is to be found in Hungary, a small NATO member. On the neoliberal front, the ultraneoliberalism of Bolsonaro's Chicago boy can hardly be matched elsewhere. Yet, privatizations have been taking place across these countries. For example, Erdogan's first years were decisive to deepen neoliberalization in Turkey. In Hungary, although some nationalizations took place, Orbán implements a low, flat income tax rate and super low corporate tax rates, while a new wave of financialization was allowed and social subsidies were cut back.

The particular way each of these governments articulates nationalism and neoliberalism speaks a great deal about their *modus operandi*, which is detailed in the country chapters. But, there is common ground: given the impossibility of economic-grounded nationalism as envisaged during the import substitution industrialization days, the battleground of nationalism is displaced to the realm of culture. As such, the pursue of the nation is likely to be enacted through a variety of cultural wars.

While neoliberal social reproduction dynamics further compromise social bonds based on formal work and social rights (minimal as they might have been in some of these countries), alternative networks and identities tend to be reinforced. In India, social bonds of caste and religious identity are being restrengthened, both by the explicit politics of Hindutva, and because economic collapse has increased reliance on existing social networks. The same can be said about the sweeping growth of conservative Christian sects in Brazil, particularly evangelicals. At the same time, conservative family values, often connected with conservative religious interpretations, are invoked: the fact that these leaders are all macho figures, should not go unnoticed. All in all, it is as if the moral could bind together what the economy dissolves.

Under these conditions, nationalism does not appeal to people through the concept of citizenship, which entails universal values. Rather, it mobilizes specific cultural, religious, ethnic or family values. Facing the impossibility of building a nation through the integration of citizens bestowed with a job and social rights, these politics displace the grounds of national belonging in favor of subjective, exclusionary criteria. No wonder human rights either have to be redefined (as in Hungary) or dismissed (in all other cases), being despised as a Western construct in Turkey, India, and the Philippines. In any case, rights are for 'good' citizens, whatever that means: therefore, they are not universal. These identitary ideologies speak to a social dynamic that produces disposable surplus population on a massive scale. It is an ideology that fits societies where not everyone fits.

Politics of hate do not aim to change this scenario, but rather reinforce it. Rather than producing social inclusion, it intends to legitimize and ultimately to naturalize social exclusion.

None of these governments have social amelioration schemes as their hall-mark, although cash transfer programs were not discontinued under Duterte or Bolsonaro. Erdogan did promote social schemes and Orbán launched a public workfare initiative, but in every case a clientelistic and not a universal rights approach prevailed. Overall, these politics do not aim to solve or mitigate the social production of despair. On the contrary, they further intensify social and economic dynamics that engender it.

3   Between Spectacle and Falsification

The previous sections demonstrate that although the regimes analyzed in this book rose to power in contexts of crises of legitimacy of the then-prevailing politics, once in charge they produced no substantial change in economic ori-entation nor in social policies, in the sense of foiling neoliberalism. If there was change, it was not in direction but rather in intensity. Furthermore, these regimes' popular prestige does not stem from successfully addressing the people's grievances, nor from outstanding economic performance. Even if Erdogan's first decade or Duterte's first years benefited from economic growth spurs, consistent paths for capital accumulation beyond dispossession or cro-nyism have not been blazed. Orbán did reshuffle business conditions to the benefit of sectors of the domestic bourgeoisie, but manufacturing is run by German capital. In India, even when the economy was faring comparatively well, it was marked by jobless growth.

In fact, there seems to be a disconnection between livelihood conditions and popular support to these leaders' benefit. In all cases, but most starkly under Modi, Duterte and Bolsonaro, there is little concern for policy delivery: their political efficacy seems to reside elsewhere. Under the circumstances, a ques-tion has to be posed: under what conditions does this detachment between popular support and policy delivery take place?

These leaders do not innovate on the economic nor the social policy fronts. Instead, novelty lays in their political form, as social resentment is politicized through various shades of hatred politics. These politics involve the constant fabrication of internal and external enemies targeted by hate speech, setting the stage for political polarization and the enactment of cultural wars.

As a consequence, this political form is dearly concerned with public image and media performance. Again, they did not invent politics of the spectacle, but the disconnection between reality and the alternative narratives these governments promote reaches unprecedented heights. Fact distortion is not restrained to the realm of ordinary political propaganda, which selects specific features from reality to portray a partial, favorable picture of governmental deeds. The detachment between public performance and policy delivery is stretched to a point that capsizes ordinary parameters of political efficiency. The de-monetization carried out by Modi is a case in point: although this arbitrary state action resulted in devastating economic effects, the alleged narrative that a crusade against corruption was taking place successfully engaged many. The political efficacy of de-monetization did not lay where the government claimed (a corruption crusade), but rather in boosting political cohesion: Modi's support increased in the elections that followed. A second example is Bolsonaro's staunch popularity despite his criminal stands on the Covid crisis.

A paramount example of narrative paradoxes is that these leaders claimed not to be corrupt but once in power, corruption has reached unparalleled levels. This increased corruption, however, has not affected them, with the exception of Orbán. On another level, alternative narratives lead to historical falsification, which informs Ottoman revivalist nationalism and Hindu nationalism, such as when Muslims are portrayed as invaders in India. Similarly, albeit on a different scale, the praise of Cold War dictatorships in the Philippines and Brazil, and of the interwar proto-fascist Horthy regime in Hungary, signals that historical revisionism is under way there too.

Disregard for the truth also has implications for science. In India, much space is given to nonsensical claims by religious heads and so-called practitioners of indigenous medical traditions as opposed to rational, evidence-based debate and policy making. Anti-science policy making thrives. Unlike Hindu nationalism, Orbán's politics are not anti-science, but it does try to capture the academe and universities to put science in the service of his own agenda. Human rights are subject to a comparable approach: rather than attacking those values, Orbán's politics gives them a different meaning in order to capture and instrumentalize them. A radical version of these redefinition operations is to be found in the Philippines under Duterte's or Brazil under Bolsonaro, where human rights are allegedly for 'good citizens' and not for criminals, implying that rights are not universal, or criminals are not humans. Under Erdogan, the dismissal of human rights and freedom discourse in liberal and socialist forms is framed by a broader rejection of secularist enlightenment-centered modernity, which is replaced by claims of justice and humanism based on religious morality. At the same time, as in Hungary under Orbán, the scope for dialogue or real debate around political decisions has died out. In all these countries, institutions that can support data-based policy making (such as research centers or statistical bodies) have been despised, defunded, co-opted, or directly challenged and drowned out by executive narratives.

Overall, these regimes approach to history and science replicate their approach to politics, in the sense that as with democracy, truth matters only to the extent that it fits their narratives and enforces their power projects. Should that not be the case, truth is subject to distortion through redefinition or falsification, just as liberal democratic institutions have to be undercut or manipulated. Otherwise, they should be silenced. This approach reveals no commitment to science, truth, human rights or democracy as such. In short, these regimes have no commitment to universals, unless when redefined in religious or nationalistic idioms by their brands of hatred politics and weaponized to legitimate the production of exclusion – that is to say, to be twisted against universal values. Unlike liberalism, there is no pretense of allegiance to values and institutions larger than themselves – values and institutions who might counter them. In that sense, they exude absolutism.

4   Governing through Crisis

Between the invention of alternative narratives and flat-out coercion, the culture war is the preferred means to dispute and recast the boundaries of public discourse, but it is also a key governance device. The culture war is not only about content; it is also about form. The constant fabrication of conflict distracts public attention while displacing political debate from economic to cultural or moral grounds. In the meantime, neoliberalism is hardly disputed, even if it is rhetorically targeted by illiberal ideology in Hungary.

Besides being instrumental to shift the boundaries of public discourse and to generate political distraction, cultural wars are key to cultivate these leader's image as outsiders who fight the system. All these five leaders were first voted as going against established elites. However, once in power, this was never done in a consistent manner. Hungary experienced a constitutional reform and a deep reform of the electoral and judicial system, but these were driven by power design rather than structural change. At most, new elites were fostered but the "system" as such, was far from challenged. Nevertheless, the lens of the culture war portrays them in permanent opposition: potentially, they are outsiders forever. As in other fronts, this can be a very contradictory stance, as the Hindu right for example, also claims that Hindus are the only "insiders".

When the constant fabrication of enemies that routinizes conflicts is linked to a political rationality where public performance supersedes policy delivery, we are faced with a political novelty. Instead of a crisis management approach driven to contain or undo whatever stirs a crisis, we are facing a political form that produces and surfs on crisis: these leaders govern through crisis.

Their subversion does not lay where it claims to be, but elsewhere. Although these regimes do not act against the "system" as they claim, this political form is anti-establishment oriented in a certain way. Since social reproduction underpinned by capital is not questioned, their anti-establishment orientation can only be superficial, in the sense that it is restricted to the political realm. Moreover, as it depletes institutional checks and balances that restrain power concentration while regulations that contain capital's rapaciousness (such as labor reforms) are lifted, social disembeddedness is further intensified rather than countered.

In the 20th Century, Karl Polanyi wrote that since market relations cannot create societies, in times when market forces spread unhindered a social backlash tends to take place, in order to re-embed economy in society. Liberal institutions could be invoked to that end, as in Roosevelt's New Deal or under Welfare states, but they could also be subverted, as in socialist projects. Despite emerging in times when neoliberalism further eroded social bonds, these 21st century regimes do not seek to counterbalance this trend: no Polanyan backlash takes place. On the contrary, subversion takes the form of disregard for the prevailing liberal democratic framework, but in the name of less democratic politics; contempt for political liberalism in rhetoric and in practice, but dressed in Cold War anticommunism; attacking economic and political elites, but to make room for cruder versions of crony capitalism embedded in corruption; bashing intellectuals and enlightenment-related values, but to stage culture wars while social despair is intensified. Not only is subversion devoid of any potency to modify social structures, but the dynamics of disembeddedness that produce social despair in massive scale, are intensified. Subversion is perverted, while these anti-establishment political forms reinforce the establishment, further blurring the borders of truth.

5   Governance for Whom?

As previously noted, there is a striking disconnection between policy delivery and popular support, particularly among the "late comers" Modi, Duterte and

Bolsonaro, whose mandates have been notably marked by bad governance. Incidentally they are the strongest in social media, as if virtual prowess could compensate incompetency.

Erdogan and Orbán arguably have something to show in the delivery side, no matter how flawed this may be. The first has benefited from economic growth during his first decade in power, while the second successfully supported sectors of national capital while driving the country in the aftermath of the 2008 crisis. These early successes have certainly been important to renew their support in the elections that followed. Nevertheless, after two decades under Erdogan and more than one decade under Orbán, it can hardly be argued that these regimes strength lies in solid improvement of people's livelihood. Good governance in their terms, means the successful implementation of power projects which rely on the capture of state institutions.

Although all these governments have strived to centralize power, none of them has crossed the line to discard a democratic façade so far. Despite overt displays of distaste for the parliament and for the judiciary when these cannot be commanded, institutions remain open and working even in Erdogan's Turkey, where growing loss of legitimacy has been countered by growing repression. A democratic façade is valuable and can indeed be interpreted as a sign of strength and not of weakness of these regimes.

In fact, authoritarianism is produced otherwise: institutions are seized from within, mostly through the appointment of loyal cadres, although rewards and punishment, funding and defunding, threats and privileges are also at play. In the Philippines, institutions are so weak that Duterte has used the power of the presidency to co-opt or stifle the opposition and institutions, combining money and violence. In Brazil, Bolsonaro appointed over three thousand military officers to top government posts while in constant fight with a judiciary he was unable to control. On the parliamentary front, the Brazilian president resorted to ordinary horse-trading politics to buy the loyalty of congressmen. Orbán never had this problem, as he has benefited from parliamentary super majorities for over ten years. Of the five countries studied, Hungary has witnessed the most acute forms of institutional centralization of power, which include a new constitution and reforms in the electoral system. Centralization in Hungary can only be potentially matched by that in Turkey, where the drive towards centralization has been boosted since the Presidential system was instituted in 2017, a maneuver devised to prolong Erdogan's reign while giving him massive powers as the executive president. State capture in both countries – simply understood as taking over state institutions to advance a political project – has not been limited to occupying institutions. Rather, the institutional framework itself has been reformed.

Furthermore, in Hungary the government commands a heavily centralized political system that reaches the municipal level, holds a supermajority
in parliament, supervises the judicial system, and has total control over the
state media. These and other features that, *mutatis mutandi,* are to be found
in Turkey as well, reveal that checks and balances to executive power are
seriously compromised under these regimes. In contrast with the Brazilian
case, where constant tensions between branches of state power are at play,
in Turkey and Hungary these institutional tensions have subdued, signaling
that Erdogan and Orbán's power projects have advanced to another level. India
under Modi is evolving in a similar direction. As state capture paves the way to
recast the institutional framework befitting these regimes power aspirations,
institutional frictions wane and a new stability makes headway. Albeit tensely,
a new hegemony has been established.

6   Violent Democracy

This brand of authoritarianism leans on the liberal democratic framework to
undo liberal democracy from within. As no coups are staged and no open institutional ruptures take place, their international status is ambiguous. These
leaders may be despised (as Bolsonaro) or not (as Modi), but in any case, their
governments are not susceptible to political pressure the way Cold War dictatorships once were, nor to economic sanctions as Nicolás Maduro's Venezuela
currently is, although European Union membership implies some level of
external constrains in Hungary. This dubiety stems from the fact that these
regimes expose the ambivalences of liberal democracy as such. Therefore,
nobody is in a position to cast the first stone and unambiguously blacklist
them – certainly not the US that elected Trump.

Accordingly, violence is clothed in different forms, starting with the role of
the military, who in the days of the Cold War ruled Turkey, the Philippines and
Brazil for long time spans with US support. Nowhere is this difference plainer
than in Turkey, as under Erdogan the long-lasting political relevance the army
held since Kemal Ataturk's days is now gone. In Brazil, even if Bolsonaro was
formerly an army captain, the role played by the armed forces in his government is akin to that of a political party, rather than touring tanks in the streets.
Shifts in the forms of state repression are captured well in the Filipino case,
where the military is given policy concessions and an increased budget to fight
communist and Islamist-linked groups, an old-time obsession. But, the military is not the primary arm of popular repression, which under Duterte takes
the form of a drug war staged by the police.

Indeed, the police is a key actor of state violence and violent forms of social management in all cases, except under Orbán. As a rule, the police have always exerted petty authority and brutality with little respect for legality or discipline in these countries. In Modi's India, the police force and its respective brutality has now been captured by the Hindu right, becoming openly communal. It is the chief agent of surveillance, evidence planting, and violent repression of democratic forces. In the Philippines, Duterte controls the police (but not the army), which is the implementer of state-based violence. As in Brazil, unpunished random acts of violence became commonplace while opaque connections with the criminal organizations that the police are supposed to confront, blossom. The so-called drug war does not target regime-friendly politicians nor Chinese nationals who run the business. Beyond repression, the police in Brazil is being engaged in the production of politics. Fueled by mounting budgets, links with booming illegal activities and the spread of a "good criminal is a dead criminal" mentality, the Brazilian police aspires to become a political force of its own.

Another difference when compared to Cold War dictatorships is that these regimes mobilize mass support, while in the past, order meant demonstration-free countries. In fact, Erdogan and Modi have colluded with riot production as new and old paramilitary organizations (like the RSS in India) have been boosted, taking politics of hate from talk to action. Bolsonaro has consistently called on his supporters to demonstrate, albeit not always successfully. The Brazilian president is not backed by an ideologically-driven paramilitary organization, but he does count on the support of the so-called militias (a kind of criminal organization comprised mostly of retired and active duty police, firefighters, and military men), who were behind the murder of the young, black, bisexual Rio de Janeiro city councillor, Marielle Franco, in 2018.

Marielle's murder was an extreme case that predated Bolsonaro's presidency. As of 2021, civil liberties were preserved in Brazil: ordinary citizens were not afraid to speak out their views, massive street demonstrations against the government took place in a regular basis and major media outlets are staunchly critical of the government. The institutional tensions that mark this government are echoed in the public space. As a paradox, civil liberties were also preserved in Hungary. If they did not fear losing their (public) jobs, people could openly advocate opposition views, although these views may not appear in proper media outlets, as many have been captured by Fidesz-affiliated groups. Under Orbán, opposition is not criminalized, but it is effectively silenced via political means. As an antipode to the Brazilian case, the subsiding of institutional tensions in Hungary corresponds to low levels of contestation in the public space. Bolsonaro cannot afford to silence the opposition while Orbán does not need to do so.

In the other three cases, civil liberties are seriously disrespected and there is fear to speak out. Under Erdogan, leaders and MPs of opposition parties, mass democratic organizations, independent media outlets and journalists are marked as enemies and are repressed through 'terror trials'. Beyond appearances, a *de facto* "one party and one man regime" is in place. In India, a closing down of the liberal public sphere and of the right to speech and expression accompanies attacks on and arrests of activists from a range of movements, including human rights, Dalit, Adivasi, citizenship, farmers, environmental, as well as lawyers, journalists, and academics who work in their defense. In the Philippines, state repression reaches both high-level political targets and random ordinary individuals.

At the same time, the mainstream media is mostly hostile to Duterte, although it practices self-censorship as well. This has also been the case with Bolsonaro, who portrays journalists as part of the establishment he confronts, while relying heavily on social media – as do Duterte and Modi. The media is broadly supportive of the government in Turkey as well as in India, where some English newspapers that try to be more middle of the road are threatened in multiple ways, including income tax raids and not getting government adds, making them pliable. In Hungary, corporate media has been divided, but state propaganda is very strong and in certain areas it almost has a monopoly.

Altogether, the role of violence in these regimes is uneven, but they are all different from Cold War authoritarians. There are notable differences related to the institutional façade, the role of the military and the police, riot production and popular mobilization, and civil liberties and media censorship, among others. To name a conspicuous difference, political exiles have been rare. Variances between these regimes have to do with historical and institutional particularities, so that the role of the military in Hungary or India is incomparable to that in Turkey or Brazil. But, they may also be a matter of time and political effectiveness, as Bolsonaro or Duterte would certainly like to be in Erdogan's shoes.

In any case, none of these leaders conceal their authoritarian ambitions nor their will to move from words to action. But, differently from Cold War authoritarians, they rely on the ballot to reach power and on the build-up of popular support to further advance their authoritarian landscapes. They lean on violent democracies to produce popular autocracies.

7   Social Base and Class Shifts

Maintaining popular authoritarianism implies the need to build up loyal political bases beyond these leaders' original electoral constituencies. The leaders' positions and accomplishments in this respect also vary. Orbán and Modi count on highly organized and embedded social organizations, which in the Indian case stems from century-long activism (the RSS). They are also sustained by solid political parties that are key vehicles for state capture: in practice, both cases have been evolving toward one-party states in countries that were one-party states (of sorts in India) during the Cold War. Furthermore, it can be argued that both the Hungarian and Indian leaders have national projects, as Orbán reorganized patterns of capital accumulation in order to promote national capital while the BJP intends to "saffronize" India, including its crony capitalism.

In contrast, Duterte and Bolsonaro have little organic bases of their own. Although the Brazilian leader has often called for demonstrations in his support, he has shown little concern for organizing his followers. As of 2021, Bolsonaro was not even affiliated with a political party while Duterte was informally affiliated with several, making him *de facto* affiliated with none. Neither leader espouses any vision for the future of his country, no matter how flawed (as Orbán's) or delirious (as Modi's) that might be. Their political instincts are driven by short term interests and no strategy beyond sheer accumulation of power and wealth are to be found. The drug war led by Duterte and the dismantling of the New Republic undertaken by Bolsonaro serve no grander cause. Their *modi operandi* are, at their best, destruction, not construction.

We observe a third position in Turkey. After two decades in power, Erdogan's leadership has gained a life of its own, outshining organizations that once supported him. In the past, the AKP's grounding in the grassroots Islamist movement was instrumental to enable Erdogan reach out to the working class, but more recently Erdogan has undermined his own party. Likewise, the now president pretends to be a defender of Islam while dragging down the gulanists that once backed him. All in all, the Turkish leader shows no firm ideological commitments, but rather keen political instincts to remain in power: everything that does not kill, makes him stronger. Erdogan blends staunch popular support with a bigger than his party leadership, and despite health issues, has been striving to create his own fascist-like basis.

Entrenched social support is not only instrumental to sustain these regimes' legitimacy, but such support also suggests that the regime types will outlive their leaders' stint in power: no matter how charismatic Modi is, Hindu nationalism is much larger as a social phenomenon. The Turkish case suggests a more weaker version of organized support, as it tends to revolve more around Erdogan's personality. Yet, this has been effective in its own way. In this vein, Duterte and Bolsonaro lag behind: they still rely on highly personalized brands of politics but without organic bases of their own.

Beyond strategic moves to enlarge their electoral constituencies, visible class shifts have taken place in Turkey and Hungary where a crisis of accumulation was under way, further entrenching Erdogan and Orbán's political basis. In Turkey, the Anatolian tigers and new construction players have challenged an Istanbul-based industrial and financial bourgeoisie that prospered after the foundation of the Turkish Republic and during the isi-led developmentalist era of the 1960s. In Hungary, Orbán reconfigured alliances with international capital for the benefit of national capital. It is the only case where deindustrialization did not accelerate but, on the contrary, reindustrialization took place, albeit led by German capital.

If any pattern is to be devised, it should be expected that India's provincial, propertied capital class, and Gujrati's big capitalists in particular, will play a growing role under Modi. In the Philippines, Davao-based crony capitalists have made it to the national scene, but this does not point to major class shifts. In Brazil, burgeoning evangelical corporations and illegal economic networks have been empowered by Bolsonaro, but not at the expense of financial capital or agribusiness: on the contrary, their ability to cohabit is part of his success.

Other than shifts at the top, these regimes have counted on the staunch electoral support of the middle classes. In some cases, new middle classes have been actively promoted. They were given ample opportunities under Erdogan. Orbán devised a comprehensive set of policies to cement their support. Duterte has legislated a tax reform designed to lessen the burden on middle-class taxpayers while clearly promoting middle-class conservative values. Bolsonaro and Modi also promote conservative middle-class values. It should also be recalled that enthusiastic diaspora support has been relevant in the Indian and the Filipino contexts. Although this cannot be leveled as "middle class" support, the diaspora often embody and inspire middle class aspirations at home.

As Turkey and Hungary happen to be where politics of hate have been in power for longer, it may be hypothesized that producing shifts in the bourgeoisie and building middle class allegiance is pivotal to these regimes long-term sustainability. This point can be stated the other way round: successful reconfiguration of upper-class alignments while cementing middle class support should be key to Modi's, Duterte's or Bolsonaro's long term power goals, in addition to solidifying their organic social bases.

8   Singularities and Generalities

At this point, it should be clear that these governments have differences among themselves. However, as a group they also differ markedly from standard liberal democracy as well as from Cold War authoritarianisms. This last point is further demonstrated by geopolitics. While Cold War-era dictatorships in the Third World were largely backed by and aligned to the United States while socialist countries (sometimes also repressive) were largely backed by and aligned to the Soviet Union, this is not necessarily the case now. Bolsonaro's servile stand to the U.S. is not a norm across cases. Duterte sides with China while Erdogan successfully plays the rivalry between the US and Russia to his benefit. Similarly, Orbán plays on China's and Russia's interests, although not at the expense of its ties with the U.S. Modi's India projects itself as a "democratic" pillar in the region and is part of the Quad alliance (US, Japan, Australia, India) aimed at containing China in Asia.

On the same note, these leaders do not seek to cooperate between them. Although links can be traced between extreme right beacons across these countries, as Dan Geary points out in his chapter in this volume, these are informal personal connections or temporary cooperation between particular state institutions, but not state projects. Perhaps the competitive neoliberal rationale that underpins these various bogus nationalisms is not conducive to international cooperation. Or, perhaps it makes little sense to pursue ideology-based cooperation in a world ruled by economics. At any rate, these leaders display themselves as friends rather than allies.

All in all, geopolitics does not unite these regimes. What does bring them close is a comparable political form. This form took shape as a response to the crisis of the liberal democratic framework, mobilizing hatred politics into power projects that rely on state capture and the production of spectacle to intensify ongoing violent economic, social, and cultural trends. On one hand, this political form is not entirely uniform. We have seen that these governments differ on civil liberties (still in effect in Brazil and Hungary); the role of violence (not central in Hungary); riot production (in India and Turkey); the role of the police (key in Turkey, the Philippines and Brazil); their relationship with corporate media (highly critical of Duterte and Bolsonaro); constitutional changes (carried out under Erdogan and Orbán); an anticorruption image (damages Orbán but not the others); an organized social base (highly organized in Hungary and India); political parties (irrelevant for Duterte and Bolsonaro); the role of religion (a minor factor in Hungary and the Philippines but crucial in Turkey or India); the restoration of past greatness (mobilized in Turkey and India); hostility to secularist 'enlightenment'-centered modernity (in Turkey and India); openly negationist about Covid (Bolsonaro); anti-science policy-making (Modi); the role of the diaspora (relevant in India, the Philippines and Turkey); and geopolitical stands, among others.

168 BARBOSA DOS SANTOS

On the other hand, common features include: liberal economically, illiberal politically; nationalism linked with neoliberalism; the politicization of social resentment; pretending to confront old elites; the perversion of subversion as anti-establishment feelings are manipulated; hate speech; concrete and symbolic violence; the fabrication of enemies; culture wars; politics as spectacle; governing through crisis; poor policy delivery; the centralization of political power; state capture; crony capitalism; high levels of corruption; democratic façades; rely on elections to build legitimacy; popular constituencies; masculine leaderships; the intensification of social and economic disembedding; the production of social despair and its weaponization; disregard for the truth; and the redefinition of human rights and universals being particularized.

Although Orbán's Hungary shares all these features, its political economy is to some extent exceptional. It is the only government that attacked the austerity policies of his predecessors while promoting economic regulation, internal market protection (of the financial sector), some nationalization of industry and some degree of reindustrialization. Likewise, it is the only country in this study where labor formality increased, and the unemployment rate is low. These measures were conceived in order to unleash a new regime of accumulation, implying the intention to effectuate class shifts that have been successfully carried out. Leaving aside that the content of this agenda implies a national strategy, it should be remarked that this level of strategizing is way beyond the capabilities displayed by the likes of Duterte or Bolsonaro.

On the political front, we have seen that in Hungary, civil liberties are not threatened, the police play no relevant role, there is no riot production and the opposition is not criminalized (as opposed to Turkey, India and the Philippines). Neither social media nor fake news is significant. Instead of blunt lies, Orbán's regime focuses on building alternative narratives. Accordingly, science is not despised while ideals of equality, freedom, fraternity and human rights are not denied; rather, they are captured. Instead of clashing with the parliament (as Bolsonaro does), Orbán uses the body, and the constitution has been rewritten to fit the regime's designs. Even the content of his hate speech is peculiar in comparison to the other regimes in this volume in that it targets immigrants. Hungary built a wall that can be seen as an extension of the barriers the West has been building against the "wretched" of the Earth. Although many Hungarians do migrate, they are unlikely to be found in the same side of the wall as most Turks, Indians, Filipinos and Brazilians.

At some level, the particularities of the Hungarian case can be traced to its history. The country has no colonial legacy comparable to that of India, the Philippines or Brazil and was never part of the Third World as Turkey was. In fact, none of these four countries were closer to building a cohesive society underpinned by wage citizenship as state socialist Hungary was, despite all its handicaps. At the same time, the specificities of Orbán's political economy may be a sign of its effectiveness: as it has more to show on the delivery side, it leans less on truth distortion and state repression, although this might change if contestation rises. If popular authoritarianism blends coercion and consent, perhaps Orbán's Hungary can afford to dismiss violence as it primarily relies on consent. Furthermore, that the principal opposition it faced for a while stemmed from the right (the *Jobbik party*) is a sign that the regime has successfully reordered the boundaries of public debate. All in all, an argument can be made that Orbán's Hungary is the most consolidated of these regimes, as it relies less on coercion and more on consent to establish hegemony.

9   Oppositions

As with state capture, the role played by the opposition can be seen as a marker of these regimes' entrenchment. In all these cases, there is little vocal opposition stemming from the upper classes. In India and Brazil, there is concern that the culture war may become dysfunctional to capital as it stirs political instability. Nevertheless, in spite of visible unease and discomfort, capitalists have not yet openly thrown their weight behind the opposition. A similar stand can be found in the Philippines, where despite individual discontent, no big taipans are vocal oppositors. If in the 2022 elections another candidate seems to have a chance to defeat the Duterte candidate, they are likely to donate money but will not openly speak or mobilize. In Turkey, traditional big capital and Erdogan became increasingly confrontational with political illiberalization and the AKP government's socially conservative maneuvers. Their seeming partnership came into open contention during the 2013 Gezi uprising, which was followed by the 2016 coup attempt. Repression escalated as Erdogan came out victorious, quenching the military and gulanists. Hungary's small ruling class is behind Orbán with a few individual exceptions, while the United States-based billionaire George Soros became an iconic target of hate speech. Overall, the upper classes are either supportive or complicit with these governments.

On the other edge, popular dissent has been visible in some cases. Duterte faced mass protests in his early years (2016 and 2017) but these have since subsided. The contrary happened under Bolsonaro, where mass demonstrations have picked up since 2021, while the president also tries to bring his own followers to the streets. In India, anti-Muslim social engineering during Modi's second term has triggered lasting street occupations that only the pandemic was capable of undoing. Meanwhile, Farm Laws triggered a massive farmers movement that marched to Delhi despite Covid, while trade unions also put up a fight against labor legislation reforms. On the other hand, the streets have been quiet in Turkey since the Gezi days and the failed coup attempt. Popular opposition to the regime is headed by the Kurds who, in turn, are the primary target of state repression. In Hungary, only seldom do mass protests confront the government. They are mostly staged by urban cosmopolitans in the cities or by the far right in rural areas.

The level of mass contestation can be seen as another indicator of these regimes' grip on power. The streets are still vivid battlegrounds in Brazil, where Bolsonaro is openly contested, as well as in India, where Modi's policies have triggered broad and sustained resistance. However, in Turkey and Hungary, the streets have been silent. As they do with institutional tensions, these regimes strive to subdue organized protest by increasing the costs of explicit opposition. As both the institutions and the streets die down as political battlegrounds, contestation as a whole is subsided, which is as a sign of their authoritarian effectiveness.

Have Erdogan and Orbán been in power for so long because they are not contested, or are they not contested because they have been in power for so long? Although we can never know what is coming next and rebellions burst unexpectedly, the Turkish and Hungarian cases suggest the latter: surviving for as long as the Erdogan and Orbán regimes have been in power has allowed them to defeat the opposition, but it has also modified the social conditions where organized resistance might emerge. That is so because beyond their illiberalism, the social disembeddedness that nurtures politics of hate in the first place, has been further intensified.

Under these conditions, the relevance of left parties and trade unions is undermined and no competitive opposition has emerged from the left – except in Brazil and to a lesser degree in Turkey, where the Pro-Kurdish HDP emerged as a novelty and did well in the 2015 elections, but state repression has hit them hard since. Nonetheless, the Brazilian PT is perceived as part of the liberal democratic framework, which is widely discredited, similar to the liberals and socialists in Hungary, the Indian National Congress, and the Filipino Liberal Party. To some extent, the intellectuals are in a comparable position, associated with the privileged "elites" these regimes feign they are fighting. The critical stands of the intelligentsia do not seem to affect these regimes, as intellectual life is discredited as well.

In these circumstances, opposition tends to take the form of political fronts that react to these regimes, rather than opening new landscapes. Ever broader fronts emerge to defend ever smaller rights and liberties. In some cases, these fronts may be led by old-fashioned, discredited parties such as the PT in Brazil or the Indian Congress, while in Hungary, it may include the far right, as Jobbik is the principal opposition force of an eclectic coalition comprising old social democrats and new liberals. Even a left-leaning front led by the HDP in Turkey is constrained to a defensive stand beyond their Pro-Kurdish position. Overall, political imagination seems to be captured by these regimes staged culture wars. As the form and content of right politics evolve while those of the left remain stagnant, the end of history seems to unfold as a one-sided trend.

10   Deadlock

As neoliberalism intensified the social disembedding trends inherent to capitalism across the globe, the never-fulfilled promise of wage citizenship lost its historical ground in countries on the margins of capitalism, undermining liberal democracy as a framework to build nations founded on cohesive societies. In the process, conventional vehicles of left politics, such as trade unions and worker's parties, eroded. This erosion occurred against the background of a broader discrediting of enlightenment-related values and concepts, ranging from human rights to intellectual work and the status of truth.

Meanwhile, right-wing politics found new forms which capture social malaise. The social and cultural dynamics that brought politics of hate to the limelight in the first place have been reinforced. These regimes enact culture wars and exacerbate the dynamics of individualism and competition that preside over social reproduction. The policies they implement reinforce the dissolution of social bonds that made the politization of social resentment feasible in the first place.

As the violent production of social disembedding is inherent to the modes of capital accumulation that these regimes accelerate, these politics are further propelled by the ongoing dynamics of social reproduction. In other words, these presidents were elected under social conditions that they reinforce. The social production of despair is thus accelerated, further engendering hate, fear and indifference, which in turn, these regimes weaponize. As such, what at first was an electoral reaction to a crisis of legitimacy, comes to achieve a deadlock between neoliberalism and liberal democracy, as conditions where hatred politics thrive are deepened. A dynamic comparable to an autoimmune disease unfolds, in the sense that the social disembeddedness that nurtures illiberal politics is intensified, while the conditions that could enable organized resistance are undermined. As a consequence, a Polanyian backlash becomes ever more unlikely.

Meanwhile, the boundaries of public debate and political dispute are distorted: what initially emerged as an extreme reaction against the establishment becomes the new normal. It is one thing to elect a politician of hate as an outsider, but to reelect him is a very different matter. Furthermore, as the Turkish and Hungarian trajectories show, class shifts reinforcing the foundations of new hegemonies may take place. As those who once embodied a rejection of the establishment (whether or not they did so earnestly) recast the norms, a new normal takes root: the bogus antisystemic figures reorder the system.

Without a doubt, resistances are to be found everywhere, and we see ourselves as part of them. However, it must be admitted that these valuable efforts have not been up to the challenge so far. In fact, if politics of hate owes its pervasiveness to the violent dynamics of capital reproduction that underpin the neoliberal way of life, these structural trends have to be addressed in order for a consistent alternative to arise. Electoral defeat is unlikely to unroot hatred politics as a global phenomenon, just as it will take more than vaccines to avoid future pandemics. Alternative modes of production and reproduction of life have to emerge, the seeds of which are to be found around the globe, although scattered.

For the time being, hatred politics contrives to normalize the violent social dynamics that produce it, while their electoral opponents try to contain its effects. The winds of history blow the sail of hatred politics while its opponents swim against the tide. It seems that unless these social dynamics are challenged as a whole, the future of this present belongs to them.

CHAPTER 8

The Pandemic as an Opportunity

Daniel Feldmann, Cecilia Lero, Devika Misra, Ágnes Gagyi, Tamás Gerőcs and Ilhan Can Ozen

1 Introduction

Daniel Feldmann

For the governments under analysis in this book, Covid-19 was first and foremost viewed as an opportunity, aiding their agendas of the politicization of social hatred and resentment. The global pandemic that broke out in 2020 brought about a situation analogous to war. In war, internal and external enemies must be mercilessly confronted, and authoritarian and repressive measures are more easily justified. Moreover, that the enemy in this context is a virus that potentially everyone could carry, surveillance and control could reach all citizens. If the state of alert must be total, the justification for employing extreme measures increases, as does the legitimacy of potentially authoritarian measures.

From this point of view, there is an affinity between authoritarian neoliberalism and the political use of the pandemic. The processes of dissolution of collective bonds, of individualization, and of promoting the competition of all against all, create a favorable terrain that is akin to a civil war. Just as everyone is a potential carrier of threat during a viral outbreak, neoliberalism creates a contaminated social dynamic in which everyone is a potential threat and the tendency to view others with fear, hatred and indifference is reinforced. The outbreak of the pandemic allowed these social characteristics to be further exploited and manipulated by the right-wing governments analyzed here, who managed to strengthen their bases of support and their ideological projects. The exceptionality of COVID-19 allowed governments to accentuate their rhetoric of a permanent state of exception. This enables leaders to appear as generals in a fight for national regeneration, a fight conducted in the form of a grand spectacle in mass and social media that take different forms in each country.

The most important point of reflection is not the obvious demagoguery that is a central characteristic of these governments. It is more significant to understand why such practices appear as legitimate and just to important parts of the population. The progressive ideals of democracy, citizenship and equality sound increasingly fictitious and distant in the face of objective economic and social processes that deny these ideals on a daily basis. These governments do not propose to defend these ideals – not even rhetorically. Rather, they govern through a logic of conflict and self-cleansing. Hence, they appear as 'authentic' and 'true' to so many: if there is really no place for everyone, then let there be, without subterfuge, a general and destructive war of all against all. Or, faced with the imminence of war of all against all, such governments try to appear to offer protection, stimulating collective identities in a way that is reminiscent of fascism. The marriage between neoliberalism and authoritarianism steers their countries towards the brutality of a permanent crisis of capitalism whose effects are always more acute in capital's periphery.

1.1   Facets of War

Common among these governments is that they announced war against the pandemic and employed this position to justify authoritarian and repressive measures against sectors of their own populations. Thus, Orbán in Hungary took advantage of the war against the virus to create a state of emergency to expand his powers, while simultaneously implementing measures to reinforce the monopolization of capital that had begun before the pandemic. Modi, on the other hand, proclaimed India as a world champion of 'science' and 'vaccine diplomacy' even as he has encouraged pre-existing divisions in society and intensified repression against informal temporary workers who were totally unprotected while living far from their home communities. Duterte in the Philippines adopted another authoritarian tactic, where the alleged non-compliance with one of the toughest lockdowns in the world provided the justification for the arrest of over 100,000 people. These people then ended up even more exposed to disease in the conditions under which they were detained. Even with such a strict lockdown, the government has intensified its 'war on drugs,' considerably increasing the number of killings carried out by security forces.

The pattern described above was not the only strategy that enabled these leaders to use the pandemic as an opportunity for repression and the consolidation of their own political agendas. Erdogan in Turkey, like the other leaders, also sought to strengthen his authoritarian and repressive power in the name of fighting COVID-19. Most striking, however, is the way that the government sought to conduct the supposed return to normality after the first wave of the pandemic. The return to free movement privileged the spiritual base of the AKP, which was soon able to resume its religious events, while restrictions without scientific basis, such as restrictions on alcoholic beverages, were implemented to limit others. In the case of Brazil, however, what was observed was a totally different scenario. The pandemic was minimized or even denied in the name of prioritizing the continuation of economic activities above all. Bolsonaro's strategy was to claim that the risk of economic disaster was much greater than that of the health disaster, blaming the media and local governments that insisted on lockdowns for the increase in unemployment. Moreover, Bolsonaro sought to present the lockdown as an 'elitist' measure that would be inviable for a large part of the workers who live in informality. The Brazilian exception confirms the more general rule of declaring a state of war. Even if in this case the war was not against the pandemic, but the economic war continued by all means ...

1.2   *The Spectacle and the Reality*

The capacity to use fiscal and monetary policies to respond to the crisis is undoubtedly much more limited in these countries than in richer countries. Additionally, tax structures tend to tax the richest at relatively low rates, leaving few resources for policies that favor the poorest. This induced governments to propagandize and emphasize the spectacle of their measures, while, in actuality, health systems proved to be saturated and social policies were absent or insufficient to contain the increase in poverty. An emblematic example is Modi promoting India as a major world exporter of health care products, while internally, a large part of the population visibly struggled for access to these products during the much-publicized onslaught of the second wave of the pandemic.

At the same time, the absence of resources to ensure minimum social protections for all induced governments to act selectively, reinforcing clientelism and creating a climate of dispute between different sections of the population. This is illustrated by the case of Turkey, where the AKP's great difficulty has been to organize the distribution of scarce government resources in order to accommodate the different sectors of its broad political base. In the Philippines, the distribution of relief resources after the pandemic was organized by corruption and patronage, prioritizing certain support bases, while extremely poor people were left to fend for themselves. In Brazil, there have been reductions in health spending, while the government has made huge increases in the military budget and channeled resources without any oversight to deputies in order for Bolsonaro to consolidate his parliamentary support base in the face of increasing threats to his legitimacy and popularity.

Therefore, it is not only a matter of capitalizing on successes as every government does, but of making adversity a means of actively doing politics, consolidating loyalties on one side and stigmatizing opponents on the other. Social precariousness and instability are no longer roadblocks to be overcome, but rather have become tools for these governments and their projects of ideological affirmation. The structural impossibility of an economic and social dynamic that ensures the integration of populations and dignified lives generates a set of tensions that are the object of populist exploitation. In this way, the idealization of a glorious past, common in all cases, is not a mere return to the past, but rather symbolizes a real regression that must be lived with full intensity in the present and projected as an unavoidable horizon for the future. Thus, the result is a programmed release of social malaise. In summary, this chapter suggests that the effects of the Covid-19 disease can only be fully understood in these countries if we also consider the disease of social corrosion that strengthens a new extreme right that is not a passing phenomenon, but rather is here to stay for a long time.

2   The Brazilian Singularity in the Pandemic

Daniel Feldmann

Brazil is a peculiar case in the pandemic. In addition to the catastrophic scenario that make it rank second globally in deaths, what is unique in the country is the way in which negationism was elevated to state policy. Unlike other far-right governments that sought to take advantage of the situation to institute a rhetoric of national salvation from Covid-19, or governments that took advantage of lockdown measures to intensify social repression, the Bolsonaro government deliberately refused to organize any major actions against the virus. Even when it did act, its actions were so irrational that they raised suspicions that the government deliberately acted to spread the disease.

The government's strategy to let the pandemic follow its course with limited to no intervention can be observed through various events: the resignation of the Minister of Health who defended containment measures, the attempt to prevent the mandatory use of masks and lockdowns by local governments, spending on ineffective medical treatments with harmful side effects, and refusing the advance purchase of vaccines that could have greatly advanced innoculation in the country. Simultaneously, the government created a 'Parallel Cabinet' outside formal institutions with the backing of politically close doctors who have not hesitated to suggest actions totally contrary to the scientific consensus. Additionally, the president himself has created a media spectacle of explicitly promoting negationism and indifference to Covid-related deaths, even when the pandemic was already reaching devastating proportions. When asked about the deaths, Bolsonaro responded with "So what?" or "We can't be a country of faggots". Explicitly refusing to get vaccinated, Bolsonaro justified his position by stating that contamination was the best way to produce immunity against the virus.

2.1   The Significance of the Negationist Strategy

Bolsonaro had a plan in mind when he was propagating the 'herd immunity' approach that has greatly increased the number of deaths. Although internationally isolated and ridiculed, especially after Trump's defeat, and with reduced popular support in domestic opinion polls, Bolsonaro has consolidated power with his negationism emerging as a truly national movement. Although this negationism is espoused by a minority, it has managed to have a great impact on a society stunned by Covid.

There is a social force that supports Bolsonaro's refusal to govern the country in a way that minimally contains the damage amid the storm. Behind the madness, Bolsonaro's rationality can be expressed as follows: the economy must work above all, laissez-faire economics must become absolute, and the capitalist social machine cannot be interrupted under any circumstances. With this, Bolsonaro sought to exempt himself from responsibility for the worsening economy under Covid-19, arguing instead that the blame should be placed on local governments with their restrictive measures and the media that supported them. In addition, Bolsonaro could argue that the lockdown was an elitist practice, claiming it was inviable for a large part of the population that needed to continue working outside the home.

Bolsonaro and his movement embody the paradox of an anti-systemic dynamic that seeks to push to the limit the systemic compulsions of capitalism in crisis. His anti-systemic character – destroying institutions, norms, and regulations – emulates the systemic desire of capital to come to fruition as a pure and destructive force of self-expansion. Even more, this reconfigures Brazilian capitalism, with no means of resuming a 'normal' capitalist accumulation process, as well as no means of reproducing workers' lives in a 'normal' contractual form with recognized rights. Bolsonarism feeds on very objective social tendencies that render opaque the distinctions between what is formal and informal, between democratic-legal rights and their objective denial in everyday life, between the role of the state and the private sector, and finally, between what is legal and illegal. The logic of the norm and the contract, which has never been fully cemented in Brazil, has become even weaker amidst an economic and social impasse that has been dragging on for decades. The more that practices considered civilized are weakened and demoralized by the prevailing forms of the reproduction of social life, the more that confusion between rules and their exceptions is reinforced.

Thus, the agenda of destroying environmental and labor protections, as well as privatizatizing at full speed, gain support among small and large capitalists. Even layers of the working class, atomized and immersed in informality and precariousness, adhere to Bolsonarism because they consider it more authentic. Bolsonarism corroborates the savage and lawless war that has become the world of labor, unlike parts of the left that advocate for what appears to be a fantasy world of more protected work. Furthermore, particular social sectors are empowered by the confusion between rules and their exceptions. These include religious leaders who strengthen themselves by promoting social assistance at the expense of the responsibilities of a welfare state, farmers and gold miners who illegally occupy lands to the detriment of rules that should preserve indigenous areas, internet activists who disseminate fake news while promoting themselves as a new source of information to the detriment of journalistic ethics. They also include the police, who, during the pandemic greatly increased violence against blacks and poor people whose right to life should be safeguarded and the militias, closely linked to Bolsonarism, that combine private security activities with the direct extortion of the communities they control. Not to mention the encouragement on the part of the government to release access to weapons (whose sales have exploded in Brazil), encouraging everyone to use violence in private. Behind a moralistic discourse, Bolsonarism strengthens groups that do not hesitate to circumvent all norms.

An emblematic episode is the scandal of the private hospital group, Prevent Senior, which adulterated the number of its patients it reported to have died from Covid-19 and even used patients as human guinea pigs to test medical treatments recommended by Bolsonaro and his entourage. This group acted in collusion with Bolsonaro's 'Parallel Cabinet' without any oversight, seeking to maximize their profits while also maximizing contempt for medical standards and for the very life of their patients. This collusion is even more scandalous if we bear in mind that funds for public health would fall in the coming period in the name of 'fiscal austerity.'

2.2   *The Silent Majority versus the Noisy Minority*

The health chaos, the social degradation of the country, and the growth of famine have increased feelings of opposition to Bolsonaro. In society at large, Bolsonaro is in the minority and opinion polls indicate that Lula is the favorite to win election in 2022. At the same time, a large part of the elites has incisively attacked the government. But to what extent does this indicate the effective defeat of Bolsonarism?

On one hand, it can be said that the same disruptive behavior of Bolsonaro that is in line with the destructive impulses of capital, also creates problems for the institutional order without which capitalism itself cannot function. In this sense, Bolsonaro's negationism ends up being counterproductive to the very logic of business that demands a minimum of predictability and agreed-upon norms. By turning the country into an international health and environmental pariah, damaging the economic recovery with the exaggerated prolongation of the pandemic, and, finally, creating institutional chaos that resulted in capital flight and made it impossible to carry out the very pro-market reforms proposed, Bolsonaro raised hostility from powerful sectors.

However, only the future can tell what Bolsonaro's electoral outcome will be, or whether he will be judicially punished for his role in the pandemic and other serious accusations. Without giving up the rhetoric of confrontation, Bolsonaro also plays the venal political game that his campaign promised to fight. Through the distribution of unregulated funds to the 'Centrão" – an opportunistic group of parliamentarians without ideological or personal loyalties – his government has managed to avoid impeachment. This is reinforced by the fact that the elites, despite their discourse against the president, have no disposition for a real confrontation: at most they demand that Bolsonaro moderates his 'bad manners.' Deep down, everything in Brazil is now channeled towards elections, from the left to the right. Even the street mobilizations for "Oust Bolsonaro,' which had had some impact, have weakened considerably as elections near, as political parties are more concerned with the 2022 polls.

In this scenario, the noisy minority of Bolsonarism expands its strength before a silent majority that cannot give adequate expression to its repudiation of Bolsonaro. In this sense, Bolsonaro had full success with his policies during the pandemic, consolidating his social base. Moreover, there is the aggravating factor that thousands of military personnel occupy the government, not to mention the direct support that Bolsonaro has in the police and militias across the country. All this reveals that Bolsonarism is not a mere historical accident, but rather something that feeds on the deep contradictions of Brazilian capitalism. This form of capitalism, by driving a dynamic that reiterates social violence and seeks to transpose any kind of norm or normality, finds a fully adequate and rooted expression in Bolsonarism. Like Covid-19, Bolsonarism is a persistent disease that is here to stay for a long time.

3   The Duterte Administration and the Covid Crisis

Cecilia Lero

The Duterte administration's response to the Covid-19 crisis can be characterized by the contrast between, on one hand, using the crisis as an opportunity to further concentrate power in the executive and close democratic space, and, on the other hand, abdicating power to deal with the crisis, instead shifting responsibility to local governments and the private sector. This response reinforces the theme that the Duterte administration is more concerned with rhetoric, theatre, and opportunities for personal wealth accumulation than actually governing. It also demonstrates that at a time of global crisis where a strongman's efficiency could arguably be useful, in Duterte's case it has proven completely inutile.

Whereas other countries in the region, including Taiwan and Singapore, implemented travel bans from the Chinese mainland as the virus spread in Wuhan province, Duterte refused to declare a ban until the day after the Philippines confirmed its first case (a Chinese national from Wuhan visiting the Philippines on holiday) on January 30th, 2020. That patient would become the first confirmed Covid death outside China. Despite this declared ban, subsequent senate investigations revealed that flights carrying Chinese nationals continued to enter the country. This hesitation reflects the administration's overall deference to the Chinese government in foreign and domestic affairs.

Despite this initial inaction, the ensuing months would witness one of the harshest lockdowns in the world. Although some measure of lockdown was certainly necessary to contain the disease's spread, the National Task Force to address Covid-19 was dominated by retired military generals instead of health professionals. Accordingly, the government's response took a punitive approach instead of a health- or community-wellbeing centered approach. Since March 2020, the government has imposed various forms of lockdown. The constant change in variations of lockdown and its accompanying rules, as well as variations in implementation across local government units, have resulted in confusion, mismanagement, and unnecessarily harsh and counterproductive treatment, especially of the poor. Whereas prior to the onset of Covid, the government's language and attitude placed the blame for the country's profound woes on the figure of the 'addicts,' thus justifying their extermination, during the Covid crisis, the government at times sought to blame its failure to bring the virus under control on the '*pasaway*' (undisciplined). This is despite mobility data showing high rates of adherence to the lockdown and mask-wearing. In the first two months of the lockdown, the Commission on Human Rights received 368 complaints and requests for assistance. As of September 6, 2020, 100,486 people were arrested for allegedly violating lockdown.

Those arrested were often detained in conditions not in accordance with social distancing requirements, likely exposing the detained, as well as arresting officers, to even more risk of infection. There have also been instances of inhumane and violent treatment towards alleged quarantine violators, including placing quarantine violators together in dog cages, detaining quarantine

violators and forcing them to sit in an unshaded area at midday, where tem-
peratures can reach over 40 degrees Celsius, beatings, and forcing LGBTQIA+
people to kiss each other and perform a 'sexy' dance as punishment. At least
two people have been killed by police after confrontations for allegedly violating lockdown regulations.

This inhumane treatment of ordinary citizens, especially the poor, stands
in stark contrast to government officials who not only violate quarantine,
but also encourage others to do so. In May 2020, photos surfaced of police
General Debold Sinas having a birthday party at a police camp with at least
fifty attendees. Sinas was defended by both the Philippine National Police
and the Department of Interior and Local government and has received no
institutional sanction. In April, Deputy Administrator of the Overseas Workers
Welfare Administration, Margaret 'Mocha' Uson gathered a crowd of repatri-
ated overseas Filipino workers in a quarantine facility for an event. The administration defended her actions.

The Duterte government has also been able to use the Covid as an opportunity to take legal measures to limit democratic institutions and human rights
protections. In addition to avoiding calling for street mobilizations to avoid
spreading the virus, the opposition has been overwhelmed with providing
food relief, medical supplies, and other basic services to communities in need,
thus providing ample opportunity for the government to act with even less
resistance. At the administration's behest, Duterte-allied leaders of the House
of Representatives railroaded the passage of the Anti-Terror Law of 2020. The
law greatly expands the definition of terrorism and allows the government to
surveil a person for up to ninety days without pressing charges and imprison
a person for up to 14 days without a warrant, with the option to extend the
imprisonment to a total of 24 days without charges. Shortly after the law was
passed, Randall Echanis, a longtime activist and peace consultant was killed
in his home, his body exhibiting signs of torture. His body was later forcibly
taken from the family's chosen funeral home by members of the Philippines
National Police.

Freedom of speech came under direct attack as Duterte allies refused to
renew the franchise of the country's largest broadcast network, ABS-CBN, effectively closing the station down. Duterte had held a grudge against the station's
owners since the 2016 election, when the station allowed an attack ad against
him to run. Duterte's attacks against ABS-CBN and any non-administration
news sources continued as they reported on drug war killings and corruption
allegations. The shutting down of ABS-CBN occurred together with some incidents of local police arresting ordinary citizens for Facebook posts criticizing
the government or hyperbolically threatening the president. At the same time,

the administration and armed forces ramped up 'red-tagging' or identifying journalists and activists as Communist party members and therefore enemies of the state.

Finally, the Covid-19 pandemic has not seen less killings related to the so-called "war on drugs," but rather more. According to government-provided data, 155 people were killed during police anti-drug operations from March 31 to July 31, 2020. This is a 50% increase from December 2019 to March 2020 indicating that police killings justified by the so-called war on drugs' have not subsided despite strict lockdown and the understandable shift in public attention towards dealing with the pandemic.

While the Duterte regime used the Covid crisis as an opportunity to justify expanding the repressive apparatus of the state, it did the opposite when it came to actually dealing with Covid. Instead of assuming additional power and thus responsibility to, for example, procure and distribute hospital equipment, tests, and vaccines and implement a widespread financial amelioration program, the Duterte administration largely left these to local governments and the private sector. By May 2020, the government stated outright that it did not foresee having the capacity to conduct mass testing and was instead relying on the private sector. Local government units and private corporations, likewise, purchased their own vaccines as the national government lagged behind. When the Duterte government lockdown suspended public transportation, private companies and the Office of the Vice President (who is part of the political opposition) arranged their own shuttle busses for workers, including healthcare workers. Duterte's transportation secretary responded by stating that they were operating illegally and needed to apply for public utility vehicle permits.

In March 2020, the Philippine Congress approved social amelioration payments granting two PhP 5,000–8,000 monthly payments (approximately USD 100–160, less than the minimum wage) to low-income families, the Duterte administration left it up to local government units to distribute the money in cash according to lists created without national government oversight. As expected, the distribution was plagued by corruption and patronage as many of those in need but without a contact at city hall did not receive payments whereas other families received multiple payments. In response to widespread hunger and government inaction, "community pantries" where private citizens collected food for distribution to needy families sprung up around the country in May 2021. Instead of supporting the initiatives, some government officials, particularly those from the military and communication arms, warned that the pantries were a ploy for communist recruitment intended to instigate anger against the government. There were many incidents of pantry organizers being harassed by police, and Duterte himself warned that food distribution may turn into super spreader events.

In short, Covid has shown both the extent to which the Duterte administration is willing to amplify repression and close democratic space, as well as its total ineptitude in dealing with actual crisis. Throughout the crisis, it has sought to make itself felt in the everyday lives of citizens through the harsh repression of banal activities in the name of maintaining quarantine, yet it has washed its hands of the responsibility to implement some of the most important and obvious anti-Covid measures.

4   India during the Pandemic: Arena for Ideological Entrenchment

Devika Misra

By the end of 2021, the Indian government with much fanfare, announced the record number of vaccinations it had achieved. In his monthly communiques, where Modi talks to the people, if not with the people per se, he heralded a new era of post-pandemic recovery for India, espousing great faith in the government's policy of '*Sabko Vaccine Muft Vaccine*,'[1] where the superlative statistic of total vaccinations was itself emblematic of India's victory against Covid. Couched in the language of capability and achievement, Modi underlined the 'science-born, science-based and science-driven' character of the Indian vaccination program, where this forward-thinking land was poised for a remarkable economic recovery, heralding a future that would be *Made in India*. Capacity, capability and leadership all seemed uninterrupted, completely successful and sovereign, brooking no room for doubt.

The solidity of the narrative however, purposely worked to undercut the fractures evident in this tale. For example, the catch-all slogan of free vaccines was, itself, outrightly misleading, given that earlier government dictums had laid down payments for vaccinations, with a large stake afforded to private players in the process. Similarly, even as Modi distinguished himself from other alleged autocratic leaders like Trump and Bolsonaro by emphasizing not only his direct "attack" against the pandemic, but reliance on scientific temper in informing this attack, most notably, the Ayurvedic giant Patanjali grew by leaps and bounds during the pandemic, peddling its Coronil as a Covid cure. While the blurring of fact and fiction is hardly a novelty in the rise of the

---

1   Vaccine for All, Free Vaccine.

regimes under discussion in this text, it was the pandemic that allowed the Modi government to not only dissipate doubt, but drown it. The exigencies of the pandemic allowed opportunities for the Modi government to propel itself into prominence following a twofold strategy: entrenching its ideological narrative and furthering the growth of crony capitalism in order to further the consolidation of its political power.

4.1 Pandemic as Opportunity: Entrenchment of Ideology and Consolidation of State Authority

Despite claims of 'Sabka Saath, Sabka Vikaas,'[2] the BJP and its ideological agenda of Hindutva have promoted an increasingly exclusionist vision of India, where religious polarization has been defended in the name of promoting development that the 'right' kind of citizenry demands. India's pandemic management was emblematic of this where public health and public protection were in fact, weaponized to sanction unilateral public policies to further marginalize the dispossessed. The migrant exodus during the first lockdown is a prime example of this.

India imposed a nationwide lockdown overnight, allegedly a visible demonstration of the government's preparedness, alertness and hardliner attitude towards managing the pandemic. Stranded migrant workers and suddenly unemployed informal workers found themselves in alien urban climes, with no job, housing or food security. Policed by an unempathetic state machinery in the guise of observing public safety laws, their state-led persecution was aided and abetted by a vigilante enforcer society, where the logic of the pandemic exposed the pre-existing inequality and class divisions in Indian society. When heart breaking images of stranded migrant workers walking back home, hounded by those that should have helped, flooded television screens, the logic of promoting public health allowed the state to justify its actions despite the visibility of the plight of migrants forced into exodus by state policies. Their exodus was marked as a focal point for public outrage, as the government argued that political misinformation had incited rebellion amongst those who were not deemed smart enough to recognize their own destitution. Pro-government media channels found new pawns for the firmly established anti-national rhetoric and mounted it against all and sundry who mildly forayed into the realm of dissent against the law of the land, even if to survive a deadly disease.

---

2 With the Support of Everyone, Development for All.

Similarly, the pollution-purity binary that has traditionally upheld the vicious exclusionary violence of the Hindu caste system was reproduced in state-sanctioned modern logics of the pandemic. This was most prominently demonstrated in the demonization of the Tablighi Jamat, a transnational Sunni Islamic missionary movement that organized an event in Delhi during the first wave, where some dozen travelers tested positive. This breach of rules by a small congregation was weaponized to castigate a much-persecuted Muslim community where the media established a pandemic version of an alliance between non-Hindu religions and anti-nationalism. Not only did these narratives of hate grant legitimacy to the government project of dismantling the Anti-Citizenship Amendment Act[3] protest sites, which had outlasted overt state violence in the past, they also seemed to grant social and legal approval to an unfettered state in its prosecution of civil society dissenters, students, journalists and activists. Strangely, the same logic that the state effectively mobilized as an enforcer of public health to dismantle protest, was conveniently voided in its role as a provider of public health, as was palpably evident when the same dissenters argued for their rights during a pandemic in prison.

This legitimation of state authority with the entrenchment of the Hindutva agenda came home to roost when on August 5th, 2020, in a highly televised ceremony, and on the first-year anniversary of the abrogation of Article 370 that revoked the state status of Kashmir, Modi, along with the high and mighty of the BJP and the RSS, laid the foundation stone for *Ram Janmabhoomi*[4] in Ayodhaya. The metaphors were potent and deadly in their insinuation – the solidification and sanctity of the Hindutva agenda appeared complete.

4.2   *Pandemic as Opportunity: Expansion of the Crony Capitalist State*
The Indian government announced emergency responses of providing food grain rations and other help in May, after devastating losses had been registered in the labour market. Despite this much delayed response, by the end

---

3   The BJP introduced an amendment to the Citizenship Act of 1955 on December 11, 2019, bringing the Citizenship Amendment Act (CAA) into force. The CAA on the face of it, appears to only offer formalisation of citizenship of persecuted asylum seekers from its neighbouring countries, specifically only offering this amnesty to non-Muslim immigrants and was coupled with the intent to formalise the National Register of Citizens, It sparked protests across the country especially against the introduction of religion as a marker of citizenship.

4   The birthplace of Lord Ram, a deity in Hinduism. The struggle for this temple was preceded by the demolition of the Babri Masjid in 1992 which was followed by massive communal riots across the country. The issue has remained central to Hindutva since.

of 2020, the government had begun internationally promoting its narrative of optimum pandemic management. It began with provisions for PPE kits and pharmaceutical help abroad, with Modi uncharacteristically bridging home-grown ideological political divides through his participation in the SAARC[5] and NAM.[6] India's pandemic aid abroad, supported by assertions of global responsibility and India's morally sound internationalism, underlined the desire for recognition on the international stage. The morality rhetoric and Indian magnanimity were clearly in opposition to the petering out of domestic food grain assistance, despite acute shortages by the end of 2020. India's moral rhetoric of its vaccine diplomacy and status as global health provider grew in a rising crescendo in 2021, where at the Davos Summit of the World Economic Forum, Modi publicly claimed India's successful management of the pandemic not just for its own people, but also its success carrying out its global responsibility of helping the world fight the pandemic by functioning as the "pharmacy of the world". This internationalization was supported by aggressive campaigning domestically, especially to ensure BJP's success in the upcoming state legislative assembly elections, where protocols were often flouted by senior BJP leaders, amidst grandiose predictions of the national government's capability and competency.

The insistence on the rule of the law and state authority, if not the aggrandizing propaganda, might lead to the conclusion that the Indian state was completely efficient in managing the pandemic. However, as the second wave proved, the Indian state suffered serious setbacks in safeguarding its population. As the healthcare system of India crumbled with SOS calls and massive oxygen and medicine shortages reported all over the country, the dissonance between the claims of the government and efforts on the ground seemed to violently erupt.

This dissonance was nevertheless diffused, disrupted and managed by the Modi government. Citizen accusations about the crumbling state of healthcare infrastructure were piled at the door of the previous governments. At the same time, the Modi government emphasized its ability to build capacity by highlighting the foreign aid that came into the country in order to defend itself against criticisms that vaccine drives prioritized international recipients over domestic ones. Claims of scientific success visibly manifested into active propaganda, as vaccination certificates carried large images of Modi. The alteration of Covid data continued, and most potently, towards the end

5   South Asian Association for Regional Cooperation.
6   The Non-Aligned Movement.

of 2021, the Rajya Sabha or the Upper House of the Indian Parliament, auda-
ciously denied the death toll of the second wave. Meanwhile, links between
the business community and the neoliberal state became further entrenched
as the prodigal Poonawala, the CEO of the Serum Institute of India was feted
by the Indian government, weeks after the organization's domestic and internationally publicized crisis where it defaulted on its ability to manufacture
and supply vaccines it had committed to partners across the globe. This murk-
iness between facts and public statements was already exemplified by the 'PM
Cares' fund, which provided little to no information about how much these
funds amounted to and how they were utilized. Amidst rising inflation and
unemployment, the heavy costs of the Central Vista Redevelopment Project,
which includes a new parliament building that many consider a vanity project, were pitted against an increasingly dispossessed and marginalized population's clamors for support. These clamors included, among others, demands
made by primary healthcare ASHA workers and widescale farmers' protests
when changes were introduced in important supportive measures offered by
the government to India's most vulnerable sector, followed by long protracted
silences against farmer suicides in both government and media. The plight of
farmers was exacerbated by the dilution of important legal safeguards like the
Environmental Impact Assessment, allowing the expansion of neoliberal development projects in the country. The National Education Policy was a prime
example of this dissonance between the country's vision for development, and
its disregard for reality on the ground when, amidst staggering dropout rates in
schools and colleges, the NEP gave greater impetus to online education. This
was blaringly manifested in the public psyche via BYJU's advertisements, a for-
profit edtech venture, supported by the corporatization of education and the
increasing footprint of private universities in the country.

Coming back to the stupendous vaccination figure, the entirety of its success was marketed as brand-building for Prime Minister Modi. It is not that
dissonances to this propaganda were not registered, but rather that the government has been creative in its diffusion of criticism. Major criticisms of
the continuing inflation, unemployment and public distress have been effectively managed by Bollywood scandals, Indian Premier League (IPL) tourna-
ments, standard misdirection and huge privatization drives as symbols of a
rebranded and rebuilt India. There have been a few victories for the dissenters, as evidenced by the accommodation of the farmers' movement demands
by the government, where Modi's capitulation was an acceptance that hardliner leadership was becoming less relevant to an angry populace. In the face
of accusations of poor governance and, most importantly, the electoral pressures of the various state elections in 2022, the paternalistic bowing down

to 'warring children' was being increasingly marketed as a being symbolic of change, compromise and flexibility. Nevertheless, it is not a stretch to suggest that the pandemic and its own self-proclaimed success in its management has allowed the government to play in superlatives of undifferentiation, ignoring the inherent unequal social and economic realities of its people, no matter the violence and destruction unleashed. Its management allowed for the adoption of warlike metaphors where Modi's savior image continued to grow, as did concomitantly, the image upheaval in the Prime Minister's visage with the growth of his white, Tagoresque beard, and consequently, his leadership and prestige.

5   Pandemic Measures in Hungary between 2019 March and 2021
       October

Ágnes Gagyi and Tamás Gerőcs

5.1 *Further Centralization of Power: Protecting and Expanding National Capital's Maneuver Space through Pandemic Measures*

Right after the outbreak of the pandemic, the Hungarian government was initially hesitant to undertake serious healthcare measures, and the first propaganda reactions still attempted to link Covid to the official discourse on migration and George Soros. However, the regime soon turned course to make maximum use of the broader space for state interventions opened up by the situation in order to accelerate internal capital concentration and increase centralized control over its external and internal conditions. In his notable speech in the parliament before introducing the emergency regulation, Viktor Orbán said: "I need 133 brave people, the 133 bravest in the country. And that is you here on the government's side and I ask that you not be shaken, do not retreat, do not succumb to uncertainty." Using its parliamentary supermajority, the governing Fidesz party voted for a state of emergency regulation that allowed the government to rule by decree. This has greatly extended the Prime Minister's authority. While the period of rule by decree was closed after the first wave of the pandemic, the emergency situation has remained in place until today.

The government's steps to further centralize power during the pandemic happened in a context where swift global capital concentration (aided by state measures) motivated preemptive steps to enhance and protect domestic capital's positions, and where the approaching 2022 elections showed a slight but possible chance for a win by the united opposition, to which the regime reacted by stepping up measures to secure state-backed domestic capital as

private capital. Expanding earlier tendencies, the regime provided new benefits to multinational manufacturing, sped up the expansion of domestic oligarchic capital in domestic service industries (squeezing out foreign actors from
the market), fed domestic oligarchic concentration from the crisis of smaller
domestic companies, while further flexibilizing labor and keeping crisis allowances to an extreme minimum.

This concentration of capital was especially peculiar in the hotel and catering industries where government-affiliated businesses rapidly overtook the
market, enjoying the help of the state by the reallocation of EU-funds. This
capital concentration was further propelled by a wave of privatizations in the
domestic services sectors where the state had previously extended its shares
(including energy, telecommunication infrastructure, and banking).

5.2   Diversifying External Capitalist Alliances – Geopolitical and Business Deals with Russia and China

The Hungarian government used the opportunity of the pandemic to deepen
its economic ties with new geopolitical allies and push for a quick global recognition of their vaccines ahead of European or US approval. Russia and China
in particular are the most important allies in this geopolitical space. Hungary
was the first European country to officially approve both China's Sinopharm
and Russia's Sputnik vaccines. The country also gained access to vaccines distributed by Western suppliers, however, government propaganda explicitly
recommended Chinese and Russian vaccines to the general population. Prime
Minister Viktor Orbán himself got vaccinated by Sinopharm, and senior government officials stated that they believed the Chinese vaccine was the most
efficient amongst all other types. Because of the large variety of vaccines available to the public, there have been political discussions and speculation about
the efficiency of the various types of vaccines, with liberals and social democrats accusing the government of risking the health of senior citizens by promoting the Chinese vaccine.

5.3   Using Pandemic Measures to Weaken the Opposition

In the 2019 local elections, the united opposition won a significant number
of local governments, including that of Budapest. Weakening opposition local
governments' space to maneuver was an important aspect of the government's
pandemic measures.

The centralization of local industrial taxes was a significant blow to local
governments. To compensate for the revenue loss after the centralization and
confiscation of tax receipts, the national government allocated special subsidies to local governments. However, political selection criteria favored those

municipalities that remained loyal to the central government. They received the majority of funds, whereas opposition local governments were allocated only a disproportionately small amount of money, which led in some cases to their day-to-day operations being jeopardized by selective and discriminatory emergency measures. The opposition governments' situation was further worsened by an obligatory contribution to the state emergency fund by all parties, as well as by local measures like the temporary suspension of collecting parking fees in Budapest and other major cities (a major income source for local governments).

5.4   *High Death Rate despite High Vaccination Rate*
Due to several factors, the two most often cited of which are the relatively late lockdown and the dire conditions of the public health care system, Hungary was hit very hard by the pandemic. While number of cases and death rate during the first wave in the Spring of 2019 were still relatively modest, following the pattern of other EU countries, the second and particularly the third and fourth waves had devastating effects, putting Hungary among the highest ranked death per capita global figures. Altogether, 30 thousand people are estimated to have died from Covid in a population of less than 10 million. There have been 822 thousand active cases registered between 2019 March and 2021 October.

5.5   *Social Measures Kept Minimal*
An extension of the 2019 'slave law' allowed companies to temporarily lay off labor without compensation, while at the same time obliging it to work heightened hours of overtime (when needed by capital). Hungary did not introduce a pandemic-related unemployment benefit, and wage subsidies related to lockdowns were kept at a maximum of 23%. The lack of protective gear at workplaces, and especially in the healthcare and educational systems, became a source of tensions, eased somewhat by workers' skepticism about the virus, fueled by social media sites.

The crisis of the healthcare system, an underfunded and crumbling structure awaiting reforms and pointing towards privatization already before the pandemic, became highly visible during the pandemic. Like elsewhere, pandemic measures repressed non-Covid related care functions, and put extreme pressures on women who were expected to substitute for institutional healthcare and education at home. However, even despite peaking death rates and wide-ranging personal experience with the system's inadequacies, the healthcare issue seems to have been erased relatively successfully from public debates after the third wave, reflecting the government's strong media power. Deteriorating conditions in schools, however, remained in the public discourse.

Two social aspects of the crisis that continued pre-pandemic characteristics of the Hungarian labor force were those of household debt and migration. The boom of forex mortgage lending, fueled by Western capital during the 2000s, led to an especially deep penetration of mortgages among lower-income Hungarian households and after 2008, caused a mortgage crisis that stood out in its social consequences within the region. While the Fidesz government used debt crisis measures to save better-off debtors and reconfigure the banking sector to the benefit of national capital, a large part of lower-middle class and worker households with forex debts were pressed towards work migration to be able to sustain their payments. Next to the flexibilization of work to support manufacturing FDI after 2008, forex debt was a leading cause of the work migration boom of the 2010s, which created a serious labor shortage locally. Like elsewhere in Eastern Europe, pandemic measures pressed migrant labor back from Western workplaces, creating a situation where households deprived of significant chunks of income were left to take care of their reproduction at home. A moratorium on debt enforcement was key to tackling the symptoms of this crisis. Analysts expect that the lifting of the moratorium could unleash a spiral of a new debt crisis at the same level or even higher than that of 2008.

5.6   *Ideological Repressions Hardened*

While the Hungarian government and Viktor Orbán personally maintained an image of strong men not afraid of the virus, but instituting security measures out of responsibility (i.e., for being able to restart the economy), official discourse did not question medical interpretations of the virus and maintained a pro-vaccine standpoint. By introducing Russian and Chinese vaccines ahead of their EU acceptance, reaching a high vaccination rate, as well as making immunity cards mandatory for participating at public events, the government successfully created an image of itself having used its decision-making power to efficiently tackle the pandemic. Pandemic-related tensions are played down by government communication – the healthcare crisis is represented as a hard but successful struggle, the pressure on women is reframed as men responsible for the economy thanking women for playing their due role in household work during the pandemic, and popular income anxieties are linked to promises to restart and expand the economy. Other than classic ideological topics, like opposing Brussels for pressing liberal values on Hungary, anti-migration and threats linked to George Soros, the run-up to the 2022 campaign also included repressive measures targeted against LGBTQ communities, a new minority group drawn into the center of government's hostility propaganda with the aim to create a symbolic majority on the side of Fidesz

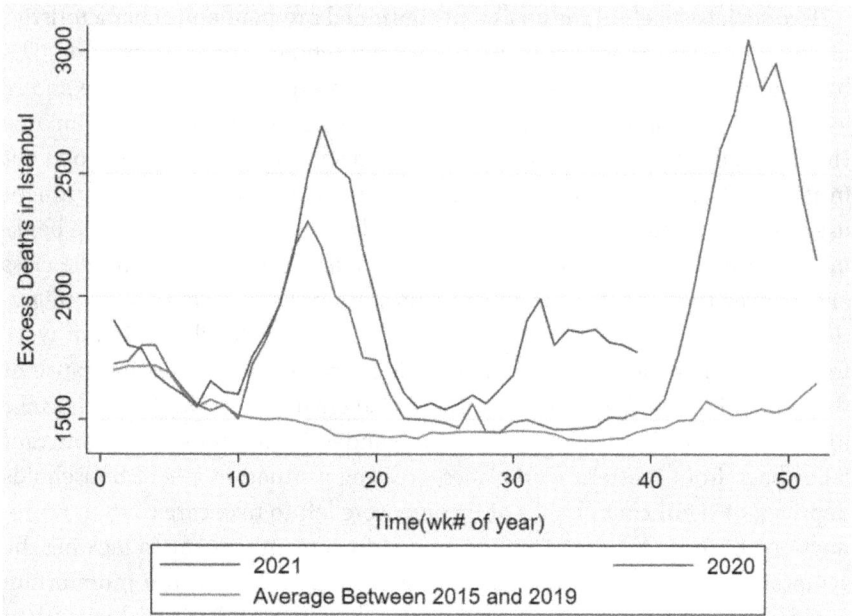

FIGURE 8.1   COVID-19 graph with first second third wave (weekly distribution within years)
Note: Istanbul Municipality Cemeteries Branch (2021)
SOURCE: ISTANBUL DAILY DEATH DATA 2015–2021 (ISTANBUL MUNICIPALITY
DEATH RECORDS (2021), ISTANBUL,TURKEY.)

6   Turkey's 'Long' Covid: The Analysis of the Sources of Economic and Health Failures during the Covid-19 Crisis

Ilhan Can Ozen

In 2002, the economic crisis and the health crisis had created significant popular support for a replacement. The AKP utilized this electoral and political opportunity by continuing the institutionalization of the already introduced economic liberalism, and introducing the new, and more powerful institution of the Health Ministry, and the General Health Insurance Fund. The interesting historical irregularity is that while the AKP and Erdogan gained power on the waves of a well-known economic crisis in 2001, and a latent health coverage/service crisis, they have been unable to manage the more current explicit health crisis, and a latent economic crisis, in the 20th year of their rule. I will look at the reasons why while they were able to use the opportunity to garner support for their new era of rule, and expand their political base in the early

2000s, and why they were so unable to use the opportunity window created by this new situation to manage the dual crisis in the 2020s.

I am going to focus on the post-2016 period, where the AKP has passed to a different governance stage characterized by much more pronounced populist tendencies and social support based on support based on an alliance[7] between the urban poor and the businesses which have been attached to AKP through extensive and ongoing contracts and long-term PPPs.[8] The question will be, how has the specific economic and social structure that came out of the COVID-19 crisis make this coalition's internal and external dynamics less or more sustainable?

The first Covid-19 case was recorded in Turkey on the 11th of March 2020. As the cases in Italy had reached their peak around the same time, the first wave was a quite controlled period, with government sanctions starting at the national level on the 3rd of April. Although it did not stop the first wave, the length and pace were much more controlled compared to the second and third waves, which started in November 2020 and March 2021, respectively. The epidemic was also largely present in Istanbul (Istanbul also has the highest quality healthcare system), rather than being present nationwide as it was during the second and third waves. Covid control policies were quite successful and internationally commended when they prioritized protection, but faced their biggest struggles when a relaxation policy was not effectively implemented in the tail end of 2020. Significant changes in publicly available data policies were undertaken on 29 July 2020, and then the protective policies instituted to control the second wave were relaxed in March 2021.

The AKP's quasi one-man rule struggled with Covid's societal effects, health effects and the critical public transfer and social support system that undergirds the party's political base. Three problems that the AKP brought to the Covid era further complicated strengthening its political base: 1- the loss of municipal centers as public fund transfer agencies has meant that there were less discretionary funds to use, and only at the national level, 2- The lower output growth that has been achieved since 2014, with significant and growing vulnerability in foreign exchange markets, compounded by bad macroeconomic policies depleting the foreign reserves, and 3- The growing inflation/higher interest rate equilibrium that was fueled by the capital flight crisis has threatened the financial liberalization-higher consumption-real estate bubble

---

7 As has been argued in Esen and Gumuscu, 2021.
8 Public-Private Partnership (PPP)'s have increased in numbers and relative size of the economy during the AKP Era, with a specific jump after 2011.

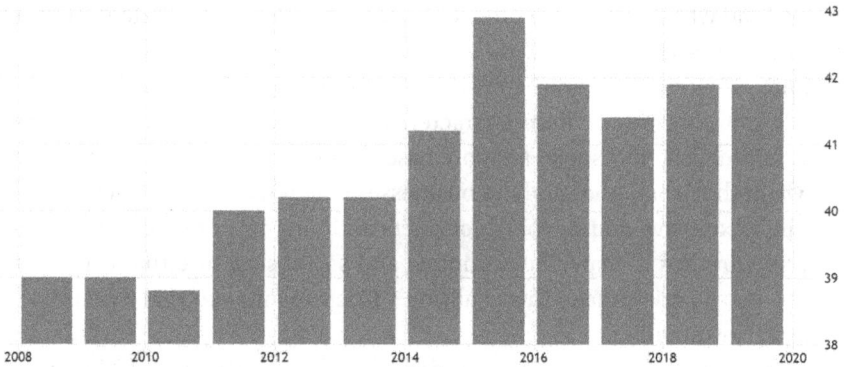

FIGURE 8.2 GINI coefficient of Turkey from 2008 to 2020
SOURCE: INCOME-LIVING CONDITIONS SURVEY DATA (TURKSTAT, 2021)

chain that had defined the first 12 years of AKP rule, with a brief interlude during the 2008–2009 crisis.

Income distribution has worsened, and substantial poverty (especially urban poverty) has been on the rise since 2014[9], with a significant jump in the Covid period.[10] The AKP government has not been consistently hurt in the polls from increasing inequality (though an argument can be made that its breakthrough performance was in 2007 with the lowest inequality in the last 30 years (Figure 8.2), but the high level of inequality is making the distribution of the support base more polarized and harder to pacify with the same economic policies.

Developing countries like Turkey have much more limited fiscal space to push their economies out of recessionary equilibrium[11]. However, Turkish discretionary fiscal space to deal with the Covid crisis (Figure 8.3) was curtailed even further as the AKP government fostered growth in the post-2017 period mainly through additional fiscal space use and delivering ever greater guarantees to attract scant foreign investment. The limited choice environment created a situation where the AKP had to prioritize certain portions of their support base.

The international winds are becoming less precipitous for countries like Turkey because of: A – the well documented change and decline in capital inflows starting in the first quarter of 2020, making debt refinancing much

---

9   Turkstat (2021).
10   Bayar et al. (2022).
11   IMF (2021).

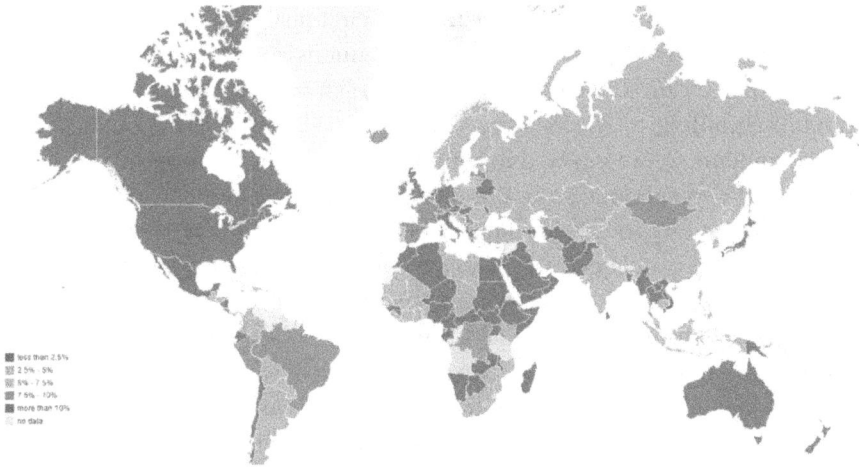

FIGURE 8.3   Global budgetary fiscal support to people and firms
SOURCE: FISCAL POLICY DATABASE (IMF, 2021)

more difficult,[12] and B – the changing global distribution of COVID related health problems, that became an external threat, and with the failure of containment policies, a problem of internal organization and health provision.

Control over the pandemic in March through May 2020 was effective, though uncommonly nationalized, with minimum regional variation despite the epidemiological and socioeconomic characteristics of the regions being significantly different. Integration into the European system, especially of the scientific community, was crucial. It meant that Italy`s devastating experience with the virus, as well as Germany and other EU-West countries aggressive pandemic control actions were integral in driving the first round of restrictions and its multi-scope, multi-sector, all-nation[13] nature.[14] Sector-by-sector and local-to-local differentiation did not occur at all, but the epidemiological benefit to economic cost ratio was high, with the economic costs comparable to the European average.

---

12   Kalemli-Ozcan et al. (2020).
13   In terms of the stringency index, this period represented the policymakers at their most vigilant.
14   All the crucial and correct decisions that are in force to this day that both control the COVID epidemic spreading further and ameliorating the resulting health and economic inequality from infection, which is full public coverage for all COVID patients, and public reimbursement of their health expenditures as related to COVID were also made in this period.

Together with the strained economic circumstances, what made the epidemiological-economic balance more tenuous were: 1- Wrong opinions held about the causality chain between the high interest rate and high inflation rate equilibria, 2- The idea that the health system of Turkey could control Covid epidemic more easily than European countries because of its health system and demographic structure 3-The idea that the difficult social coordination required by NPIs (Non Pharmaceutical Interventions) to prevent the spread of Covid could be achieved in a context where the information coming from the government authorities was either conflicting, or highly misleading, especially after lifting the initial lockdown.

The interest rate debate in Turkey has a political economy dimension, but I am more interested in the products of error, rather than rational political economy. Table 8.1 makes clear that Turkey has a high nominal interest rate and high inflation rate (higher than its comparison countries), which might be related to the two erroneous points of view that policymakers currently hold: 1- That the interest rate can be reduced in order to reduce and control inflation, and 2- That reducing the Interest rate is unconnected to the ongoing domestic currency depreciation, and the domestic currency depreciation is unconnected to the growing inflation.

The result of these two errors is that as the state decreases the real interest rate, the inflation rate skyrockets,[15] and the nominal interest rate (the decreased real interest rate plus the ascending inflation rate), as a total increases (Table 8.1). The government's policy choices have become significantly more suboptimal in this challenging economic environment because the quality of inputs that the economic bureaucracy that has to offer the decision-making process has been severely depleted in the last 5 years due to skill loss and skill mismanagement.

Skill mismanagement among the health bureaucracy (which, when not circumvented, is quite highly capable), has come to the fore during the Covid crisis in Turkey. Changing from reporting Covid case numbers to reporting Covid hospital admissions, which is a less sensitive measure, over the summer of 2020, meant that the decision makers were not alert enough to change their social policies in the direction of greater control.[16] This, in turn, put

---

15   The alternative inflation calculation organization ENA Group has measured, in October, the highest yearly inflation rate in the AKP era with 49.87% (Inflation Data (ENA Grup, 2021).
16   Whereas clearly the international literature is showing that at the country level, the better the ability to track an epidemic, the better the country's ability to control the wave-length of the epidemic (Ssentongo et al., 2021).

TABLE 8.1   Global inflation rate, interest rate and CDS premiums[a]

Country	Inflation rate	Interest rate	CDS premium
China	0.8	2.9	47.5
Indonesia	1.6	6.4	84.2
France	1.9	0.2	20.4
Greece	1.9	0.8	76.2
UK	3.2	1	9.4
Germany	3.9	-0.2	9.3
USA	5.3	1.5	12.7
Mexico	5.6	7.6	96.1
Russia	6.7	7.3	86.2
Brazil	9.7	11.1	200.1
Turkey	19.3	18.8	415.5

Note: Credit default swaps (CDS) are a zero-sum game that is concluded through a bilateral contract agreement. The premium associated to enter the game is priced in order to insure against a credit event of a reference entity which has issued a bond or has taken out a loan. The CDS of a country is associated both with the financial healthiness of the firms and financial entities that exist within the country, and the macro-economic and macro-political stability, which determines the certainty of the macro-economic environment.
a   World Government Bonds (2021)

Turkey's Covid numbers outside the acceptable dimensions in September and October 2020.

Non-pharmaceutical interventions, including social distancing, wearing masks, and washing hands, can only be as effective as the knowledge spread among the population. The more correct information is spread equally among different groups,[17] the more effective the coordination and reaction of society at large will be. It is here that the new culture of secrecy, censored data, and restricted data hampered the government's own effectiveness. It also led Turkey to be eliminated from the green tourism zones for EU citizens, that in turn further hampered the country's tourism revenue at a crucial time for scarce foreign exchange. This happened in 2020 and in 2021, until the government shared clearer epidemic data with its international partners.

---

17   This has been stated in (Alsan et al., 2021).

From its first period in power, the most important linchpin of the AKP's promise to provide justice in the age of capitalism was undergirded by the health system. Providing access to health services and security to the masses that had neither could only be achieved by the reform of the health system, and the AKP's reforms did give public health access to a huge group of previously unprovided, or under-provided mostly urban masses.[18] So, the Covid crisis with its specific problems around health inequality, health provision, and health insecurity, created a problem in the hallmark of AKP-style neoliberal integration. There are four facets that are important to consider. First, it was exactly in the procurement of protective equipment and private-public partnerships that the AKP has been most obviously a failure. Second, the issues of security and protection in the Covid era were mostly run through the Internal Ministry, rather than the Health Ministry. Third, taking into account that the AKP rose to power in the early 2000s amidst a dial economic and health crisis, opinion polls show that the health administration and health matters are perceived to be the most successfully run part of the administration.[19] However, this relative popularity is not shared by the efficacy of the lockdown administration, nor the economic administration. Finally, the integration of primary healthcare, switch to protective healthcare, and then increased focus on surveying the population's health, have become especially glaring weaknesses during the Covid crisis. The takeaway for us is that any part of the institutional solution that AKP brought to the 2002 dual crisis, is still operational, and is popular even during Covid. Every part of the de-institutionalization process that AKP's current leadership clearly prefers, has made the dual crisis not easier to manage but actually harder to manage, with greater collateral damage, and less stable social support.

References

Alsan M, Stanford F C, Banerjee A, Breza E, Chandrasekhar A, Eichmeyer S and Duflo E (2021) Comparison of knowledge and information-seeking behavior after general COVID-19 public health messages and messages tailored for black and

---

18   Atun et al. (2013).
19   Please consult the Turkey's Report website to look at the recent opinion polls, where only 23 percent of the survey participants believe that Turkey has deteriorated in terms of health performance in the last 10 years. For all other performance dimensions, the evaluations are much lower, with 68.4 percent saying the economic performance has deteriorated Turkey's Political Perceptions Data (Turkiye Raporu, 2022).

latinx communities: a randomized controlled trial. *Annals of Internal Medicine*, 174(4): 484–492.

Atun R, Aydın S, Chakraborty S, Sümer S, Aran M, Gürol I and Akdağ R (2013). Universal health coverage in Turkey: enhancement of equity. *The Lancet*, 382(9886): 65–99.

Bayar A and Günçavdi Ö (2022) In the Wake of the Outbreak, Income Distribution, and Poverty in Turkey. In: *Turkey and the Post-pandemic World Order*. Kentucky: Lexington Books: 89–111.

ENA Grup (2021) Inflation Data (ENA Group-Inflation Research Group, Year Ending Report 2021. Accessed From: https://enagrup.org/bulten/202110ea.pdf?v2.

Esen B and Gumuscu S (2021) Why did Turkish democracy collapse? A political economy account of AKP's authoritarianism. *Party Politics* 27(6): 1075–1091.

IMF (2021) Database of Fiscal Policy Responses to Covid-19. Accessed from https://www.imf.org/en/Topics/imf-and-covid19/Fiscal-Policies-Database-in-Response-sto-COVID-19.

Istanbul Municipality Cemeteries Branch (2021) Istanbul Daily Death Records 2015–2021 (Istanbul Municipality Death Records (2021), Istanbul, Turkey. Available at https://www.turkiye.gov.tr/istanbul-buyuksehir-belediyesi-vefat-sorgulama.

Kalemli-Ozcan S, Gourinchas P O, Penciakova V and Sander N (2020) COVID-19 and SME failures (No. 2020/207). International Monetary Fund.

Ssentongo P, Fronterre C, Geronimo A, Greybush S J, Mbabazi P K, Muvawala J and Schiff S J (2021) Pan-African evolution of within-and between-country COVID-19 dynamics. Proceedings of the National Academy of Sciences, 118(28).

Turkiye Raporu (2022) Turkey`s Political Perceptions- Differences in the Last 10 Years Report. Available at: https://www.turkiyeraporu.com/arastirma/son-10-senede-neler-degisti-2-5421/.

Turkstat (2021) Income-Living Conditions Survey Statistics. Available at: www.tuik.gov.tr.

World Government Bonds (2021). CDS and Macroeconomic Balance- Historical data. Accessed From: https://www.worldgovernmentbonds.com/cds-historical-data/.

CHAPTER 9

It Can't Happen Here

Trump Viewed from the Margins

Daniel Geary

Shortly after Adolph Hitler came to power in Germany, the American novelist Sinclair Lewis (1935) published *It Can't Happen Here,* the story of how a fascist dictator came to rule the United States. After Donald Trump was elected president in 2016, the American intelligentsia posed the same question Lewis had eight decades prior: could fascism triumph in the U.S.? The debate over whether or not Trump was fascist yielded important insights and helped alert Americans to the real danger he posed. Yet there was something strange about making 1930s European fascism the point of comparison. After all, the global rise of authoritarianism was already evident prior to Trump in Hungary, India, Turkey, and the Philippines. Why, then, were intellectuals so focused on the "lessons of the twentieth century"? (Greenberg 2021; Snyder 2017).

When Trumpism is viewed in contemporary global perspective, it is usually in relation to Western Europe, especially Brexit in Great Britain (Geary, Schofield, and Sutton 2020). Yet the comparisons can be extended to other parts of the world as well (Vorman and Weinman 2021). With typical imperial hubris, most Americans presume that history develops from the Global North outwards. When Jair Bolsonaro was elected President of Brazil in 2019, he was depicted as the "Trump of the Tropics." Trump, however, was rarely depicted as following in the footsteps of Rodrigo Duterte, Recep Tayyip Erdoğan, Victor Orbán, or Narendra Modi. What if we examined Trump's rise from the perspective of places that most Americans view as on the margins of global development? What would we gain if we compared Trumpism to the new authoritarianism in the Global South that predated his presidency? Unlike the fascist comparison, doing so allows us to understand Trump as a response to a particular historical conjuncture marked by the global crisis of neoliberalism.

While American intellectuals compared Trump with Hitler, Trump himself recognized a kinship with Bolsonaro, Duterte, Erdoğan, Modi, and Orbán. Though it didn't necessarily mean that his administration offered more favorable treatment of these leaders' nations, Trump's professions of affinity were still significant. Such professions were reciprocated and were typically expressed by both parties as a friendship based on mutual admiration of strong leadership rather than a commitment to a shared ideology.

Bolsonaro endorsed Trump's 2020 presidential campaign and supported his baseless claims of election fraud after he lost. Trump returned the favor, endorsing Bolsonaro's 2022 re-election bid (Klawans 2021). In 2017, Trump trumpeted his "great relationship" with Duterte. This was a marked shift from Trump's predecessor, Barack Obama, who criticized the Filipino leader's extra-judicial killings and cancelled a meeting after Duterte called him a "son of a whore" (Gayle 2016; Holmes 2017). In spite of geopolitical tensions with Turkey and his anti-Muslim racism, Trump considered Erdoğan "a friend" and a "hell of a leader" while journalists hailed their "bro-mance" (Pamuk and Coskin 2021).

Trump and Modi similarly admired one another. In September 2019, Trump appeared with the Indian leader at a "Howdy, Modi" rally of 50,000 Indian-Americans in Houston, Texas; when Trump visited India a few months later, Modi hosted a rally for him in Ahmedabad that attracted 100,000 (Menon 2020). Trump also enjoyed a very warm relationship with Orbán. One of his top advisors at the start of his administration was the Hungarian-American Sebastian Gorka, a former Orbán ally who now helps lead the right-wing opposition to Fidesz.

Going beyond Trump himself, there are deep ties between the American Right to these other authoritarian regimes. Indian and Filipino migrants to the U.S. offer crucial financial and political support to the Modi and Duterte regimes. In 2022, Mehmet Oz, the crackpot celebrity doctor and television star, was the Trump-endorsed Republican U.S. Senate candidate in Pennsylvania. The son of Turkish emigrants, Oz has substantial business and political ties to the Erdoğan regime (Baird 2021). Jair Bolsonaro's son, Eduardo, has successfully rallied support for his father's government among American conservatives (Nicas 2021). The Conservative Political Action Committee, a leading organization of the American Right, held a 2019 conference in Sao Paolo. In 2022, it met in Budapest. Indeed, ties between the American Right and Fidesz have only deepened since Trump's exit from office; popular Fox News host Tucker Carlson has visited Hungary and frequently cites Orbán's example (Zerofsky 2021). The case of John O'Sullivan suggests the need to triangulate connections between Trumpists and Brexiteers. The Eurosceptic Anglo-American, former editor of the leading American conservative magazine *National Review* and once a special advisor to Margaret Thatcher's government, now heads the pro-Orbán think tank, the Danube Institute.

Taking seriously the Trumpist Right's affinity with Bolsonaro, Duterte, Erdoğan, Modi, and Orbán leads to an examination of decidedly twenty-first century dynamics. Like these other leaders, Trump responded to a legitimation crisis of neoliberalism. Yet like them he offered no real alternative to it. Rather, he both emerged from and exacerbated neoliberalism's competitive logic. The roots of Trumpism lie in the distinctive history of the U.S. and in its current position as a declining global hegemon. Yet, like similar movements in these other nations, it represents authoritarianism with a democratic façade.

Trump represents a racial nationalism with a long tradition. The United States was founded as a white supremacist settler republic rooted in the genocide of indigenous peoples and the exploitation of enslaved African labor. Racist and xenophobic movements have persisted throughout American history. They did not disappear after the civil rights era of the 1960s. The resurgence of white nationalism in recent years, of which Trump's emergence is part and parcel, has much to do with the dissolution of social bonds under neoliberalism. As with the other leaders studied in this volume, Trump's rise cannot be understood apart from the plummeting popularity of previous governments identified with neoliberal policies.

Though notoriously difficult to define, neoliberalism can be understood as an ideology supporting the free flows of capital, people, and goods across national borders. In practice, neoliberalism is a form of class warfare entailing the upward distribution of wealth and power and increased economic precarity for the majority. While offering a limited challenge to the ideology of neoliberalism, Trump embodied its deeper logic as a starkly competitive world split between "winners" and "losers" in which the drive to compete displaces any sense of social obligation. At the core of the neoliberal project has been an attack on the notion of social citizenship and the universal guarantee of a basic standard of living. In the U.S., social citizenship is best associated with President Franklin Roosevelt's New Deal. In the 1930s, Roosevelt introduced a number of policies to protect citizens from what he called the "hazards and vicissitudes" of life in a capitalist society including old age pensions, unemployment insurance, and the right to unionize. Though sharply conscribed by gender and race and hence hardly universal in reach, New Deal measures enjoyed broad political legitimacy. Social citizenship was further expanded during the 1960s largely due to pressure from civil rights and feminist movements.

The rise of neoliberalism can conveniently be dated to the 1970s. The United States was both a key site for the development of neoliberalism and a central global actor in pushing it abroad. In 1971, President Richard Nixon took the US dollar off the gold standard, introducing a floating exchange rate system that ended the Keynesian system of controls that had been agreed at Bretton Woods in 1944. Thus began the unleashing of finance. In 1973, the CIA backed a coup d'état in Chile by General Pinochet against the government of socialist

Salvador Allende. US interference to protect American business interests was hardly new, especially in Latin America. But in this case with US support and under the influence of the "Chicago boys" – economists from the University of Chicago – Pinochet's brutal dictatorship introduced a series of liberalizing measures that set a template followed elsewhere: privatization of state enterprises, removal of tariffs, repression of labor unions, and abandonment of social welfare protections. Shortly thereafter, a dramatic retraction of social citizenship occurred in the largest U.S. city, New York, which nearly declared bankruptcy in 1975. In exchange for bailing out the city, bankers demanded that it dismantle the expansive social-democratic system it had built since the 1930s (Freeman 2000). Signalling the ascending political power of Wall Street, the bailout entailed a wage freeze and layoffs for public workers, a hike in subway fares, and the introduction of tuition at the City University of New York (Harvey 2005).

At the national level, policies such as Social Security (old age pensions) and Medicare (health insurance for the elderly) remained too popular to dismantle. Nevertheless, since the 1970s, national politicians from both parties found other means of undermining social citizenship (Gerstle 2022). Though a Democrat, Jimmy Carter, President between 1977 and 1981, broke with his party's New Deal tradition. He gutted legislation sponsored by members of his own party that would have guaranteed employment as a federal right. He initiated the deregulation of airlines and other industries. Most significantly, in 1979 he appointed Paul Volcker to head the Federal Reserve. Volcker raised interest rates to draconian levels to control inflation, pushing millions of people out of work.

In 1980, the unpopular Carter was defeated by Ronald Reagan, who professed right-wing economic views that would have made him unelectable a decade prior. Congressional opposition prevented Reagan from achieving the kind of sweeping reforms put forth by Pinochet or even by Thatcher in the UK. Nevertheless, Reagan accelerated the deregulation of industry and slashed taxes on corporations and the rich; during his eight years in office the top tax rate on corporations fell from 46% to 34% while the top rate on individuals plummeted from 70% to 28%. Reagan also helped cement a new celebration of anti-social individualism. It was during this period that Trump first achieved celebrity as one of several businessmen whose accumulation of wealth supposedly demonstrated the opportunities Reagan's America offered to those bold enough to seize them.

The Democratic Party largely accommodated itself to Reagan's reforms. Bill Clinton, who became president in 1992, had positioned himself on the Democratic Party's right wing and backed the North American Free Trade

Agreement (NAFTA) opposed by environmentalists and organized labor. Nevertheless, for a short period, it seemed that an expansion of social citizenship was possible. But Clinton failed to get his plan for universal health insurance through Congress and acquiesced in neoliberalism's acceleration after Republican congressional victories in 1994. In 1996, he famously declared, "The era of big government is over." He signed a bill eliminating the Aid to Families with Dependent Children (AFDC) program, popularly known as "welfare," which was the most vulnerable remnant of New Deal legislation because it disproportionately aided poor African American women. Clinton also supported the deregulation of banking. Meanwhile, under Clinton and his predecessor George Bush, the US pushed neoliberalism as the only alternative for post-Communist states. American diplomats backed rapid selloff of state-owned industries and the stripping of social safety nets in Eastern Europe and Russia while also abetting the transition of China to state capitalism.

Significant political opposition to neoliberalism first emerged during the second term of President George W. Bush. Surprisingly, it came not from the left but from the right, among members of Bush's own party. First, congressional Republicans stopped Bush's planned immigration reform because it would have provided a pathway to citizenship for undocumented immigrants. Second, during the 2008 economic crisis, Bush needed the support of congressional Democrats to pass emergency legislation allowing the U.S. Treasury to purchase toxic assets from the U.S. banking industry. Republican opponents of such legislation had become so extreme in their opposition to state interference that they pursued it even when it was overwhelmingly backed by American business leaders and necessary to the preservation of global capitalism. These legislators were merely responding to the massive unpopularity of big finance among their constituents as a rift grew between the Republican base and neoliberal corporate elites. Anti-immigrant and anti-government forces coalesced in subsequent years as the "Tea Party" movement which was the most immediate precursor to Trumpism.

Barack Obama, president from 2009 to 2017, proved a reliable ally for American capitalists, providing steady management of the 2008 economic crisis. Instead of backing a substantial overhaul of the country's financial system, Obama aimed to keep its institutions intact. He promised unpopular and ungrateful bankers that he would stand "between you and the pitchforks" (Obama 2019: 297). Obama offered the biggest expansion to social citizenship since the 1960s through his health insurance plan, but this remained far short of the universal healthcare rights enjoyed by citizens in every other nation in the Global North; it was, in fact, based on a model initially introduced by conservatives as an alternative to universal healthcare. Most importantly, the complicated half-measure failed to mobilize any constituency for further progressive reforms.

Neoliberalism manifested itself not simply at the level of federal policy but in the growing power of economic elites at the expense of workers. The results were devastating to the living standards of most Americans. Union density in the private sector decreased from 24.5% in 1973 to 6.5% in 2016 as a result of a sustained business offensive enabled by declining legal protection for labor rights (Mischel, Reinhart, and Windham 2020). Real wages failed to rise in line with productivity gains, increasing just 12% from 1973 to 2017 while productivity increased 75%. While the real wages of the top 10% of workers increased 32.3% from 1979 to 2017, they actually fell for the bottom 50% of workers (Gordon 2018). Despite continued belief in the "American Dream," class mobility in the US lagged considerably behind that of most other nations in the Global North. Inequality reached obscene levels with three men (Jeff Bezos, Warren Buffett, and Bill Gates) possessing as much wealth as the bottom 50% of the American population. Meanwhile, as social welfare provisions decreased, the punitive arm of the state increased, most notably in the exponential expansion of the carceral state. Between 1970 and 2010, the U.S. prison population increased fivefold with African Americans and Latinx Americans suffering disproportionate rates of imprisonment.

Economic shifts exacerbated geographical differences. Some metropolitan areas such as New York City and California's Silicon Valley thrived due to the presence of finance and technology industries. States in the Southern and Southwestern "Sun Belt" prospered on a low-wage, non-union, service sector model best embodied by the rise of the Arkansas retailing giant, Walmart. However, millions of unionized manufacturing jobs were lost in the "Rust Belt" of industrial cities of the Northeast and Midwest. The effects of economic decline and inequality were felt in the weakening of social bonds and an epidemic of drug addiction. Distrust of elites became widespread. In 2015, trust in American government fell to 18%, a figure half that recorded in 1974 in the wake of the Watergate scandal (Pew 2021).

By 2016, the neoliberal consensus that had characterized American politics for four decades was fracturing. A democratic socialist, Bernie Sanders, mounted a surprisingly strong primary challenge to the presumed Democratic nominee, Hillary Clinton. Though the center ultimately held in the Democratic Party, it collapsed in the Republican Party. Most of the Republican Party establishment was hostile to Trump, but he succeeded by voicing the concerns of the party's disaffected base.

Trump offered a limited challenge to neoliberalism. He opposed free trade deals such as NAFTA and proposed protectionist measures to defend American manufacturing jobs.

Most of all, Trump campaigned on openly racist opposition to immigration. Trump's opposition to immigration departed from the stance of established Republican elites such as the Bush family who had supported immigration both because it benefitted American corporations and because they hoped to woo Latinx voters. Trump offered a coherent narrative that attributed American national decline to non-white immigration. Announcing his presidential candidacy in 2015, he declared, "When Mexico sends its people, they're not sending their best. [...] They're sending people that have lots of problems, and they're bringing those problems with us. They're bringing drugs. They're bringing crime. They're rapists. And some, I assume, are good people." Trump articulated overtly racist thoughts that previous Republicans had only implied. He courted the support of white nationalist groups, who became some of his staunchest backers.

Trump was never as popular as the other leaders studied in this volume. At no point during his presidency did he have the support of a majority of Americans. He narrowly defeated Clinton in the 2016 election because she was nearly as unpopular as he was and because the political system enabled him to win despite losing the popular vote. Yet Trump was popular in the sense that his success fed off considerable grassroots support. He attracted tens of thousands to rallies and not only during his electoral campaigns. Not since Reagan had a Republican leader generated such enthusiasm and loyalty.

Because the 2016 election was so close, the votes Trump received from industrial workers in Midwestern states helped put him over the top. Trump won as much as 62% of the "white working class" vote according to one measure, but this was not a sudden spike. Rather, Republican support among this demographic had been rising since 1992 and hence constitutes a longer-term trend (Carnes and Lupu 2021). The best explanation for this trend is the erosion of the Democrats' working class base due to the party's embrace of neoliberal policies. A related factor is the steady decline of trade unions, the crucial institutions linking working-class voters to the Democratic Party, which had once reliably delivered industrialized Midwestern states. After decades of neoliberalism, the dominant political sentiment of the working class – which can be crudely defined as those who work for hourly wages rather than yearly salaries – is disengagement and disgust with a system rigged against them. Trump's outsider status appealed to some working-class voters, but they voted for him mostly by default and not because they were enthusiastic about Trump in particular (Silva 2019).

It is thus mistaken to identify Trump's base of support as the "white working class," as many lazy commentators did. To be sure, there is little doubt about Trump's racial appeal to whites. He received considerable support from whites of all classes except the poor (defined as a family income less than $30,000). In 2016 Trump won the support of 62% of white men as against 32% for Clinton and the votes of 47% of white women as against 45% for Clinton (Pew 2018). Similarly, Trump's patriarchal persona drew considerably more support from men than from women. Despite Trump's crudeness – video emerged prior to the 2016 election in which he bragged about groping vaginas – his embodiment of male authority proved a point of appeal to a key Republic constituency of religious conservatives.

Trump's base is not the working class. The average income of Trump supporters was higher than that of Clinton supporters and considerably higher than that of the average American. In the 2016 Republican primaries, the median household income of a Trump supporter was approximately $72,000 as compared to a national average $56,000 (Silver 2016). Trump's base is the "petit bourgeois," a group with small property holdings. In the U.S., these are typically homeowners and consist of groups such as retirees with pensions, small business-owners, and lower-middle-class salaried employees such as policemen and border agents (both of which supported Trump in huge numbers). These are not the have-nots, but those anxious to protect what they have. Their material wealth may be considerable when considered in global perspective, but of course the Global South is not their point of comparison.

The economic anxiety of this strata is very real, yet its stake in the social order enables its resentment to be projected downwards toward immigrants and recipients of government welfare deemed to be a drain on their tax dollars. The antipathy it projects upwards directs more typically to the professional-managerial class, members of whom they encounter within daily life, than to the corporate elite. The other authoritarian leaders in this volume similarly draw support from the precarious lower middle class, which of course was also the base for historical fascism. The existence of a large petit bourgeoisie is not a new development in the U.S. as it is in the Global South, but its political dynamics are similarly rooted in hatred and fear of lower classes (Myerson 2017).

Trump also found considerable support among regional bourgeoisie, large property-owners scattered throughout the nation who measure their wealth in the millions rather than the billions (Wyman 2021). Trump had fairly limited backing from the wealthiest capitalists given that he ran as the representative of the most pro-capitalist party. Nevertheless, he benefitted from the support of reliable bastions of the Republican Party such as the extractive industries.

In addition, he had the backing of some savvy ultra-rich donors such as hedge fund managers Lee Hanley and Robert Mercer who presciently saw the declining popularity of the party's agenda and the need for an outsider candidate who could effectively mobilize discontent without representing any real danger to corporate interests (Green 2017).

In 2016, Trump won the support of 64% of voters without a university degree but only 38% of voters with one (Pew 2018). Many analysts confused education level with class, but the large gap in support by education level is nevertheless significant. For most Democrats, educational credentials are a path to social advancement. The party's middle-class supporters believe in meritocracy, an ideology embodied by leaders such as Obama and Clinton who tout their ability to rise above the limits of race and gender through talent and hard work.

Trump, however, has his base in those who reject meritocracy as a sham. He appeals both to the grievances of those left out of a system they feel is rigged against them *and* to those who feel they owe their success to their natural place in the hierarchy because they are white, male, and/or inherited their wealth. He appeals to those who fear losing status by promising to "make America great again." Clinton's claim that America was already great rang hollow outside of its thriving metropolises; Trump spoke to those who perceived a world more sharply divided between haves and have nots. His simple division between "winners" and "losers" reflects a world in which the hypercompetitive logic of neoliberalism pervades daily life.

When in power, Trump persisted in his racist anti-immigrant agenda, musing before other politicians about why the US couldn't attract more migrants from Scandinavia than from "shithole countries" such as Haiti. Despite the horrifying realities of Trump's anti-immigrant policies such as the separation of families at the Mexican border, much of Trump's agenda remained symbolic, notably in his unfulfilled campaign pledge to build a wall between the US and Mexico and to have Mexico pay for it. In economic policy, Trump nixed the free trade Trans-Pacific Partnership Agreement negotiated in the Obama administration and started some low-key trade wars with China and the European Union. But, otherwise, his challenge to neoliberal flows of people, capital, and goods was fairly limited. Manufacturing jobs continued to decline.

Steve Bannon, a top political adviser who ran Trump's political campaign and drafted his inaugural address, had proposed a more thorough challenge to what he called "globalism" by combining harsh anti-immigrant measures with a program of state investment in infrastructure designed to boost employment. But Trump ultimately rejected that path in large part because of the accommodation he reached with the Republican establishment that dominated the U.S. Congress. Under Trump, Republicans continued to pursue the same conservative agenda they had pushed since the time of Reagan. While an attempt to repeal Obamacare failed, the signature economic policy of the Trump presidency was another round of tax cuts that favored the wealthy. Meanwhile, Republicans continued to populate the federal courts with hard-line conservatives, appeasing both their religious conservative base and their wealthy donors. These judges were not only opponents of abortion rights, they also pledged to block or overturn policies designed to enhance social citizenship and promised to preserve the right of the rich to make unlimited political donations. Under Trump, federal courts, including the Supreme Court, moved significantly to the right further insulating property rights from democratic will, a central aim of neoliberalism.

In addition, Trump sought to undermine the regulatory capacity of the federal government and cripple the power of its civil service. He advanced a curious sort of anti-statist nationalism that seeks to capture state power only to dismantle it, thereby unfettering corporate power. Even Bannon, with his close affinity with neo-fascist movements in Europe, called for the "deconstruction of the administrative state." The tragic consequences of this assault on federal government capacity were most apparent during the COVID-19 pandemic. Like the other authoritarian leaders studied in this volume, Trump was slow to respond to the threat posed by the virus. The Trump administration had already ripped up the pandemic plans put in place by the Obama administration. When the pandemic hit, Trump undermined the authority of the federal Center for Disease Control, leaving states and localities to fend for themselves. He personally dismissed the seriousness of the virus and made refusing to wear a mask into a political gesture of defiance against educated elites. As a result, at least 400,000 Americans died of COVID while Trump was President. According to one public health analysis, 40% of these deaths could be attributed to Trump's mismanagement of the crisis (Woolhander 2021).

Though Republican elites had initially opposed Trump, they soon discovered that the spectacle he produced as president allowed them to pursue their unpopular agenda outside of the spotlight. As other chapters in this volume have shown, authoritarian neoliberals rely on spectacle to hide the fact that their policies mainly intensify the neoliberalism against which they campaigned. For Trump, running for president had been a publicity stunt designed to enhance his brand. He had debated whether to run in the Republican primary or to return for another year as star of the reality show, *The Apprentice,* and was likely as surprised as anyone that he actually won the presidency.

In the U.S., the same dynamic of spectacle hiding corporate power had prevailed in the presidency of Reagan, a film star. But whereas Reagan presented a genial persona to cover up his shredding of the social fabric, Trump laid bare the asocial violence of neoliberalism in his narcissistic and hateful character. While Reagan had emerged from classical Hollywood, a medium that presented a consensual American dream (Rogin 1987), Trump was a product of cable news, reality television, and social media. In all of these forms, outrageous and extreme acts were prized for helping to draw in viewers. Spectacle was good for business; as a head of a major television network confessed in 2016, the Trump candidacy "may not be good for America, but it's damn good for CBS" (Bond 2016).

Before his presidential candidacy, Trump was best known to Americans as the star of a reality show in which contestants competed for a role in Trump's company. Like other reality shows, *The Apprentice* presented a stark division between winners and losers; at the end of each episode Trump would famously meet with the losing contestant and gleefully declare, "You're fired." An avid consumer of cable news, Trump became a figure on the political right as a regular contributor to the conservative Fox News network. In this role, he pushed the racist conspiracy theory that Obama had been born abroad and was hence ineligible to be president (Poniewozik 2019). With its algorithms amplifying the most extreme views, Twitter became an ideal platform for Trump's statements, enabling him to reach his base directly without any danger of his claims being checked for factual accuracy.

While the other authoritarian leaders studied in this volume led nations in the global semi-periphery, Trump presided over the world's foremost global power. Paradoxically, because of this power, Trump was able to enact some mildly protectionist policies challenging neoliberalism without fear of the U.S. suffering any significant economic consequences. Yet he also tapped into fears of the U.S.'s declining hegemony coincidant with the global crisis of neoliberalism. Many Americans are conscious of their country's loss of power especially to the rise of China. Part of the rancor that fed into Trump's popular support lay in his promise to rectify the fact that the U.S. was increasingly becoming a "loser" on the global stage. He promised to enhance American power against its geopolitical rival, China, and to make Americans "winners" again. At the same time, Trump promised a change in direction from the military interventionism associated with both parties but especially the Republicans. The U.S. effort to project its power in the Middle East with its 2003 invasion of Iraq backfired spectacularly and fractured the once bipartisan consensus that had underlaid decades of American foreign policy. Moreover, disillusioned veterans of the "forever wars" in Iraq and Afghanistan swelled the ranks of diehard white nationalist supporters of Trump such as those who stormed the U.S. Capitol on January 6, 2021.

Trump faced more political opposition than did any of the other leaders studied in this volume. He was the first of them to lose power when his 2020 bid for re-election failed. Though Trump retains a large active and loyal base, he has never enjoyed broad public support. His approval rating hovered around the 40% mark throughout his presidency, averaging well below that of any President in their first term (Gallup 2022). Though Fox News was strongly pro-Trump, most coverage of Trump in the mainstream media was critical throughout his presidency. Even mainstream works of popular culture were critical of Trump; for example, the 2021 children's film, *PAW Patrol: The Movie,* is a transparently anti-Trump allegory. Especially after the events of January 6 many corporations disassociated themselves from Trump. He was permanently suspended from Twitter.

By and large, most corporate elites are more comfortable with a centrist Democrat such as current president Joe Biden than with Trump. The Democratic Party has shifted markedly to the left in recent years. Yet only a minority of its members, such as Senator Bernie Sanders and Representative Alexandria Ocasio-Cortez, advocate an open challenge to corporate power and a clear break with neoliberalism. The left is revived, yet still weak, even as Biden has adopted some aspects of its domestic agenda as his own. Accordingly, most economic elites have little reason to back authoritarianism as an alternative to socialism.

Unlike the other nations studied in this volume, the U.S. possesses a long and unbroken history of constitutional self-government. It has operated under much the same constitution since 1789 and this remains a considerable source of national pride even as the document is interpreted in radically different ways. On the one hand, one could rightly hail constitutional provisions as a key impediment to Trump's authoritarianism. The document was specifically designed to prevent tyranny by dividing power among different branches of government and between federal and state governments. It is impossible to amass total power.

On the other hand, the Constitution makes it very difficult to enact the kind of measures needed to expand social citizenship and strengthen the social bonds whose dissolution under neoliberalism aided the rise of Trumpism. Reforms designed to improve the living conditions of ordinary Americans are remarkably difficult to enact and have historically required Congressional super-majorities. As such, though Biden managed to increase spending on domestic programs during his first two years in office, it is likely that more ambitious efforts to expand social citizenship will fail. The consequence may be a further erosion of trust in the American government helping to feed

Trumpism's appeal. Trump himself seems likely to run again in 2024 but if he does not his replacement will likely be in the Trumpian mold.

The Constitution, which long protected the political power of slaveholders and segregationists, has considerable anti-democratic potential. In the long run, Trumpism is perhaps best understood as a minoritarian effort to exploit that potential. Republicans are well aware of the fact that changing demographics have made it difficult for them to win lasting electoral majorities. They have ensured their continued hold on power by packing the Supreme Court, gerrymandering Congressional districts, and passing state laws designed to suppress voting. Republican success is based on a combination of a highly mobilized minority of voters with a willingness to ruthlessly employ anti-democratic measures that block or even override the will of the majority.

American Presidents are still chosen via an archaic electoral college system rather than by popular vote, a system that overrepresents voters in smaller and more rural states and thereby advantages the Republicans. Republicans have only won the popular vote once since 1992 and won two of the past five presidential elections despite having lost the popular vote. They are currently seeking to further their advantage by passing laws enabling state legislatures to overturn the results of close elections, laws that are deeply undemocratic yet perfectly constitutional because the electoral college relies upon states to choose their own electors. Trump and the majority of his party refuse to admit that he lost the 2020 presidential election not only to assuage their anxiety that they are "losers." Baseless charges of voter fraud lay the ground for future efforts to overturn an election.

The real danger to American democracy is not that of a violent coup depicted in the novel *It Can't Happen Here*. It lies rather in the long-standing democratic deficit in the U.S. political system exploited by a Republican minority feeding off petit bourgeois resentment exacerbated by decades of neoliberalism. A successful coup of the kind attempted on January 6 remains highly unlikely, yet the disturbing political violence evident on that date normalizes and distracts from the efforts of Republican politicians to capture democratic institutions from within. As with the other countries studied in this volume, a facade of democracy is maintained.

Though the authoritarian danger may manifest itself in peculiarly American ways, it cannot be understood without a global perspective. Trump may not be an American Hitler, but the political tendency he represents is similar to that represented by Bolsonaro, Duterte, Erdoğan, Orbán, and Modi. Americans should pay closer attention to what is happening in those countries because they may discover that it can indeed happen here.

References

Baird B (2021) Behind Dr. Oz's Curtain. *National Review*, Dec. 23, 2021 Available at: https://www.nationalreview.com/2021/12/behind-dr-ozs-curtain/ on 19 January 2022.

Bond P (2016) Leslie Moonves on Donald Trump. *The Hollywood Reporter,* Feb. 29, 2016 Available at: https://www.hollywoodreporter.com/news/general-news/leslie-moonves-donald-trump-may-871464/.

Carnes N and Lupu N (2021) The White Working Class and the 2016 Election. *Perspectives on Politics* 19: 55–72.

Freeman J (2000) *Working-class New York: Life and Labor Since World War II.* New York: New Press, 2000.

Gallup (2022) Presidential Approval Ratings. Available at: https://news.gallup.com/poll/116677/presidential- approval-ratings-gallup-historical-statistics-trends.aspx.

Gayle D (2016) Barack Obama cancels meeting after Philippines president calls him 'son of a whore'. *Guardian*, Sept. 5, 2016. Available at: https://www.theguardian.com/world/2016/sep/05/philippines-president-rodrigo-duterte-barack-obama-son-whore.

Geary D, Schofield C and Sutton J (2020) *Global White Nationalism: From Apartheid to Trump.* Manchester: Manchester University Press.

Gerstle G (2022) *The Rise and Fall of the Neoliberal Order: America and the World in the Free Market Era.* New York: Oxford University Press.

Gordon C (2018) Growth (or not) in Real Wages. *Economic Policy Institute*, March 1, 2018, Available at: https://www.epi.org/blog/growth-or-not-in-real-wages/ accessed on November 22, 2021.

Green J (2017) *Devil's Bargain: Steve Bannon, Donald Trump, and the Storming of the Presidency.* New York: Penguin.

Greenberg U (2021) What Was the Fascist Debate? *Dissent* (Summer 2021) Available at: https://www.dissentmagazine.org/article/what-was-the-fascism-debate.

Harvey D (2005) *A Brief History of Neoliberalism.* New York: Oxford University Press.

Holmes O (2017) Trump Hails 'Great Relationship' with Philippines' Duterte. *Guardian*, Nov. 13, 2017. Available at: https://www.theguardian.com/us-news/2017/nov/13/trump-hails-great-relationship-with-philippines-duterte.

Klawans J (2021) Donald Trump Endorses Jair Bolsonaro as Brazil Senate Recommends Charges Over Pandemic. *Newsweek*, Oct. 26, 2021 Available at: https://www.newsweek.com/donald-trump-endorses-jair-bolsonaro-brazil-senate-recommends-charges-over-pandemic-1642912.

Lewis S (1935) *It Can't Happen Here: A Novel.* Garden City, NY: Doubleday.

Menon S (2020) League of Nationalists: How Trump and Modi Refashioned the U.S.-Indian Relationship. *Foreign Affairs,* September/October 2020, Available at:

https://www.foreignaffairs.com/articles/united-states/2020-08-11/modi-india-lea
gue-nationalists.

Mischel L, Rhinehart L and Windham L (2020) *Explaining the Erosion of Private-Sector
Unions.* Washington DC: Economic Policy Institute.

Myerson J (2017) Trumpism: It's Coming from the Suburbs. *The Nation,* May 8, 2017,
Available at: https://www.thenation.com/article/archive/trumpism-its-coming
-from-the-suburbs/.

Nicas J (2021) The Bolsonaro-Trump Connection Threatening Brazil's Elections. *New
York Times,* Nov. 11, 2021. Available at: https://www.nytimes.com/2021/11/11/world/
americas/bolsonaro-trump-brazil- election.html.

Obama B (2019) *A Promised Land.* New York: Crown.

Pamuk H and Coskun O (2021) Behind Trump-Erdoğan 'bromance,' a White House
meeting to repair U.S. – Turkey ties. *Reuters,* Nov. 12, 2021. Available at: https://www
.reuters.com/article/us-turkey-usa- trump-Erdoğan-idUSKBN1XMoFo.

Pew Research Center (2021) Public Trust in Government, 1958–2021. May 17, 2021.
Available at: https://www.pewresearch.org/politics/2021/05/17/public-trust-in-gov
ernment-1958-2021/.

Pew Research Center (2018), "For Most Trump Voters, 'Very Warm' Feelings for him
Endured," Aug. 9, 2018.

Poniewozik J (2019) *An Audience of One: Donald Trump, Television, and the Fracturing
of America.* New York: Liveright.

Rogin, M (1987) *Ronald Reagan, the Movie, and other Episodes in Political Demonology.*
Berkeley: University of California Press.

Silva J (2019) *We're Still Here: Pain and Politics in the Heart of America.* New York: Oxford
University Press.

Silver N (2016) The Mythology of Trump's 'Working Class' Support. May 3, 2016.
Available at: https://fivethirtyeight.com/features/the-mythology-of-trumps-work
ing-class-support/.

Snyder T (2017) *On Tyranny: Twenty lessons from the Twentieth Century.* New York: Tim
Duggan Books.

Vorman B and Weinman M (2021) *The Emergence of Illiberalism: Understanding a
Global Phenomenon.* New York: Routledge.

Woolhandler S et al. (2021) Public Policy and Health in the Trump Era. *The Lancet*
397: 705–53.

Wyman P (2021) American Gentry. *The Atlantic,* Sept. 21, 2021. Available at: https://
www.theatlantic.com/ideas/archive/2021/09/trump-american-gentry-wyman-eli
tes/620151/.

Zerofsky E (2021) How the American Right Fell in Love with Hungary. *New York Times,*
Oct. 19, 2021.

Index

www.ingramcontent.com/pod-product-compliance
Lightning Source LLC
Chambersburg PA
CBHW070105030426

42335CB00016B/2020